PENGUIN AFRICAN LIBRARY
Edited by Ronald Segal

The Discarded People

COSMAS DESMOND, O.F.M.

Cosmas Desmond was born in Stepney in 1935, and went
to Cardinal Vaughan School. Having joined the Franciscan
Order in 1952 he was ordained in 1959, and went straight
to South Africa to work among African miners in the
Ladysmith district. In 1967 he moved to the
Maria Ratschitz Mission at Ermelo and later became a
South African citizen. He began to travel around the
African 'homelands' to investigate conditions among
people resettled there by the Government. Recently he
applied to the authorities for a passport to visit his family
in England. He was classified as 'communist' and his
application was refused.

COSMAS DESMOND, O.F.M.

The Discarded People

*An Account of African Resettlement
in South Africa*

*Preface by Lord Caradon
Foreword by Nadine Gordimer*

Penguin Books

Penguin Books Ltd, Harmondsworth,
Middlesex, England
Penguin Books Inc., 7110 Ambassador Road,
Baltimore, Maryland 21207, U.S.A.
Penguin Books Australia Ltd, Ringwood,
Victoria, Australia

First published 1971
Copyright © Cosmas Desmond, 1971

Made and printed in Great Britain by
Hazell Watson & Viney Ltd, Aylesbury, Bucks
Set in Linotype Plantin

Contents

Acknowledgements

The author is extremely grateful to John Sackur for the considerable help he has given with the preparation of the manuscript of this book.

For permission to use the photographs acknowledgement is made to the following: Clifford Ranaka (Johannesburg) for Plates 1, 4, and 5; Leslie Woodhead for Plate 3; and John Seymour (Camera Press, London) for Plates 6, 7, and 8.

Preface

This is a terrifying book. It is an account of callous contempt for human suffering, the ugliness of systematic cruelty, and the self-righteousness of the oppressor.

When I first read the book, I found it difficult to believe, even to imagine, the evil which Father Desmond so faithfully and so courageously describes.

I read the book again after watching the television film which helped me to see the full horror of the events he reported.

Most of us knew before of the brutal methods of the South African Government, of the network of informers, the solitary confinement, the torture – the terrorism of oppression.

I myself, when I was a member of a United Nations commission on South Africa some years ago, heard the evidence of the stranglehold which the South African Government ruthlessly and increasingly maintains over the great black majority.

Father Desmond brings the story up to date. He shows us by his thorough and convincing reporting that the situation, far from getting better, as some, for political face-saving, would have us believe, is rapidly getting very much worse.

The picture of thousands of families uprooted, transported and then dumped, dumped like garbage, some of them in the open desert, is something no one who reads the book can forget. It must surely excite furious disgust. Those are the words Father Desmond uses to describe his own reaction : 'disgust, horror and shame'. I cannot see how anyone can feel less.

I hope the book will do more than help to stir the conscience of us all. I hope it will help to shame the hypocrites who protest their dislike of apartheid but insist at the same time on sustaining those who practise it.

I hope it will help anyone who doubts the intense feelings of Africans to realize that for them there is no issue more important than this in the world.

I hope it will help those who have advocated appeasement of the South African Government and the illegal regime in Rhodesia to understand that to side with the racialist oppressors will destroy any prospect of maintaining respect for Britain, and any hope of British leadership in the world.

I hope it will help to explain the shame which many of us feel that a British Government was prepared to flout the Commonwealth and undermine the United Nations and abandon British interests – and show itself so lacking in human compassion and an elementary sense of justice.

I like to think that the eagerness of our present Ministers to sustain the South African Government came from ignorance, ignorance of Africa in particular. Perhaps it is still not too late to change, to abandon the crazily absurd idea that a few South African helicopters or frigates could find and destroy communism in the Indian Ocean.

Perhaps it is still not too late to start again and to build confidence again in the Commonwealth.

We are all for British interest, and we want British interest to be something to be proud of. We beg our Government to make British interest something in which we can hope to prosper and rejoice.

Sometimes a book can make, can alter, the course of history. Father Desmond's book could well do so. I trust there are enough people who care enough to read his brave report. I trust that the candour and the courage of his evidence will strike home.

We should all be deeply grateful that Father Desmond has given us this challenge. I remember that it was once said that the devil with sad and sober sense on his grey face tells the rulers of the world that the ills and evils of mankind are beyond the reach of human remedy. But it was also said that a voice is raised from time to time in answer, an answer in the name of the dignity of man and the mercy of God. Such a voice is the voice of Father Desmond.

I pray that his voice may stir our compassion and shatter our complacency and save us from despair and give us a new determination, and a new militant faith and a new confidence that evil can and must be overcome.

CARADON

Foreword

Father Cosmas Desmond questioned whether he was the best-qualified person to undertake the research for and write this book, and I asked myself whether I was in any way qualified to write a foreword to it. We were both wrong; as citizens of South Africa the subject is our responsibility, and as human beings it is our concern. If, reading his book, you who live outside South Africa and are not a South African citizen question your right to judge the facts set out before you, remember that, as a human being, it is your right and your concern.

As for your qualification to judge from the facts, you know well enough to eat when you're hungry, don't you? To turn on the heating when you're cold? To choose a place to live in at a rent you can afford, on a transport route convenient to your work, your children's schools, and the pursuits of your interests? That is all the expertise needed to judge the reasonable needs of any fellow human being. Forget about his colour or 'what he was used to'; he hungers, thirsts, and must work for his living just as you do. It is too easy for apartheid apologists and their kind (and there are many in the United States and quite a number in Britain) to shelter behind the analyses of the behavioural sciences, which serve to rationalize the Americans' 'hamlet' system in Viet Nam as the 'restructuring' of society rather than the waging of war, and the crypto-behavioural theory of apartheid which rationalizes arbitrary resettlement in South Africa on the premise that affinity of skin-colour and race overrides all other human needs. The South African separate development planners have explained at length to the world *why* communities are moved; the important question that cannot be answered by any number of demographic maps is *how* communities live when they are moved. This book sets out dispassionately to give that information; after reading it, I do not think there could be any reader who does not find himself turning back to the planners with his own question: *why* should people have to live like this in a prosperous country at peace?

The forlorn and desert reality recorded in the pages that follow is the substance of that high-sounding concept, 'separate development'. Dodging about among the centuries and countries it is true that one may prove that South Africa is not the only or the first country in the world to lift people out of their homes and jobs and dump them elsewhere. On grounds of inhumanity, one may make the most obvious comparison with Hitler's deportations of the Jews; in other respects the comparison is invalid: the object in South Africa is not genocide systematically practised by a majority upon a minority group, but absolute control by a minority over a vital labour-force majority. Stalinist Russia's deportations of minorities to Siberia and Central Asia provide another precedent; and the treatment of Irish labourers in England in the nineteenth century, and the plight of the people of Manchukuo under Japanese invasion in the late thirties have certain parallels with resettlement schemes in South Africa. And then there are contemporary examples, such as the attempts to resettle depopulated areas in Southern Italy: one may contrive to lift the whole South African situation out of the context of racialism and political domination by invoking the term *decentralization* with its ring of necessity and impartiality. But this term simply cannot be invoked with honesty or accuracy to define a policy of removals decided first and last by the colour of the communities in question rather than their density. Its logic falls down completely when the community is moved from a place where people had employment to another where no employment exists.

Yes, it has been done before. What does precedence prove? That in the second richest country in Africa, in the eighth decade of the twentieth century, choosing to manipulate the lives of a vote-less and powerless indigenous majority in accordance with a theory of colour preference, South Africa is reproducing the living conditions of persecuted minorities under Hitler and Stalin, of nineteenth-century European famine victims allowed to

labour under sufferance in another country, of an indigenous Far
Eastern population under foreign invaders more than thirty years
ago? That, in a world with a refugee problem still unsolved from
the last world war and the lesser ones that have succeeded it, we
White South Africans, who have never suffered the destruction of
our own soil and cities, have created encampments of people living as the homeless refugees of Palestine, Biafra and Viet Nam
have done?

Similarly, it is often pointed out, not only by apartheid's apologists but also by onlookers eager to be disinterested and 'fair',
that great poverty and poor living conditions exist in other
African countries, and that by comparison the South African
black population in general is relatively well-off. These disinterested people should be reminded that the valid, the 'fair' comparison to be made is between the living standard of the Black
majority and the White minority within the same country and
economy – South Africa itself.

The physical conditions of life described in this book are such
an appalling desolation that one is almost unable to think beyond
bread and latrines. That is to say, the sense of urgency one feels
on behalf of people whose struggle for existence has been reduced
to a search for wood to make a fire, a bucket of clean water to
drink, bus fare to a clinic, is inclined to set the mind safely on
ameliorating such unthinkable concrete hardships. Nothing
seems to matter but that people should be quickly fed, housed,
given the opportunity to work. Indeed, it is this distress of
urgency, brought about from time to time before this book was
published, by newspaper accounts of resettlement conditions in
the few areas that came to open attention, that has led the public
of Johannesburg – for example – to do what has become known
as 'opening its heart' to pour forth from the cornucopia of White
plenty, blankets, food, medicine, to warm, feed and tend the tent-
and-hovel black 'towns'. Reading this book, many people abroad
will experience the same charitable impulse. One can only be
thankful, in the name of common humanity, that this happens.
But in the name of common humanity, how do South Africans
manage to close their minds to the implications of the resettlement policy while at the same time 'opening their hearts' to its

callous and inevitable results? How do the people of countries abroad – in particular Britain (under whose dominion South Africa's colour-bar nationhood was established) and the United States, both of whom have profited, by long tradition, from the exploitation of South Africa's natural resources and underpaid labour – open their hearts to the results of applied apartheid while closing their minds to their governments' tacit support of apartheid? It is not only in South Africa that white people may say of the victims of resettlement described in this book, 'It is enough that they show us what we have made of them for us to realize what we have made of ourselves.' [1]

Setting aside reflections on the morality of charity in the context of South Africa, the page-by-page account of the lack of basic physical necessities in village after village, settlement after settlement, strikes one in the belly, as it were, and leads one to forget that there are other needs to be satisfied in order to make life supportable. After food and shelter are secured, what then? Suppose all the settlements described in this book – even those unimaginable half-worlds, the collections of 'surplus people', 'redundant people', 'non-productive people': the desperately poor aged, the illegitimate children from the labour-pool warrens of the towns, the mentally retarded, discarded out of everyone's way, out of life itself, on the veld – suppose all these 'closer' and 'emergency' and 'transit' settlements were to provide decent housing and reasonable satisfaction of the basic physical needs of life. Suppose, in addition, no resettlement were to be set up unless it were first assured that it provided access to equal if not better employment than was available in the place from which any community was moved. Would removals then be acceptable to the conscience and common humanity of a state that designates itself Christian and democratic and a guardian of the values of Western civilization?

I do not think the answer can be anything but 'no'. For even if the material welfare of these men and women and children who are being moved out of the path of the white man were to be secured – and how remote a possibility that is can be seen in this book – they would still be deprived of something unarguably

1. Jean-Paul Sartre.

fundamental to the declared values of Christianity, democracy, and Western civilization: the right of man over his own person. Those who urge only that removals be 'better planned', carried out 'more humanely' show a preoccupation with man's animal needs that surely must be termed cynical, coming from self-appointed guardians of civilized values.

Once one has got over the first shock of the physical suffering described in this book one becomes increasingly aware of certain signs of another kind of suffering. There is an apathy, the peculiar listlessness of lack of hope shown by many people in the settlements, born of powerlessness to change their situation by any effort of their own, since all decisions about the circumstances of their lives are made for them. Even their fantasies – 'people said they had been told that dogs would be set on them if they didn't move' – are so obviously bred of the fear and bewilderment of uprooted people who do not know how their lives and persons will be disposed of next. Every human life, however humble it has been, has a context meshed of familiar experience – social relationships, patterns of activity in relation to environment. Call it 'home', if you like. To be transported out of this on a Government truck one morning and put down in an uninhabited place is to be asked to build not only your shelter but your whole life over again, from scratch.

For the hundreds of thousands who are having this experience forced upon them, there is no appeal.

As for the rest of us – if the hearts of White South Africans and, by implication, those of the White world that looks on from six or ten thousand miles away were ever really to be opened, perhaps all that we should find would be, graven there, this comment from one of the inhabitants of a resettlement: *You can't say no to a White man.*

NADINE GORDIMER

Glossary

Bantu: The 15 million descendants of the Bantu-speaking tribes who were inhabiting what is now the Republic of South Africa at the time of White settlement in the mid-seventeenth century; formerly called 'Natives' or 'Kaffirs', words (like Bantu itself) now felt to be derogatory. The word 'African' is not recognized officially. Apartheid theory holds there is no African community, but nine 'Bantu nations'.

Bantu Administration and Development (B.A.D.): The Government department responsible for all aspects of control over and relations with Africans. Formerly called Native Affairs Department, it was renamed to conform to Dr Verwoerd's presentation of apartheid as 'separate development'.

Bantu Affairs Commissioner: Has wide powers to control African community in a Reserve or magisterial district and to enforce all Government regulations affecting Africans, who have no elected representatives at Government level.

Bantustans: See 'Homelands'.

Black spots: African settlements, once secured by title-deed, tribal or mission tenure, and now to be removed from what is prescribed as the White area of South Africa.

Border industries: White-owned, state-aided industry situated near a Reserve, intended to decentralize industry, to reduce the migration of African workers into established White cities and to provide work for the Reserves.

Cattle: Once the principal means of exchange, cattle still play a far greater role in social usages (such as dowries, payment of fines) than as a source of food. All but the very poorest country people own cattle; the owner keeps them in trust for his family and heirs; their transfer legitimizes marriages and the birth of children. For a man to lose his cattle is to lose status and self-respect.

Closer settlements: New groupings of rented plots close together in Reserves, without piped water, sanitation or houses, 'for squatters from European farms, Black spots and missionary farms', e.g. Lime-hill, p. 1, Rietspruit, p. 154.

Glossary

Emergency camps: Settlements for people whose labour is needed in the town from whose 'location' they have been removed. This category of settlement is not mentioned in General Circular 25 (1967), the resettlement blueprint for 'non-productive' or 'superfluous' people; e.g. Weenen, p. 57.

Endorsed out: Forbidden to stay or work in a town, by the rubber-stamping of the Reference Book (or Pass). This is done for a variety of reasons, such as lack of residential or length-of-service qualifications, or because the individual is considered 'idle or undesirable'.

Family: African families normally include all the living descendants of the head. There will normally be three or even four generations, and the number of persons will usually range between about five and fifteen or more. In the resettlement areas, one house or residential plot is allocated per family.

'G.G.': Slang used by Africans to refer to the Government. The term is derived from the G.G registration carried by official vehicles.

Homelands: Formerly called Native areas (q.v.). A system incorporating a form of indirect rule (Bantu Authorities) is being developed in the 'homelands'. They are known colloquially as Bantustans. See also Released area, Native areas, Scheduled areas, Trust.

House: Houses built by the Government in African townships consist of four walls and a roof; no floor, ceiling, plaster or internal doors. The rents, usually ranging between R2 and R6 per month (1 rand=£0.58 sterling), sound modest. But they are calculated to pay back the capital cost and interest within a limited period.

Influx control: The mass of legislation evolved to reduce the numbers of Africans entering, living and working in the towns and cities and outside Reserves in general, enforced by police, magistrates' courts and officials of B.A.D. See Pass; Endorsed out.

Labour tenants: Africans over fifteen years who live on White farms and work for farmers in lieu of paying rent for part of every year; restricted in many ways, and scheduled for ultimate abolition.

Location: Settlement of Africans usually on the edge of a town, also called 'township'. The name is also given to the divisions of a district in a Reserve, where the community is placed under a chief or headman, responsible to the Bantu Affairs Commissioner.

Mealies (maize): The staple diet of the African community, mainly cultivated by women on lands ploughed by men.

Native area: Land apportioned for African occupation, also known as Bantustan, 'homeland', released area, Reserve, scheduled area, Trust land.

Pass: African men and women over sixteen must carry and produce

xx

on demand at all times the Reference Book containing identity card and tax, employment and residence particulars, thus making influx control possible. Over 2,500 people are arrrested daily for 'pass offences'.

Prescribed area: Any area which is stated by the Government (by declaration in the Government Gazette) to be a White area but where a large number of Africans live.

Released area: State and White-owned land set aside in 1936 for addition to the scheduled areas (q.v.) and thus for future African settlements.

Repatriation: See Endorsed out.

Reserve: See Scheduled areas.

Scheduled areas: The Reserve as defined in the Schedule to the Native Trust Land Act of 1913, in which Whites may not own land and outside which Africans may not live by right, totalling, with the Released areas, 13·7 per cent of the land surface of South Africa.

Squatter: An African tenant on a White farm paying rent in cash or kind with no security of tenure. All squatters are due for ultimate removal.

Township: See Location.

Tomlinson Report: The report of a 1954 Government commission which called for the development of the Reserves in order to make apartheid workable. The Government has not spent the money the report called for, nor has it followed the recommendations to allow African freehold tenure and White entrepreneurship in the Reserves.

Transit Camps: Similar to emergency camps (q.v.); not one of Circular 25 (1967) categories, e.g. Poll-tax Farm, p. 73.

Trust: The South African Bantu Trust, set up by the Bantu Trust Land Act 1936, administers almost all Reserves and released areas (q.v.) and can acquire land for African resettlement, e.g. Trust villages in Zululand, p. 52, Kuruman, p. 107.

1. How It All Began

Limehill is a resettlement camp in Natal, that is, a camp for people who 'become, for some reason or another, no longer fit for work or superfluous in the labour market'. Limehill was not the first, and not the worst, of these camps. Its importance for me lies in the fact that it was the place where I first entered the labyrinth of broken communities, broken families and broken lives which is the South African Government's removals policy.

For years before Limehill I had lived with an ever-increasing consciousness of the hidden world (hidden from most Whites and from the outside) of the African side of apartheid. But when Limehill was set up and my own parishioners, my own friends, were driven there, I first saw with their eyes how this policy makes homeless prisoners of Africans in their own land, with no escape from the brutality, impoverishment and hopelessness of the system.

There are, however, scores of Limehills, unmarked on any published map; scores more are planned. Each will be designated on the official plans of apartheid, the orders will be issued and the Government will fill them all, one by one, with frightened people. The most painful irony is that when these people are removed and their homes destroyed after them, they are taken to places called, in the current double-think, 'homelands'.

Limehill itself is a wretched and desolate place. There is not enough water and not enough land for even a meagre subsistence farming. There is no industry and no work within daily reach. The inhabitants struggle against disease on the edge of starvation. It is impossible to say whether the physical degradation or the mental torture of living in such a place is the more terrible.

Limehill was the experience which made me start a journey

through the provinces of the Republic. This book is the record of my journey. The facts are easy to transfer to paper. But the experience itself remains in my head as a nightmare so powerful that it still penetrates the full light of day. The conditions I witnessed are the whole boundary of life for a million of our South African people. The threat of removal covers millions more; every day, it seems, Government lorries ferry more and more of these bewildered cargoes into the empty veld.

From January 1964 until May 1967 I was priest-in-charge at Maria Ratschitz Mission in the Dundee district of Northern Natal. I had an African assistant priest and we had about 2,000 parishioners. The Mission, and the neighbouring tribally owned farm Boschhoek, were among a number of 'Black spots' in the Dundee district which were to be cleared. 'Black spots' are places outside the tribal Reserves ('homelands') where Africans live, whether as tenants, in the case of the people on our Mission, or as owners of land they have held for generations, or as labour tenants,[1] on White farms. The apartheid system demands that all 'Black spots' must be removed and the people from them concentrated in the 'homelands'.

I had heard talk of such removals for ten years past, and during that time I had seen some of the effects: the insecurity caused by the threat of removal among the people in the Missions where I lived, and the sad waste of Mission schools having to close. But, like all White people in South Africa, I had no real awareness of the full impact of these removals until the people among whom I was living at Maria Ratschitz Mission, Boschhoek and Meran were moved to Limehill. From them I learnt of the heartbreak involved in being arbitrarily uprooted from home.

The survival of family or community life is precarious at the best of times for Africans in South Africa. Wherever they live, they are forced into the White social and economic system, where they occupy the lowest and most despised status. Even in the 'homelands', overcrowded and desperately backward, Africans cannot survive without sending male members of the family

1. Labour tenants are allowed to live on a part of a White farm, paying rent in the form of labour.

as migrant labourers. Wherever they go, they are expendable, half chattel, half enemy to the White man, and harassed continually by the pass laws and countless acts of arrogance to keep them in their place.

The starkness of life under the shadow of apartheid is greatly increased by removals. I have seen the shock of simple rural people told that they must leave their homes, which were the homes of their kinsmen for generations, to go to a strange place. I have heard their cries of despair and their pleas for help.

I have seen the sufferings of whole families living in one tent or a tiny tin hut, of children sick with typhoid, or their bodies emaciated with malnutrition and even dying of plain starvation. I have seen all this in these last few years, in 1968, 1969 and 1970, in the richest, most advanced and most rapidly growing economy on the continent of Africa. It is said that the Whites in South Africa, if they are taken alone, enjoy the highest standard of living in the whole world.

I knew the Limehill area well, for we had another Mission there (which the Government was preparing to expropriate), and when the removals were announced I visited the area frequently and kept in close touch with a number of people there, especially Father Rodney Nelson, the priest-in-charge. The land at Limehill used to be European farm land and it was bought by the Bantu Trust [1] some time ago. Our Mission was called 'Amakhasi', which means 'dry leaves'. It was extremely dry. And the fact that the land is inferior is shown by the Trust giving the people from Boschhoek approximately 4,200 extra acres in compensation. Even now, nearly three years after the move, there are still vast tracts of unused land in the Limehill area, although many more people have been moved in. The official policy is that 'squatters' are not to be given grazing or arable land because there is not enough land available.

The first sign of the removal was a visit in 1965 from a man purporting to be an official of the Department of Bantu Administration and Development (B.A.D.). He called a meeting of tenants of the Mission, without my knowledge, and told them

1. The Bantu Trust is a Government body which administers the African Reserves.

they were all to be moved in July 1966. When I protested at this high-handed action to the local Bantu Affairs Commissioner, he disclaimed all knowledge of the man or the visit.

Nothing happened until in August 1967 another man came to the Mission, again without reference to the owners, and painted numbers on the doors of all the African homes in the Mission. This time the Commissioner replied to our complaint that the man was acting on instructions from Pretoria and without his knowledge. In September the Bantu Commissioner himself visited the Mission, and had the courtesy to inform the priest. He held a meeting at which he told the people that they would probably be moved in May 1968, but they would have the opportunity of building houses in the new location before they moved, and a school and other facilities would be ready for them.

On 19 October, the Commissioner held another meeting. The move was now to be on 20 January 1968. The school, he said, was not ready and would be temporarily housed in tents and the people would have to 'provide their own accommodation' while building their houses.

Then came a duplicated letter, addressed to the priest-in-charge, at the beginning of November, notifying him that, as one of the 'Black spots' in the Dundee district, the Mission was to be cleared on 29 January.

People in the adjoining farm, Boschhoek, had been receiving much the same treatment for three or four years. Twice they were told not to plough because they were going to be moved before the reaping season. Then the date was put back to November 1967; then January 1968; then May 1968. Finally they followed the people from our Mission.

During the three months before the removals I spent almost all my time interceding for the people with the Government, and liaising with the Church leaders and lawyers. A number of White people became involved in the attempts we made to prevent or postpone the removal until at least basic facilities had been provided in the Limehill area. Three months before the date fixed the only signs of development were a few dirt roads and the foundations for a school. It was obvious that the place could not be made habitable in time.

The people themselves were voiceless. Their pleas were simply of no interest to the Government. A meeting of White people was convened in Durban and attended by a large number who were disturbed by Government action. From this meeting the Committee of Church Representatives on Bantu Resettlement was formed, with representatives from the Anglican, Lutheran, Methodist, Congregationalist and Roman Catholic Churches, under the chairmanship of Archbishop D. E. Hurley. The Committee thus included all the major established European churches in South Africa, with the notable exception of the Dutch Reformed Church.

The committee entered into long and patient negotiations with the Minister of B.A.D., Mr M. C. Botha, with the hope of preventing the move if possible, or at least of having the preparations at Limehill improved. As long as there was any hope that the Government might modify their actions or in any way soften the harshest effects of the removals, we forbore to make any resort to the press, and any suggestions of publicity for our efforts were firmly suppressed in case it should harden the Government's attitudes.

It was only on 27 January 1968, two days before the first removals, when it was obvious that our efforts to negotiate had wholly failed, that we released any word to the press. The Minister had refused to receive a delegation from the committee, and had proposed himself fully satisfied with the arrangements being made by his local officials for the move. Mr Botha had even reprimanded Archbishop Hurley for bringing God into the affair!

Meanwhile, officials of the B.A.D. had given conflicting assurances to the committee. The Bantu Affairs Commissioner of Dundee assured us that the removal would be nothing like one which had taken place earlier, at Mendlo, where the people had been left in the veld with nothing but tents.

The Commissioner informed us of his plan to put all the Catholics from his district, and some from another district even, into one area in the new settlement. He seemed to visualize a Catholicstan within the Bantustan. Whether the people wanted this, or whether the Church did, was of no concern to him. He

5

had decided that this was best for all of us; evidently he thought he was doing us a favour.

We had insisted throughout the negotiations with the Government that we were acting on behalf of all the people involved and not just those from Missions. But the only result of our efforts was that the schedule of removals was changed to start with Meran, instead of the Maria Ratschitz Mission. Meran was originally fifth on the list, so the people there had presumed that their turn would not come until the middle of 1968 at the earliest.

But on Friday, 26 January, the schoolchildren were ordered to tell their parents that the lorries would be arriving on Monday, 29 January, to take them to Limehill.

Despite the Commissioner's promises, there was very little sign of preparations at Limehill. I visited it regularly and all I saw were a few boreholes being drilled and the school going up very slowly.

From this point we knew we could not influence the Government's way of carrying out its removals, or deflect them from their policy. But we could at least penetrate the cloak of secrecy which had prevented the White public seeing the truth of what was being done under this policy in their interest and legalized by their votes. So Limehill became widely publicized and one of the best documented resettlement camps in the country.

The official estimate of the number of people removed in this single district was 12,800. About 1,200 of them were from Meran, the first place to be cleared.

Early in the morning on 29 January, ten priests arrived at Meran, and waited with the people for the lorries to come. There was no sign of any activity; everyone was waiting, except for one man who was desultorily dismantling a fence.

Later the first lorries arrived, together with officials, including Special Branch men who stood all morning watching us from across the road. One of the Special Branch photographed us, shooting professionally from the hip. We priests refrained from helping the people to strip their houses and load their belongings, lest it be construed as implying our agreement with the removal.

The people were aware of why we had come and they brought us umbrellas to shield us from the sweltering sun.

The people seemed passive, though some let their anger show, especially when the Bantu Commissioner failed to arrive for a meeting which he had promised to attend. But everyone went docilely. Uniformed police appeared on the scene only to tell the priests and the press that it was illegal to take photographs because we were 'making contact with the people' – although we were on a public road in what was being forcibly proved to be a White area!

The first lorries with families left at about 11 a.m., managing to look cheerful and calling 'Sikhulekele' – 'pray for us'. Later, when Archbishop Hurley had arrived, we drove to Limehill, twenty miles away. We found the first arrivals sitting in the bare veld, surrounded by their belongings, lost and still bewildered. There was a water tank a little distance away and a pile of folded tents; these people had never erected a tent in their lives. There was nothing else.

On that first evening there was a heavy rainfall. Many of the tents were swamped, as the people knew nothing about the need for drainage trenches around the tents. Instead they piled earth around the tents, which made them insufferably hot during the day and did not keep the water out.

A few days later, in the House of Assembly, the Minister of B.A.D., Mr M. C. Botha, insulted the priests who were present at Meran with typical heavy humour; he referred to us 'in their long black and white dresses' (much amusement on the Government benches) and said 'priests had rummaged around among the maidservants'.[1] He went on to describe our activities as 'a pathetic example of how white villains' (*booswigte* was the Afrikaans word he chose) 'can come from outside to start all sorts of incitement amongst the Bantu'. The Minister insisted that the removals were voluntary and had been effected humanely and 'exceptionally well'. He had sent his personal representative, Mr Froneman, M.P., to Limehill and he had met no difficulty with the Africans there.

It is interesting to note how the Government's official news

1. Report in the *Rand Daily Mail*, 8 February 1968.

media described Limehill, reacting to the revelations in the *Rand Daily Mail*. On 12 February the South African Broadcasting Corporation quoted a South African Press Association representative as saying, 'The residents of Meran were told in August last year that the first of them should be ready to move on 29 January. ... The B.A.D. was erecting houses so quickly that in a few days there would be no need for tents ... sufficient communal toilets were provided from the first day ... none had to walk more than a quarter of a mile to purchase groceries and fresh vegetables from temporary shops ... no pupil had had cause to miss a day at school and a ten-roomed school was nearly completed.'

All these statements were contradicted the next day in the House of Assembly by Mr Blaar Coetzee, the Deputy Minister of B.A.D., in reply to questions. He said that the Africans were expected to build their own houses and latrines – no sanitary arrangements were made before the removal; the Department made no provision for the people to purchase bread, meat, milk and vegetables, but there was a general dealer two miles away and another five miles away.

The 'ten-roomed school' was in fact seven miles away and not intended for people at Limehill. When people were moved into the area of the school almost a year later it was still not completed. After a week, however, some tents were set up at Limehill for the school. Later a more permanent school was built.

At Meran the people had been tenants on three African-owned farms. They had lived at Meran for many years and were a well-established community. Their houses were neat mud-and-thatch, spaced well apart. Most of them kept cattle and planted mealies (maize) and a few vegetables. Some of the men worked in the town of Wasbank, about three miles away, and many of the women did occasional work there.

The Maria Ratschitz Mission was generally regarded by local farmers as having been one of the best farms in the district, but it was run down through over-grazing and bad farming methods. There were just over a hundred families, almost all with very neat houses, some with very good brick ones. Between them they had the use of about 6,000 acres; the Mission itself farmed very little but some was leased out. The houses were spread over several hundred acres and most families had their cattle kraal adjoining the house, according to custom, and cultivated the land near their house.

There was a higher primary school at the Mission and until the end of 1965, when it was closed by the Church, a secondary school as well. Each family paid, in theory, R20[1] a year which covered rent and Church dues. (It has been claimed in the Afrikaner press and elsewhere that we objected to the move because it would lose us income. In fact it was more profitable for us. The amount paid in rent did not cover the cost of running the school and we could have leased the whole farm for something like R10,000 a year.)

In 1964, in an attempt to rehabilitate the land and to give the people more return, the farm was incorporated in a cooperative scheme called Church Agricultural Projects and a manager was appointed.

When they were moved away many of the people were able to leave their cattle as their share in the cooperative and so receive a share in the profits. If this scheme had been given time to develop with the people it would have been possible for at least some of them to have earned their living entirely there; as it was, almost all of them were migrant workers. But it was certainly a reasonably prosperous community and it was exceptional to see a case of malnutrition.

At Limehill they were allocated for each family a tiny plot, fifty yards square. No livestock, except chickens, are allowed. There is no land for ploughing. The women have lost their income from working in Wasbank as the bus-fare costs more than they could earn. They have neither shops nor any medical services. Even elementary sanitation is lacking. Most of the men have to work in Johannesburg or Durban, several hundred miles away, so the building of the new houses had to be left to the women and children in many cases. Some people remained huddled in tents for months.

The 1,200 people moved from Meran were followed by people from other 'Black spots' in the Dundee district. The residents of

1. The South African unit of currency is the Rand which is divided into 100 cents. The Rand is equivalent to £0.58 sterling.

Alva and Amakhasi Roman Catholic Missions were put into the promised 'Catholicstan' at Uitval, about two miles from Limehill. Amakhasi was actually located within the designated 'Bantu area' and only two miles away from Uitval, but the people still had to move because their portion had not been 'planned' as a residential area. The Mission farm at Alva bordered the African Reserve on one side but the boundary, we were officially informed, could not possibly be adjusted slightly to include it in the Reserve.

Our own people from Maria Ratschitz Mission were duly moved to Limehill – and not to the Catholicstan. In August 1968 about five hundred families were moved from Boschhoek, the tribally owned farm adjoining Maria Ratschitz Mission, to a farm called Vergelegen, about three miles from Limehill. The people of the Kunene tribe had bought this 8,500-acre farm, which was good farming land with plentiful water and grazing, in 1870 and the community was four thousand strong. Officially they moved voluntarily, even though they had submitted a petition to the Bantu Commissioner asking to be allowed to remain at Boschhoek. Some of them were threatened with imprisonment if they continued to oppose the removal. As at Limehill very little preparation was made for their arrival. They complained at the type of land they had in the new place, the shortage of water and its bad taste. For five months the water was kept in uncovered tanks, some distance from the settlement, and they were warned to boil it before drinking. I saw women and children scooping water from holes in a river bed rather than drink water from the tanks.

As the months went by more and more people were moved into Limehill and the other settlements. More and more tents appeared. There were more complaints about the shortage of water for building, the difficulty of obtaining building materials and the hardship of living.

Limehill rapidly took on the appearance of a slum and acquired the nickname 'mshayazafe' – 'beat him until he dies'. The Deputy Minister of B.A.D. admitted in the House of Assembly on 14 March 1969 that there were still seventy-six families living in tents in the Limehill complex.

Two years later Limehill is still a depressing place to visit. One of the greatest difficulties is the simple fact that the people are rural people who lived by farming and now they have to adapt to a quasi-urban way of life. But there is no source of income and none of the amenities of a proper town. There is no sign of the provision of any local employment and a Government statement on 14 May 1968 said that it is not proposed to establish any 'border industry' in the area. This is not surprising, since Limehill is twenty miles from the nearest railhead, town and electricity supply and there is a chronic, perennial shortage of water.

The Limehill removals – unlike most – received wide publicity in the English language press in South Africa, and this elicited aid in the form of both money and materials. Then, after a few weeks, Limehill lost its news value. But it came back into the news even more in November 1968 when it was reported that typhoid had broken out in the area.

Officials of the State Health Department denied that there was any serious outbreak of the disease. The Regional Director of State Health, Dr Hooey, said that to his knowledge there had not been a single case of typhoid.[1] Yet I had seen the carbon copy of an official notification of a case of typhoid which had been sent to the magistrate at Dundee on 14 November. A spokesman for the Health Department told the *Rand Daily Mail* on 5 December that there had been no deaths from gastro-enteritis. Yet thirty-three people had died in the preceding month. No action was taken by the State health authorities for two weeks, despite reports of people dying in alarming numbers.

Churchmen, politicians and others called for an inquiry into the health situation. But the Minister of Health, Dr C. de Wet, denied that there had been any serious outbreak of the disease and said that the total number of deaths in the area was only nineteen, a normal figure for a population of 6,000.[2] I photographed the headstones of some sixty new graves in the five cemeteries of the Limehill complex and I learned that there were at least six others buried (illegally) outside the cemeteries.

1. *Rand Daily Mail*, 29 November 1968.
2. ibid., 11 December 1968.

Most of these people – they were mainly children – had died between October and December. Later – on 7 February 1969 – the Minister of B.A.D. admitted in the House of Assembly that there had been seventy-three deaths.

Eventually sixteen cases of typhoid were confirmed, of which one died, in the single area of Uitval, where there were only about seventy families. One family had four children ill at the same time; another had all their five children ill. Throughout November and December the press published reports of deaths in the area. But, apart from innoculating the people of Uitval alone, there was little activity by the State health authorities. Most of those who died, and hundreds of others who were ill, had the same symptoms: diarrhoea, vomiting and high fever. Almost every house had at least one sick child; in one family two children died in the same week. The people said 'a plague has struck us' and many could be seen wearing charms to ward off this unknown evil.

I accompanied Father Nelson on some of his visits to the sick and saw the emaciated, fevered children and their heart-broken parents. Yet officially there was no cause for alarm or action. The most active officials were the Special Branch, harassing and questioning Father Nelson and others keeping a continuous watch on the resettlement complex. The publicity about the sickness and deaths had one good result: a great deal of material help was given. A Christmas-time appeal in Johannesburg initiated by students of the University of the Witwatersrand brought in about seven tons of food, clothing and medical supplies. A group of volunteers left Johannesburg on 27 December and spent ten days in the resettlement area, distributing the food and clothing and helping to run a clinic; we were joined by people from Maritzburg, Durban and even further afield. By that time the number of deaths was dropping, but there was still enough sickness to constitute an epidemic. A professional assessment of the health situation by doctors who went from Johannesburg to staff the clinic at the Catholic Mission was published in the *Rand Daily Mail* on 31 January 1969.[1]

It would need a whole book to tell the Limehill story adequa-

1. See Appendix 3.

tely; to describe all the efforts by the people themselves and by others who either out of conviction or out of charity worked on their behalf to prevent the removal; to explain all the Government's actions and statements and set beside these statements the truth as I saw it. But perhaps enough has been said to show what people are subjected to in South Africa today for the sake of a political ideology. These people were moved because it had been decided that the land on which they had lived for generations was for Whites only.

On the old Mission farms, both the owners and the African tenants were content with the existing arrangement; but there was no stay of execution for them. They were not being moved from slums or insanitary conditions. They were moved to tidy the map, to separate them from contact with Whites, to lose them in the remotest, poorest land set aside for Africans. This is policy, carried through regardless of African wishes, the disruption of their lives, the ending of their livelihood and the inevitable suffering that ensues.

The question which kept occurring to me was: what happens to the hundreds of thousands of Africans who are moved to places far away from the public eye? One of the Nationalist Members of Parliament who visited Limehill remarked that he could not see what all the fuss was about as there were people living in far worse conditions than at Limehill. After visiting resettlement villages throughout the country, I can second that statement and add that it is the Government which has created such places.

When the conditions at Limehill became common knowledge I hoped that some official organization of a Christian character would back my plan to visit and report on African resettlement schemes throughout the country. But after months of trying I found that such support was not forthcoming, for financial or other reasons. My own immediate superior gave me permission to devote my time to the project and pledged his support. Other friends offered material and moral support. As a result of my experience of and involvement in Limehill, I considered the question so urgent that it had to be pursued if only privately, and therefore not so efficiently or thoroughly as it could have been had it had the backing of an organization of some standing and resources.

I started my tour at the beginning of March 1969 and in the course of the following six months covered 24,000 miles, criss-crossing the country in search of resettlement schemes. Having completed my tour, I revisited some of the settlements, for example Morsgat and Kuruman, on a number of occasions and I have followed up information or rumours of new settlements in all parts of the country. It could hardly be called an enjoyable trip, going from one place of misery to another. And one of the most distressing features was the ignorance, apathy, fear and suspicion of so many of the White people to whom I spoke. Often, the White clergy, for example, were not even aware of the existence of resettlement villages within their parish; others knew about them but saw nothing wrong. Most of the Whites with whom I came into contact were clergymen. I am deeply indebted to some of them for their hospitality (though some took a little time to overcome their suspicion about what I was doing and on whose authority). A few of them were staunch Government supporters and gave no help at all, but instead tried to get rid of me as soon as possible. One, I have good reason to suspect, reported my presence to the police; he certainly misled me with deliberate lies. But the majority were too frightened to offer any criticism of the Government's plans and actions. They fear that if they say or do anything they will be refused permission to continue their Church work within the Reserves and perhaps in the whole country, and that their schools, hospitals and other institutions might suffer. So, following rather dubious historical precedents, they prefer to remain silent and work within the system.

The physical conditions in which so many people were living were pitiful enough, but even more distressing was the mental state to which they have been reduced. They have resigned themselves, at least on the surface, to accepting whatever the White man does to them. There are very few Whites in South Africa who have not in one way or another contributed to this emasculation of the African people. There are many who, while being opposed to the Government, seem quite content to take advantage of the benefits accruing to Whites from the practice of apartheid.

But there were some redeeming features on my grim trip, dismally different though it was from the sunny South Africa safaris offered to tourists: being accepted and trusted by the people in the various settlements; the spirit and dignity of the men at Babanango; the courage of a few men at Morajo; in general, the absence of bitterness against White men as such – though there is certainly plenty of resentment and bitterness about the whole social situation, especially among the better educated and more articulate.

Some touching encounters too: being pressed to accept a few dried-up sticks of sugar-cane from a very old and almost destitute lady at Klipplatdrift, who said that she had nothing else to offer but wanted to show her appreciation of my visit; and the gift from a more prosperous person of a 50-lb. bag of sugar.

But, above all, there were frustrating moments: 'There is a resettlement village near here but everything is fine. We get on very well with the officials.' 'Oh yes, there has been a lot of resettlement around here, but I don't know exactly where.' 'I have heard, but I am not too sure of the facts.'

So it has come about that for the past three years I have been deeply involved with the resettlement areas, and for the last thirty months I have devoted all my time, first with Limehill, and since March 1969 with this project, to visiting resettlement areas and trying to make people aware of this evil. I make no apology for the fact that at a time when all the major Churches are complaining about the shortage of priests, a priest should devote his time to such work. It was only as a priest that I became fully aware of the sufferings and needs of these people, and only a priest has entrée to the resettlement areas without a special permit. Further, the whole question of removal is one of the major problems in South Africa today and the Churches accept, at least in theory, that they have an obligation to try to improve social conditions where there is need. If these people feel that their Churches have abandoned them (and some, with good reason, are already beginning to feel this), then what right have the Churches to expect any place in the lives of the people in the 'homelands'?

Originally it was planned to do an in-depth sociological investigation of the various forms of resettlement, under the direction of qualified sociologists and with trained field-workers. But this plan had to be abandoned. Apart from the great difficulty of obtaining the services of qualified personnel, one of the conditions for permission being given for research workers to enter these areas is that all data must be submitted to the Department before publication. This would have at least delayed publication, if not prevented it altogether, judging by the vehement official denials of reports on Limehill and other settlements. Nevertheless, the B.A.D. was approached for permission for African research workers to conduct a survey in some of the resettlement areas, but this was refused.

Therefore, I am simply setting out as a personal record the information I have collected and what I have seen and heard. This account does not make any claim to be a scientific study; nor does it claim to be complete. I did not approach any officials of the Department of B.A.D., apart from one or two local superintendents; I did not see that this would serve any useful purpose, as the official view is easily ascertainable from public statements and other Government spokesmen. For the rest, I think the facts and the opinions of the people involved speak for themselves and I have confined myself to the minimum of comment.

I have not set out to write a critique of the policy of apartheid or separate development as it is labelled these days. This book is quite simply a description of how apartheid works in practice. It is not the whole story by any means; it does not venture to treat the subjects of farm labour camps, prisons, the treatment of African workers, the discrimination of the law, police violence, the security measures, the deprivation of fundamental human rights, the denial of equal education, the conditions in the urban African ghettoes, the migrant labour system, the climate of hostility and contempt which Africans meet in the White world. All these aspects of South African society and apartheid have been illustrated by both Black and White writers. I hope my book will help to complete the picture, grotesque and tragic as it is, by showing what has been happening to the silent thousands, whole communities, who have been removed from sight.

The response of White people in South Africa to the reports in the *Rand Daily Mail* of Limehill and of starvation in the Tswana 'homelands' at Kuruman was some sign of an awakening conscience. Many were horrified and showed that once they were made aware of what was happening they were sufficiently concerned to give material aid. This is already something, and let us hope that a fuller awareness, if this book can get through to more people, will move them further. But giving can also be too little. Many would agree that the migratory labour system, repeatedly condemned by various Churches and leaders of all communities, is wrong. But there seem to be very few Whites who draw the obvious conclusion from this: that there must be something inherently wrong with a social system under which these atrocities can take place.

The poverty, suffering and broken families caused by the resettlement schemes are not accidental, they are an inevitable consequence of the policy of separate development. They are allowed to happen because they are part of the price of White wealth. There are few, if any, Whites in South Africa who do not benefit from this wealth, and who do not share in the responsibility for the steps taken to ensure it. We cannot absolve ourselves from guilt simply by handing out relief or calling on the Government to improve the preparations for moving people.

The Government is responsible for applying apartheid. But the rest of us are also responsible for perpetuating a social climate in which such things can happen with no effective opposition. There would be far greater opposition if White people were subjected to a fraction of the indignities which Africans suffer daily. If we are used to seeing Africans living in hovels in our back gardens, cooped up in a location, or being treated as medieval serfs on White farms, then we will not be too horrified when we see them dumped in the veld and left to fend for themselves. We are liable to become so conditioned by our social environment that we just do not think of applying the same standards for Africans as for Whites. Sadly this was illustrated by the Roman

Catholic Bishop of Queenstown, who considered a tiny one-roomed hut at Sada to be quite adequate for an African family.

The resettlement camps are sometimes at places whose names reveal with unconscious irony the bitterness of the experience for those who have to live there. To read the grim litany of these names – Limehill, Morsgat (messhole), Weenen (place of weeping) and Stinkwater – is to share something of the spirit of the places. Mr M. C. Botha explained that these names were 'unfortunate'. 'They are nearly all the names of old farms where the settlements are being carried out,' he said. Mr Botha also assured us on the same occasion: 'The Bantu people like being moved. ... The Bantu people like the places where they are being resettled.'[1] Can the Minister really believe this? Of course, the people are careful not to complain to Government officials. Nobody who is aware of this situation should expect them to let themselves be listed as 'troublemakers'. Some say there is simply no point in complaining to Government officials, others admit that they are frightened to criticize.

Time and time again on my tour I was told: 'We are suffering.' 'We have been thrown away.' 'We have nothing.' 'But what can we do?' 'We are only Africans, there is no one to hear us.'

1. *Star*, 21 November 1969.

2. Why Removals?

Traditional Nationalist Party doctrine was simple and clearcut, namely, to achieve total social and political separation between the White and non-White peoples of South Africa. The Whites were the master race, and the Afrikaner Volk were divinely chosen to lead the way to a permanently entrenched racially pure White state.

This vertical form of apartheid is easier to understand than the newer, more subtle, developments of policy under Dr Verwoerd, who set out to show that the Africans could be kept apart economically and territorially as well. Changes in the economic and international environment demonstrated that the policy could not be maintained simply by continuing to ignore not only the rights but even the existence of Africans. The White economy depended on the availability of plenty of cheap African labour. Whites were not prepared to do heavy manual work or forgo their African servants and their wealth. Dr Verwoerd's sophisticated embellishments of Afrikaner doctrine were formulated as separate development, based on:

(1) African self-development in separate client-states, the Bantu 'homelands' or Bantustans, as they have been labelled.

(2) The establishment of White industries on the borders of the Bantustans to draw labour from them.

(3) The clearance of all the smaller African residential areas ('Black spots') within the White areas and the consolidation of African populations in the Bantustans.

(4) The reduction of the numbers of Africans living in (White) urban areas.

(5) Complete segregation – in all possible aspects – of White

19

and non-White wherever non-Whites are still required in White areas.

One of the comforting beliefs held by many people who recognize the fundamental moral wrong underlying the policy of apartheid is that the whole programme of the Nationalist Party is contrary to the impersonal forces at work in the economy and the society, such as the need for a growing labour force and market for industrial goods, and that the policy is therefore a dead letter. It is believed that after a period of repression, as we are undergoing today, with the enactment of Draconian laws, the Terrorism Act, the Sabotage Act and the rising terror of arrests and imprisonment of Africans for pass offences (this is known by another master-stroke of double-think as 'petty' apartheid), the Nationalist Party and the White electorate will be caught up by the tide of these impersonal forces and will gracefully bow to them. In this book I will describe how the South African Government is pressing ahead with the implementation of apartheid, in spite of any impersonal forces. Such forces ultimately prove to be fictions, and while it is undoubtedly true that economic needs obstruct and hamper the application of apartheid doctrines, the determination and ruthlessness with which removals of Africans are carried out prove that the Government has the power largely to shape the economic and social forces in the country to its own ends.

The Government has in fact made it clear that economic considerations are subservient to political and ideological ones. For example, Mr Viljoen, the Deputy Minister of Labour, said in February 1970: 'Important as the growth rate may be it is not the most important factor. It does not weigh up against the position of the White worker. It can be said that such an outlook is contrary to the economic laws but it should be understood that this is the policy of the Nationalist Party.' And there is ample evidence of the Government using its power to prevent economic pressures from bringing about any significant change in the apartheid system.

The resettlement schemes with which we are dealing here have their origin in two of the requirements of the Government's policy, the clearance of 'Black spots' and the reduction of the urban African population.

The clearance of the 'Black spots' might be called the completion of the process of White takeover and settlement in South Africa:

The policy of the present Government is to consolidate as far as possible all Bantu land into consolidated blocks, i.e. by excising smaller scattered areas out of scheduled or released areas and giving compensatory land of equal value contiguous to the larger Bantu blocks. ... When all these 'Black spots' and isolated scheduled and released areas are once removed, the chess board pattern of Bantu Areas and White Areas in South Africa will also to a great extent be eliminated.[1]

A glance at the first map at the end of this book shows how much sorting out of land is needed to eliminate the chess board pattern. When the whole process is finished, Africans, numbering fifteen million at the last census, will have 13·7 per cent of the land surface. Whites, numbering about three and a half million, will have 86·3 per cent. In the meantime, Africans do not have even as much as their promised 13·7 per cent; what they have is in large degree economically marginal land – too mountainous, or too dry, or too remote from markets and means of transport to be productive. As for the compensatory land being of equal value, the Government has never consulted African views on this. If they were prepared to listen to the people after they had been moved, they would have heard that the places where they have been resettled are all too frequently lacking in water, too far from towns or main roads, out of reach of hospitals or clinics, or unsuitable for cultivation. In short, the land is rarely of equal value.

It is accepted Government policy that the Bantus are only temporarily resident in the European areas of the Republic, for as long as they offer their labour there. As soon as they become, for some reason or another, no longer fit for work or superfluous in the labour market, they are expected to return to their country of origin or the

1. Address by Mr G. F. van L. Froneman, M.P., Deputy Chairman of the Bantu Affairs Commission, to the Institute of Citizenship, Cape Town, on 30 May 1968.

territory of their national unit where they fit in ethnically if they were not born and bred in the homeland. . . . It must be stressed here that no stone is to be left unturned to achieve the settlement in the homelands of non-productive Bantu at present residing in the European areas.[1]

For those who live and work in the White towns (albeit they live in segregated satellite townships) this policy is no mere change of home – it is a removal from the urban life which many of them have known for generations to a totally different environment. The African dormitory townships outside the cities are being transferred from teeming, slummy but still somehow living communities to giant barracks for regiments of industrial serfs.

Apologists of the Nationalist Government are fond of explaining their racialist policies as a solution to the allegedly special and unique South African problem of populations which cannot mix or share a polity. But in fact these Government policies are not purely Nationalist Party policies, and do not represent a radical change from the past. If they were, there would be grounds for hoping that they would wither away when the implications became clear.

The real horror of the South African situation is that the present Government's policies are acting out the same sick, violent drama as those of their ancestors. The South African trap is made of attitudes which were formed in the old seventeenth- and eighteenth-century Cape Colony, when the original Hottentot inhabitants were either pressed into bondage or liquidated. The way of life evolved from the mixture of slave-owning and primitive Calvinism has been modified only in outward form in the last two centuries; the lot of African workers today has been described as 'paid slavery'. The banning of the institution of slavery by the metropolitan power in the 1830s was met by the Afrikaner Treks into the interior, away from the jurisdiction of the overseas government. The Afrikaner colonists established their republics, taking over vast areas of land and suppressing African resistance by the destruction of the Africans' herds of cattle and

1. The Secretary for Bantu Administration and Development's General Circular No. 25, 1967.

crops. English settlers and the colonial powers protected the Boers indirectly by containing and finally crushing the main concentration of African resistance on the Eastern Cape frontier and in Natal.

The economic revolution created by diamond and gold finds in the late nineteenth century and the political revolution in the wake of the Boer War were incidents between groups of White men. They did not fundamentally alter the relationships of White and Black, though they ended forever any possibility of keeping the White and Black economies separate. The interlude during which South Africa was a dominion of the British Empire and Commonwealth could have been a period in which irreversible changes were made; but the weakness of the liberal, internationalist group in the coalition of White interests which ruled ensured that nothing vital changed. All that was new was hope: African political and trade union movements and White opposition groups with various political sympathies were born. But the law still discriminated against Africans in every sphere, and rigid caste barriers kept them apart from the society and economic opportunities of the Whites. When the Nationalists were elected into office in 1948 there was no counter-revolution; merely a strengthening of the will to maintain the old way of life. Today, continuing the unbroken custom of the country, the normal form of address by an African to a White man is 'Master' or 'Baas'.

Twenty-six years before the Nationalist Party came to power, in 1922 Stallard Commission had recommended that an African should only be allowed to enter the urban areas, which are essentially the White man's creation, when he is willing to enter and minister to the needs of the White man, and should depart therefrom when he ceases to minister.

From this recommendation the basic system of 'influx control' and the removal of surplus persons in White urban areas was established, with the passing of the Natives (Urban Areas) Act of 1923. From that date on, the construction of the elaborate battery of regulations and prohibitions circumscribing African life and removing their basic rights has been continuous, reflecting the increasing complexity in the economic and social interaction of White and Black communities since the nineteenth century.

In 1937 the Native Laws Amendment Act limited the right of Africans to acquire property and provided that all institutions serving Africans – churches, schools, etc. – must be in African locations.

The Bantu Authorities Act of 1951 created a pyramid of purely tribal councils in the 'homelands', on which Africans appointed by the Government would serve. There is provision for some posts to be elective. This Act represented the final separation of all Africans from the White political institutions and processes of the country.

The Natives (Abolition of Passes and Coordination of Documents) Act of 1952 required all Africans to carry at all times reference books (passes) containing proof of employment and permission to be in an urban area.

The Native Laws Amendment Act of 1952 extended the system of influx control to women as well as men, and established labour bureaux in the African 'homelands' to control the movement of work-seekers.

The Native Trust and Land Amendment Act of 1954 was designed to limit and register annually all African 'labour tenants' and 'squatters' on White farms. Labour tenants are Africans who occupy parts of White farms for which the rent is paid by working for the farmer for a part of the year varying from three to nine months. Squatters are Africans who live on part of a White farm in return for a share of the produce they raise, or, occasionally, for a cash rental. The Act removed a previously binding obligation on the Government to find alternative land for squatters or labour tenants who were displaced.

The Native (Urban Areas) Amendment Act of 1956 enabled urban authorities to order Africans out if their presence was considered detrimental to peace and order; and the Native (Prohibition of Interdicts) Act of 1956 provided that no court may issue an interdict to suspend the execution of a removal order. This Act has been applied to removals of Africans from urban areas, and to those ordered to leave White rural areas.

The Native Labour (Settlement of Disputes) Act of 1953 redefined the term 'employee' in the Industrial Conciliation Act to exclude all Africans, prevented White unions from having African members and prohibited strikes by Africans. African trade unions were denied the right to registration. The 1956 amendment to the Industrial Conciliation Act made provision for the reservation of specified categories of work for specified racial groups.

The Physical Planning and Utilisation of Resources Act of 1967 empowered the Minister of Planning to control the use to which all resources, including labour, may be put. All employers must apply for permits for each African employee. The Minister is also enabled, after declaring a White rural area 'controlled', to de-register labour-tenants and squatters and enforce full-time labour practices on White farms.

There are many other Acts regulating African conditions, but the above list should suffice to show how the removals policy is inextricably bound up with the treatment of Africans in every sphere of the South African system – in ensuring White economic supremacy and political domination, in job reservation and en-suring the control of African labour, in maintaining 'law and order'.

The Minister of B.A.D., Mr M. C. Botha, told parliament in a speech describing what he called the Government's 'Dynamic Third Decade': 'Among the most striking successes we as a National Party have on our record book, I mention the tightening-up of influx control and the organizing of our countrywide system of labour bureaux.' He defined the task for the 1970s as 'the very exacting one of further checking and re-ducing the influx of Bantu to the White areas, and to establish in their own homeland those Bantu who are in the White area illegally and to no purpose'.

The objective of Government policy is to return 5 per cent of the African population from the White areas to the 'homelands' every year. Demography and the demands of the economy frus-trate the total removal of African workers. But the policy is satisfied, through another accepted charade of double-think, with something less than the clearing-out of all Africans to the 'home-lands'. Their families are removed and the workers are turned into migrant workers. People are banished to new townships in the 'homelands', from where they must seek work through the labour bureaux. The work is still done by Africans. But the policy of reversing the influx of Africans into White areas has been upheld.

Sometimes, the trick is even simpler. Where there is an African Reserve within daily travelling distance from a White town, the whole African location is removed to the Reserve. The people still travel every day to work in the town, with the added burden of extra bus-fares, but the statistics for the reversal of African influx look impressive. For statistical purposes the important thing is that they no longer sleep in a White area; the policy is being implemented. The added inconvenience and expense to the people is of no concern to the Government; it is the policy, not the people, which matters.

The enforced splitting-up of families is probably the most evil of all the effects of the removals. Yet this is central to the policy. Mr G. F. van L. Froneman, Deputy Chairman of the Bantu Affairs Commission, said in the House of Assembly on 6 February 1968: 'We are trying to introduce the migratory labour pattern as far as possible in every sphere, that is in fact the entire basis of our policy as far as the White economy is concerned.' Thus the African worker is deprived of his right to live with his wife and family, except for one month in each thirteen. This is happening in a professedly Christian country which has a public holiday to celebrate Family Day. The migratory labour system has been condemned by all the Churches in South Africa, including even the Dutch Reformed Church, since they can see the terrible effects the system has on both the physical and moral existence of the people. But it is obvious that it is no temporary expedient.[1] It was accepted practice from the earliest mining and industrial undertakings in South Africa and it is being extended all the time. The pattern is the same throughout the country; a man who has been working in a town and living with his family in an urban location is 'endorsed out' to the 'homelands', leaves his family there and then returns to work in the town. Many of

1. Mr Blaar Coetzee reiterated in the House of Assembly on 4 February 1971 that all African labour in the White areas should be there only as migrants. He added that husbands and wives should be together 'as often as possible'.

the so-called 'towns' in the African Reserves and virtually all the rural settlements are simply dumping grounds for old people, women and children whose labour is not needed for the White economy. Apart from the people in a few African 'towns' in the homelands which are still comparatively near a White urban area or border industry and are in effect the workers' locations for those areas, I have not met one man who, after being endorsed out of an urban area, has been able to settle in the 'homelands' and earn a living there.

The women with children must depend on support from husbands working in the towns. But in practice, wage rates are too low to support the husband in the White town as well as the family in the Bantustan. Also, the men find other women as wife-substitutes, and the support dries up. The wife may then be forced to seek work in a White area herself, leaving the already fatherless children with foster parents, who will very often be near destitute themselves. If she cannot get work, the wife may resort to prostitution or illicit brewing to support the family. Children grow up with little or no family life or adult support or care. No wonder the Dutch Reformed Church, which preaches the principles of separate development, has described migrant labour in these words: 'A cancer which so rages in the lives of the African population must necessarily affect the whole social and religious life of all the population groups in our fatherland. As a result of the laws of God, the Whites will not be untouched by the disease that is destroying the moral life of the Africans.'

The central importance of migrant labour in the apartheid scheme of things is demonstrated again by the latest development of policy, the Bantu Citizenship Act of 1970. At a stroke, this Act has made every African a citizen of one of the 'homelands' where he may exercise his civil and political rights. However, most Africans have to work in White South Africa, and so the rights they are granted are purely theoretical. Dr P. Koornhof, Deputy Minister of B.A.D., explained:

I am afraid to say that the ... African males from the homelands have no rights whatsoever in South Africa. Their rights are in their own homelands, and they are in South Africa only to sell their labour.

To establish the elaborate legal fiction of the 'homelands' the Government has had to devise historical doctrines about the African population. The 'homelands' are supposed to represent distinct territories for separate 'nations'. Officially, therefore, segregation in South Africa is not based on race but on nationalities.

The Bantu are in fact divided by language, culture and tradition into several peoples or nations, namely, the Xhosas of the Transkei, and the Ciskei, the Zulus of Zululand and Natal, the Swazis of Swaziland ... the Pedi of Sekhukhuneland and neighbourhood, the Venda of the Soutspansburg, the Shangaans of the Transvaal lowveld, the Tswana of Botswana ... the South Sotho of Lesotho. ... Fortunately for each of these people or nations, history left them within the borders of the Republic large tracts of land which serve as their homelands ... the Government's policy is, therefore, not a policy of discrimination on the ground of race or colour, but a policy of differentiation on the ground of nationhood of different nations, granting to each self-determination within the borders of their homelands – hence the policy of separate development.[1]

This doctrine must ignore the much vaster tracts of valuable land now occupied by Whites, which are dotted with the graves and remains of settlements of these peoples; it must ignore the fact that the different peoples shared certain territories at certain times and intermingled; that the Swazi, Zulu and Xhosa are all Nguni peoples with variations of the same language and essentially the same culture and social structure; that the Pedi, Tswana and Sotho form another very similar and interacting population; and that there were no rigid frontiers or barriers to cooperation or intercourse between these people. The doctrine also ignores the existence, which has been the focus of much internal division in South Africa, of two White nations defined by language, culture and traditions; and it has no consistent explanation for the presence of two million or more Coloured (Eurafrican) people and Asians. Not only is the ethnic sorting-out, contrived to force out African families and deny them any rights in White South Africa, a fiction, but the 'large tracts of

1. Address by Mr G. F. van L. Froneman to the Institute of Citizenship, Cape Town, on 30 May 1968.

land' which remain as their 'homelands' are another startling piece of double-think.

The 'separate nations' theory is also used to justify Dr Verwoerd's Bantu Education system. Since 1953 African education has been planned specifically 'to play its essential part in the general advancement of the Bantu people' as an official statement puts it. This means that the English language is forbidden as a medium of instruction; each 'nation's' school must use the tribal language. The common curriculum which African schools previously shared with White schools has been abandoned. African schools now ignore history, geography and most of the sciences and teach instead manual work, gardening and housework. Most African children can expect to get a place in a school, though for only a half-day shift, and 70 per cent of them never get beyond the fourth year of primary schooling. Secondary school enrolments are a mere 4 per cent of the total. Out of more than 2·5 million children at school only 869 matriculated in 1969. The tribal colleges, which have replaced African places at South African universities, turn out graduates in subjects which fit the needs of the Bantustans, including diplomas in commerce, teaching Bantu languages and improved husbandry. The effect of Bantu education is seen above all in the changes in expenditure on White and Black pupils. In 1953 the cost of White education, per capita, was £50 and the cost of Black education was £9. Ten years later, per capita expenditure on Whites had risen to £70, but for Blacks it had *dropped* to £6 5s. (R12.63). In 1969 the expenditure was still only R13 per capita, a further drop in real terms; the ratio of state-paid teachers to African pupils changed from 1 : 42 in 1949 to 1 : 72 in 1968.

The sheer disparity in the size of the 'homelands' compared with the size of the African population has already been mentioned. The economic facts are even more disturbing. The present population of the 'homelands' is 6·9 million. Most of these people rely on money sent by workers in the White areas. The rest of the 15 million Africans live, on temporary sufferance or as migrant workers, in the White seven-eighths of the country. The population is expected to more than double in the next thirty years.

The 'homelands' consist of some two hundred scattered areas, lying round the edge of the Republic and leaving a huge white laager in the centre with strategic openings to all sea ports. All the principal known mineral resources, all industry, all cities, all airfields, main roads, power stations, nearly all the most productive and well-watered farming land, lie in the White area. The 'homelands' are typically underdeveloped, overcrowded, soil-eroded and lacking in job opportunities.

The Tomlinson Commission, officially charged with examining the development potential of the Bantustans in 1954, reckoned that, once the additional land known as the Released Areas had been included (which has not yet happened), the African Reserves could support 2,142,000 people. The Commission reported that the number which could be supported could be raised to 7 million if 50,000 new jobs outside farming could be created each year for some thirty years. By 1981, if this happened, it should be possible for 9 million (including 2 million dependants of migrant workers) to live in the Bantustans. This figure was expected to represent 70 per cent of the total African population, but it has proved to be based on a gross underestimate of the actual population growth.

However, instead of the 1,250,000 jobs required by Tomlinson, only about 1,000 have been created inside the 'homelands', and fewer than 50,000 in the border areas (it is Government policy to direct new industry where possible to areas near an African Reserve to draw labour from it). The official figure for African employment in border industries is over 100,000, but this figure includes industries in old-established cities such as Pretoria which happen to have an African Reserve nearby. The border industries in any case contribute nothing to the development of the Bantustans, being White owned and managed.

The Tomlinson figure of employment needs has been confirmed (within a comparable range of figures) recently by Dr P. Smit, head of the Africa Institute's Department of Geography, speaking at the congress of the Association of Geography Education in July 1969. He said that to absorb the natural increase of the population at present in the 'homelands' it would be necessary to provide jobs for 39,000 African men every year until

1980 and at present the border industries are absorbing only 6-7,000 men a year. Other estimates have put the need for new jobs at an even higher figure. At the same congress Dr J. H. Grobler of the Highveld Research Institute estimated that the 'homelands' hardly provided a subsistence level for two and a half million people – less than half the number who have to live there.

Tomlinson gave the average income per head in the 'homelands' as R25·8 per annum (£15). The official figure for 1969 was R22 (£13). Productivity has fallen partly because of the increased overcrowding, and partly because the resources which Tomlinson recommended must be devoted to soil reclamation were never forthcoming. Money has been spent over the years on the 'betterment areas' in the Bantustans, where the land is fenced and parcelled out into supposedly viable farm units. But even these farms produce very low incomes – far less than the R120 per annum (£70) considered by the Tomlinson Commission to be the basic minimum required for a family of five to make a living. The reasons for low incomes are many, but the most intractable is the vicious circle of lack of African buying power, lack of capital and diminishing land resources for the population of the 'homelands'. While the African population as a whole rose by approximately 70 per cent in the twenty years 1950–70, the increase in the Reserves was almost 100 per cent.

One does not have to be an economist, sociologist or specialist of any kind to see that the 'homelands' are not providing economic living standards. This is obvious from the amount of poverty and starvation that I have seen in my tour of the country. During 1969 there has been quite a lot of publicity about the extent and effects of malnutrition. One of the main spokesmen has been John Reid, Professor of Physiology at the University of Natal, who said that there are about one million young African children in South Africa suffering from malnutrition and that the position is likely to grow worse.[1] He has also pointed out that a child who suffers from kwashiorkor (a deficiency disease) never achieves full development of its mental powers.[2] And Professor

1. *Star*, 13 May 1969.
2. ibid., 10 February 1969.

Pat Smythe, after a twelve-year research programme, stated that in certain African groups there has been a general lowering of mentality due to three generations of malnutrition.[1] It seems indisputable that malnutrition in the early years of childhood causes permanent brain damage. The signs of malnutrition – pot bellies, spindly bow-legs, marks and sores on the skin – are easy to recognize and are seen throughout the 'homelands'.

Yet more and more people are being herded into these Reserves in places where they cannot possibly support themselves agriculturally, and where there is no employment. A survey in part of the Zulu 'homeland' for example showed that 91 per cent of the area had 'no soil', that the area is expected to support a population 27 per cent higher than is already estimated to be there, and that it is at present overstocked with cattle to the extent of 212 per cent of its carrying capacity. This situation is quite typical.

However, according to an official statement,[2] 900,000 Africans from White areas have already been removed to these sorts of conditions. Plans for further large-scale removals have been announced – 600,000 people settled in the Eastern Cape Province will be removed to the Transkei and Ciskei. The same process will be applied to the even larger population of Africans in the Witwatersrand complex. According to Mr G. F. van L. Froneman there were 3,807,465 'superfluous' Africans in the White cities and towns in 1969.[3] 200,000 'squatters' and 'labour tenants' are being 'cleared' from White farms. 'Black spots', like Meran, Boschhoek and the Maria Ratschitz Mission, are being ruthlessly cleared as well. Up to the end of 1968, 119 'Black spots' had been 'cleared', involving officially 83,619 people. This left a further 280 'Black spots' to be dealt with – the number of people is unknown.

We have seen that the removals hit people whose families have been living on Mission farms for over a hundred years, people

1. *Star*, 25 November 1969.

2. The statement was made in the House of Assembly on 4 February 1969 by Dr P. G. J. Koornhof, Deputy Minister of Bantu Administration. See Appendix 1, which sets out and discusses the statistics for removals available from official sources.

3. *Rand Daily Mail*, 28 March 1969.

whose forefathers bought the land in all good faith in the last century, and people who live in areas which were officially set aside for African occupation in 1913 and which until recently appeared on official maps as proclaimed African Reserves. The Deputy Minister of Justice, Mr S. Froneman, put the position clearly and starkly: 'The White State has no duty to prepare the homelands for the superfluous Africans because they are actually aliens in the White homelands who only have to be repatriated.' And 'Removal of Africans from the White areas is not dependent on the development of the Bantu homelands, except that housing facilities should be made possible for them.'

The meagre public funds spent on the 'homelands' has not been inconsistent with those principles. The money has gone mainly on making rough roads and essential works for the new townships, on fencing and dams to settle more people on the land, and on administration, including the provision of 'Bantu education' facilities and health facilities. The net effect of this expenditure is not development. It is not used to create viable industries or new jobs or to improve the opportunities for Africans to develop themselves. On the contrary, when the administration of the 'homelands' is seen in relation to the whole removals and resettlement policy, it is plain that it is steadily increasing the impoverishment of millions of people, by overcrowding and reducing their opportunities in the cash economy.

It is impossible to obtain official statistics covering the expenditure on removing and resettling people, providing the roads and 'amenities' in the new camps and townships, and compensating people for their old houses which are destroyed. It is of course also impossible to calculate the full cost of the consequent burdens placed on people – the cost of starvation and malnutrition, the loss of peasant production, the disruption of education, the breakdown of family life, the increased travelling costs and rents, the reduction in cash earnings from casual employment, and the rise in aberrant or criminal behaviour.

However, it is certain that both the direct and indirect costs of the policy are very high.[1] In fact, the costs of removals (those

1. Data on the funds for 'Bantu Development' and their connection with the resettlement policy are examined in Appendix 2.

which are borne by the State) are disguised as part of the expenditure in the 'Bantu Development Plan'. Of course, expenditure on resettlement provides no real resources: it sets back any hope of development, economic or human, for years. If the removals continue until all Africans in the White areas are migrant labourers, it will ensure that the Reserves remain permanently, chronically impoverished, emasculated and unable to develop themselves. Over South Africa as a whole more is being taken away from the Africans than has ever been given in the way of development.

The Government's latest plan for promoting investment in the Reserves involves spending R86 million over the next five years. But its potentially beneficial effects are vitiated by the fact that half of the money will go to White businessmen to help them establish agencies in the Reserves; like the border industries, these enterprises will do little more than ensure that some jobs are located in, or near, the Reserves rather than in White towns. Even the most optimistic estimate of the effects of this investment plan anticipates the creation of only 24,000 new jobs in the five years, against the assessed need of 40–50,000 new jobs each year merely to stabilize the present unemployment level – that is, to give work to the extra African men added to the pool of unemployed each year. In the Transkei, the only Bantustan with even a limited form of local autonomy, which has had its own Development Corporation for a number of years, the employment situation is as bad as everywhere else. The Member of Parliament representing the Whites in the Transkei reported: 'You should have seen them outside the Labour Office in Umtata.' (Umtata is the capital of the Transkei.) 'They were not there in hundreds, but in thousands. I saw them myself, all clamouring for permits to go out to work, because there was no work for them there.'

What a contrast this makes with the accounts of travellers who visited the coastal regions, including the Transkei, in the sixteenth–nineteenth centuries, and the interior in the nineteenth century. Their diaries, reports and books all describe a prosperous people with large herds of cattle, wide-scale trading and elaborate houses. One of the main justifications of apartheid made by the Government is that it enables the Africans to preserve their traditional culture and way of life – another example of double-think. What tradition do the resettlement camps belong to – inhabited by the old, the sick, women and children, unemployed youth, deprived of land and cattle and forced to submit to the authority of the White Government in all matters? As the official instruction puts it: 'As a result of a shortage of adequate land it is not possible to settle all these people together with their cattle in the homelands on an agricultural basis and consequently it is imperative that before they are settled in some town or settlement, they must first sell their cattle, sheep and goats.' [1]

Since it is the declared aim of the Government to preserve and strengthen African traditional life and social systems, we ought to be aware of the havoc caused to the life of the Reserves by its policies. The new settlements violate the whole structure of traditional life. They are empty of both social and economic meaning for the people, and the removals in turn cause a chain reaction of disturbance and upheaval in the existing populations of the Reserves, who must be concentrated and 'replanned', to make room for the repatriated masses.

The Government claims nonetheless that removals are voluntary. It will be seen in the following pages what circumscriptions of intimidation, legal penalties, physical methods of persuasion, and economic sanctions are applied to the tortured meaning of the word 'voluntary'. It might be thought that the insistence on the word is no more than window dressing. Yet there is an aspect of the term which deserves to be explored further: the extent to which the Government obtains an apparent acquiescence in its policies from the chiefs, the only African spokesmen it recognizes.

The chiefs are often reviled as stooges of the Government, and some who have been appointed because of their compliance have been patently self-seeking characters. But in the main, their plight deserves pity. There have been a number of chiefs who resisted Government impositions and stood out against the resettlement of their people – like the Bafurutse chief

1. Secretary of Bantu Administration and Development's General Circular No. 25, 1967.

in the Zeerust district,[1] the Sekhukhune chief [2] and the Basotho chief at Witsieshoek[3] – and they have been swept aside, every one.[4]

In the clashes between the White Government and the people of the Reserves, the chief is the man caught in the middle. If he sides with the people against the Government, he is crushed like a fly. He may be summarily deposed, or banished to a distant province to live alone and destitute, or may even be arrested. He has no possible means of representing the true interests of his people where they disagree with the Government – and even less can he act for the tribesmen who live and work in the cities, for whom a sentence of 'repatriation' to the Reserve may appear like a lingering death. No wonder, then, that most chiefs appear to acquiesce, though many do so with severely troubled consciences.

They know the anger of their people, whom traditionally they were bound to listen to in tribal councils. In Lefurutse, for example, the people felt they had no voice which would be listened to by the Government: 'How may one argue with a wall?' They were impotent before the police reprisals after any act of defiance: 'They are killing us! They are stamping us into the ground!' Their anger is therefore diverted against 'traitors' and 'collaborators', those Africans who hold office or who comply with Government orders. The scene of people attacking their own chiefs has been enacted over and over again. As conflicts worsen, the chiefs are given protection by the police or paid bodyguards, and the division between them and their people is entrenched. The opposition can be 'stamped into the ground', but even when the people have given up resisting and seem most apathetic, resentment remains and the unity of the community is finished. This is the tragic destruction of tradition which the Government has set in train, perhaps unwittingly, wherever the

1. See page 159.
2. See page 175.
3. See page 213.
4. On 1 February 1971, the chief and six members of a tribe at Manjeng in the Northern Cape who were opposed to being removed were detained by the police and charged with holding an illegal meeting. This is the latest of many similar incidents.

people of the Reserves have dared to oppose, and suffer the violent retribution that opposition brings.

The instructions contained in General Circular No. 25 of 1967[1] define the Government's policy on removals and the categories of people who must be moved:

The Bantu in the European areas who are normally regarded as non-productive and as such have to be resettled in the homelands, are conveniently classified as follows:

1. The aged, the unfit, widows, women with dependent children and also families who do not qualify under the provisions of the Bantu (Urban Areas) Act no. 25 of 1945 for family accommodation in the European urban areas;

2. Bantu on European farms who become superfluous as a result of age, disability or the application of Chapter 4 of the Bantu Trust and Land Act, no. 18 of 1936, or Bantu squatters from mission stations and black spots which are being cleared up;

3. Professional Bantu such as doctors, attorneys, agents, traders, industrialists, etc. Also such persons are not regarded as essential for the European labour market, and as such they must also be settled in the homelands in so far as they are not essential for serving their compatriots in the European areas . . .

To these categories must be added those Africans living in proclaimed African Reserves which are now considered to be 'badly situated'.

The types of settlement established in the 'homelands' are described:

(a) 'Self-contained Bantu towns . . . as substitutes for the municipal Bantu residential areas of European towns or cities situated near the boundaries of the homelands, or to provide accommodation to Bantu (and their families) employed in industries founded in the border areas.' These are proper townships with services and dwellings provided – simply shifted to a near-by Reserve to comply with apartheid theory. This book is not really concerned with these towns, which are in all but name adjuncts of White urban areas.

(b) 'Towns in the homelands with rudimentary services and housing . . . water is normally laid on only at convenient places in

1. The quotations in the rest of this chapter are taken from the circular.

the streets in pillar-faucets and cesspits are used as far as possible, whilst the houses built by the Trust usually consist of prefabricated one- or two-roomed buildings which may be either purchased or rented. . . . These townships are developed for families of which the breadwinners are usually employed as migrant labourers in European areas, or for the aged, widows and women with dependent children etc. Examples of these townships are Mountain View (Osizweni) at Newcastle, Sada at Whittlesea, Boekenhoutfontein at Pretoria, etc.' Many of the townships of this type appear in the present report and they are some of the worst settlements, having large populations, overcrowded living conditions and little local employment. The 'houses' provided in these townships are just basic shells. They have small rooms – usually about ten or twelve feet square – with rough, unplastered walls, no ceilings, very small windows, no interior doors, a tin-pitched roof and none of the amenities expected in the cheapest houses in other countries.

(c) 'More sparsely populated residential areas of one sixteenth to one eighteenth of a morgen[1] which are planned in suitable places in the homelands. Normally only a rudimentary lay-out on the basis of agricultural residential areas is undertaken and the delimitation need not be carried out by a surveyor, as the premises are not offered for sale. A common source of water where the inhabitants can fetch their water, either a borehole(s) equipped with pump(s), a fountain, river or dam is a prerequisite. The inhabitants are also expected to install their own cesspit latrines together with dwellings, traditional or otherwise. These settlements offer a refuge for squatters from European farms, Black spots and missionary farms, to whom plots are allocated on which they may erect their own dwellings. A rental of R1 per annum is payable. . . .' These places are also known as 'closer settlements'. Examples are Limehill and Rietspruit.

(d) 'On suitable Trust lands, where families are settled in accordance with a system of controlled squatting in order that they should not interfere with other developments or extension schemes there, rather than that they should remain as squatters in the European areas. They can gradually be moved, if necessary,

1. A morgen is equivalent to 21/9ths of an acre.

to any of the towns u̶ ̶ ̶(a) or (b) or to a denser residential area referred to under (c̶ ̶ ̶ ̶This appears to describe one type of Trust village i̶ ̶ ̶ ̶ ̶ ̶no mention is made in this list of 'emerg̶ ̶ ̶ ̶ ̶ ̶men, or of 'transit camps' like t̶ ̶ ̶ ̶ ̶ ̶will be seen, not all settlements ̶ ̶

The essent̶ ̶ ̶ ̶and a settlement seems to be̶ ̶ ̶ ̶r services, but the fact that in̶ ̶ ̶ ̶rchase the plot and/or the h̶ ̶ ̶and Mpungamhlophe are offici̶ ̶ ̶en though the people there ha̶ ̶ ̶no services were provided, ̶

The̶ ̶ ̶procedures for removing people ̶ ̶ ̶from White urban areas will b̶ ̶ ̶referred to under (b) or the 'denser̶ ̶ ̶ ̶They will continue to draw any pe̶ ̶ ̶eligible for. Supplementary rations m̶ ̶ ̶ase of widows and women with dependent̶ ̶ ̶ ̶no are still 'fit for employment but have no income, opportunities of employment must either be created or they must be provided with rations. The latter is an undesirable principle and must be avoided as far as possible. Consequently work must be provided for these persons, no matter of how inferior a nature, such as cleaning streets, laying out and weeding sidewalks, planting and watering trees alongside the streets and cleaning cemeteries. ... The cash wages of the breadwinner must preferably be the same throughout and it should not exceed R5 per month' (about £3).

'Squatters' families from European farms, black spots and mission stations' will normally be allocated plots in the settlement under (c) and (d). Families 'must be amply compensated for any improvements which they abandon on the Black spots or mission stations.' The cost of transport of the families and their possessions is borne by the State; rations must be provided for approximately three days.

However, I was met time and time again on my tour with complaints from the people that they had received no compensation for the abandonment of farming land – only those who farmed over 20 morgen (which means hardly anyone) are entitled to any farming land in the 'homeland'.

Even if the regulations were strictly adhered to, it would still mean that people could be dumped in the veld with only a tent and a water supply of some kind. There need be no employment, health, education or any other facilities. In practice even these regulations are not followed. For example, people from European farms have to provide their own transport and do not receive rations.

The circular insists that 'Bantu Affairs Commissioners and Magistrates in charge of districts in which homelands are situated must continually endeavour to persuade existing European or Indian traders in their area to dispose of their businesses to Bantu. . . .' But at Limehill, for example, a European was recently given a trading licence to open a store on the border of the Reserve area. There are many other examples of Europeans cornering most of the trade in the Reserves.

One last quotation from this circular expresses the style of efficient but unfeeling administration in which this inhuman policy is planned:

'I would like to stress here that the Honourable Minister has given instructions that the settlement in the homelands of thousands of superfluous Bantu families at present residing in the European areas of the Republic must enjoy the highest priority.' Then, without conscious irony: 'The human factor must, however, never be lost sight of in the process of settlement. The people must be treated with due respect and sympathy towards their problems and the impression must not be created that they are no longer welcome in the European area.'

3. Natal

After his first view of Natal from the top of the Drakensburg, on 7 October 1837, Piet Retief, the Voortrekker leader, wrote: 'From the heights of these mountains I saw this beautiful land, the most beautiful I've ever seen in Africa.' [1]

One of the earliest acts of the Volksraad (People's Assembly) of the new Boer Republic of Natal, established in 1838, was to translate into law the customary distinction between people – White men – and creatures or chattels – non-Whites. Whites could become citizens and landowners in the Republic without difficulty. Non-Whites 'had no right to be in the settled parts of the Republic at all, except as servants of White people, and then were not permitted to own land, firearms or horses, to participate in the political process, or to be at large without passes signed by White employers.' [2]

The Boers made use of African tribesmen in the Republic for labour, but in 1841, faced with the return of many people who had been absorbed by the Zulu kingdom of Shaka some years earlier, the Volksraad decided that not more than five African families should be allowed to remain as labour tenants on each farm and 'that all "surplus" Africans should be placed between the Mtamvuna and Mzimvubu rivers at the Southern end of the Republic, and instructed Commandant-General Pretorius to send them there, by persuasion if possible, by force if necessary'.[3] The Republic never had the power to implement this resolve, but it illustrates the traditional connection between Afrikaner society and ideas of segregation.

It was left to the British, who annexed Natal as a colony in

1. T. V. Bulpin, *Natal and Zululand* (Books of Africa, 1966), p. 94.
2. *Oxford History of South Africa* (Clarendon Press, 1969), Vol. 1, p. 367.
3. ibid., p. 368.

1842, to start the first resettlement schemes. A commission was appointed in 1846 to establish separate Reserves for Africans, and they set about defining 'locations' and mission reserves.

The patchwork effect of African Reserves scattered over the length and breadth of Natal is the result of the efforts of the British Administration in the 1840s and 1850s, and particularly of Theophilus Shepstone, who was Diplomatic Agent in Natal from 1845 to 1853 and Secretary for Native Affairs from 1853 to 1875. At least the degree of segregation introduced in Natal was less absolute and the Africans were not relegated such distances as they were in the more durable Boer Republics on the Highveld (Orange Free State and Central Transvaal).

But the common characteristics of the Natal Reserves today are poverty, erosion and denudation; the Reserves and the White areas are visibly different. There does not appear to be any possibility of all the Reserves being consolidated into one block because of the White farms, towns and roads interspersed between them. This makes complete nonsense of the removal schemes in Natal; yet there are still some two hundred 'Black spots' due to be removed. The people have in most cases lived there for generations and often the surrounding White farmers do not seem concerned about their presence. But for the sake of apartheid ideology they must be moved into one of the Reserves even though there is no spare land for them. There are still hundreds of White farms with more than five labour tenants; but the law is now being enforced – after almost 130 years – and the 'surplus' farm labourers and their families account for vast numbers of those who are to be resettled. According to the Natal Agricultural Union, in October 1967, the implementation of this law throughout Natal would involve the resettlement of about one million African people.

A cursory glance at the map of African Reserves might give the impression that the African population has a fair share of Natal. But when one considers that Natal has the highest concentration of Africans in the country, the highest African : White ratio (79 per cent of the population is African and 11 per cent White), and that the ports, rail-heads, industrial undertakings, sugar estates, coal mines, etc., are all in the White area, it is obvious that the African population is not so well endowed in the Province, which once belonged entirely to them. The main railway line seems deliberately to avoid entering an African area. One does not have to be an agricultural expert to see what damage the gross overcrowding has done to the Reserves. The official Agricultural Report for 1962 says: '... the position is not so acute as to cause relief measures to be instituted, but in most cases a member of the family will be required to sell his labour and seek work in the towns to earn money for food for his wife and family.' The estimated production in the Natal Reserves was about 50 lb. of grain per person. Despite the obvious inability of the Reserves to support even their present population, thousands more people are being moved into them. The Chief Bantu Affairs Commissioner for Natal, Mr T. F. Coertze, has said that there is not enough land for all Africans to be 'accommodated' on an agricultural basis in the 'homelands'. Hence the establishment of 'closer settlements' – people are moved from farms in the White areas where they had land and cattle to a place within the confines of the Reserves where they have neither. This is hardly surprising when one White farmer claims he needs 86,000 acres.

In April 1965 the Department of Information and the Department of B.A.D. announced plans for forty new African towns in the Reserves 'which were all situated as near as possible to White areas where work was readily available'.[1]

The Minister gave statistics concerning these forty 'towns' in the House of Assembly on 14 May 1968. He said the eventual planned population was 851,700. One half of the towns had no people living there at the time; the rest had a total population of 164,712. According to the Minister's figures, seventeen of these 'towns', with a planned population of 200,000 people, are not intended to serve any 'border area', the official term for industrial areas near the Reserves.

The original announcement of these towns continued: 'At all these townships full facilities would be provided, including schools, sportsfields, swimming pools, community halls, shops and parks.'

1. *Natal Mercury*, 1 April 1965.

Among the 'towns' already occupied at the time of the Minister's statement were Mondlo, Vulandondo and Mpungamhlophe; among the proposed ones was Limehill. At all of these places there were not even houses, or a proper water supply provided, let alone swimming pools and community halls and other social facilities. Furthermore, none of them serves a border area and they are from nine to thirty miles from a White area. According to the Minister's figures, some 700,000 people were to be resettled in 'towns'. Some of these 'towns' are primarily places to rehouse people from existing locations, for example Gezinsila at Eshowe and Ncotshane at Pongola, since the general trend throughout the country is to move urban locations outside the municipal areas. Others, for example Limehill, Vulandondo and Mondlo, are to house people from 'Black spots'. These are basically dormitories for the families of migrant labourers who will have to find work in distant places since the labour needs of the neighbouring White towns are already provided for by the local locations.

Natal provides classic examples of all the various types of resettlement schemes: 'closer settlements' at Limehill and in parts of Zululand; Trust villages throughout Zululand; agricultural settlements at Vergelegen and Impendle; a transit camp at Poll-tax Farm; an emergency camp at Weenen. These examples also give the lie to oft-repeated official claims, namely, that the resettlement schemes are the same as slum clearance and that they are voluntary.

Babanango

Many of the evils of resettlement schemes are exemplified in the case of the people of Babanango. They were a group of people who had been living for generations in the heart of Zululand. Suddenly they were brought into contact with White officialdom. As the old men said: 'The White men came with guns and took our land.' Here is their story, in their own words, of the efforts they made and the frustrations they met: [1]

1. My translation. The original is in my possession.

'Father, we come from Babanango. We are suffering and ask you to intercede with the Government for us so that we too may be able to live as people with sensitive souls.

'You already know something of this matter since we met with you recently. But we would like to explain to you briefly how things have gone.

'Our ancestors were living in this place at the time of Senzangakhona [the father of Shaka]. Afterwards the place fell into the hands of the White man and we gave our allegiance to them. Now we are being expelled. We do not wish to argue with the law but we ask the authorities to sympathize with us in this matter. If we are moved from here we request the Government to find us a place where we will be able to keep cattle and have fields. The reason for this is that some people here have three or four wives and others, while having only one wife, have more than ten children. There are also widows with their children and old people who have no one to look after them. All these people gain their livelihood from keeping cattle and farming.

'On 12 October 1967 we went to the Bantu Affairs Commissioner at Babanango to ask him to find a place for us since on our own we had failed. We asked him to find a place in a Reserve. The Bantu Affairs Commissioner replied: "There is no place because in the Reserve which is near you there are a hundred people for whom I have to find a place to live. But I promise to look for a place for you on farms. Do you agree to this?" We agreed.

'He sent me to a Mr Kooes to find a place. I went, but he told me that he could not take me as I came from his neighbour's place. On 13 October 1967 I returned to the Commissioner at Babanango. He sent me to another man, Mr Bill Delport. He too refused. On 16 October 1967 I went again to the Commissioner. He told me to look for a place and that he too would try. So we continued looking but without success.

'On 23 November we took our plea to Mr Boshoff and asked him whether he could find us a place. Mr Boshoff said: "You cannot get a place in Nongoma. But go back to Babanango and I will write to the Commissioner and ask him to find you a place."

'On 23 November 1967 we went to the Commissioner and lodged our plea. He replied: "There is no place; but I will write to Maritzburg. Come back on 21 December 1967." We duly returned. He said that he had not yet received a reply but that when it came we would get it through a Mr Almaan. But he emphasized that we should not stop looking as he still had a hundred people for whom he had to find a place and there were also another hundred or so people who were living illegally on the place; for these too he had to find a place.

'On 15 January 1968 we returned to report that we had not found a place. He said that he had phoned Maritzburg and they said they were still looking for a place but had not yet found one. He told us to return to Babanango and show the Commissioner the notices to quit.

'On 25 January 1968 all those who had received notices to quit sent a representative to the Commissioner with the notices. The Commissioner did not take the letters but said that no reply had yet been received from Maritzburg.

'On 31 January 1968 the owner of the farm closed the dip for the cattle of the people living there.

'On 5 February 1968 this matter was reported to the Commissioner. He said: "I already know that; the owner of the farm, Mr France, has told me. The people of the farm are summoned to appear in Court on 9 February 1968." They were charged with refusing to leave the place and were given twenty days to leave.

'On 23 February 1968 we had a meeting with the Bantu Affairs Commissioner of Nongoma, Mr Vosloo. We told him all that happened and asked him if he would find us a place. He asked us whether we wanted farms or a Reserve. We replied that we wanted a Reserve so that we would be able to live.

'Mr Vosloo said: "Go back to Babanango and find out when the surveyors are coming, and when all those who are being moved are finished there, I will give you a place in a Reserve as you want."

'On 23 February we went to Babanango. The Commissioner said the surveyors would arrive on 27 February 1968. On 27 February 1968 all those to be moved went to Babanango. The

Commissioner said: "Go away and come back on March 1st. I will see Mr Vosloo."

'On 1 March 1968 we were all present and so was Mr Vosloo. We were divided according to the different farms from which we came. Those from the farms Witklip and Nokhulu were called although we all had the one complaint. We were all called and had a great surprise. These people were assigned to a location and moreover nothing had been prepared there.

'Mr Vosloo said: "Your report is false. There is no one who has spent five years looking in vain for a place to live as you say." He asked one man to give evidence of this. He gave it, emphasizing that such people were present at the assembly and if asked could reply for themselves. Two came forward but Mr Vosloo would not accept what they said.

'Mr Vermaak said that there was a location that had been surveyed but that it would be necessary for us to build our own houses. Further, no cattle would be allowed and there were no fields. The cost of a site for a house would be £41. He further said that if anyone did not want to go there, where there would be neither land nor cattle, there were Whites who needed farm tenants at Uitlicht, Harwick and Babanango itself. Mr Vermaak's parting words were: "All the people must be off the White farms at Babanango within fourteen days. After that the owners of the farms would take a certain step."

'On 23 March 1968 the houses of two of the people were burned.

'On 20 March 1968 we went to Pretoria. We said where we came from and asked for a place in a Reserve so that we might live. Mr van der Merwe gave us a letter to take to the Commissioner at Babanango. He received it on 28 March 1968. He said that there was nothing he could do to help us. If we had the money we could buy a plot in the location that had been surveyed. He returned the letter to us and we took it with us.

'On 2 April 1968 two houses on the farm Witklip were pulled down by the South African Police. Also after 22 March 1968 each person who had not moved was fined £15.

'On 19 April 1968 the police took the letter that we had been given in Pretoria.

'Father, in all this remember us and do not tire of it.'

This account does not mention their many trips to Johannesburg, Ladysmith and Durban, looking for help. They had heard of the efforts being made for the people at Limehill and wondered whether these same people could help them. They went all the way to Johannesburg to the Institute of Race Relations, who referred them to the Resettlement Aid Committee in Ladysmith. I happened to be in Ladysmith at the time and the matter was passed on to me. Together with two other priests, I set out to find the people concerned. All we knew was the name of one man who lived in the Babanango area, but the lines of communication in Zululand are very good. We went to Babanango and the first person we asked knew exactly where the man lived even though it was some miles away.

We were directed down a track which went deeper and deeper into a valley. The road eventually petered out altogether but there were plenty of people around to point out the general direction. We drove on slowly, being passed by cyclists and even pedestrians, between boulders and across streams. After a couple of hours we began to wonder how we would ever get back, but we had gone too far to give up. We were continually assured that it was 'just over there'. We finally came to a river which we could not possibly cross (I think it was the Little Umfolozi), but a boy herding cattle, who belonged to the family of the man we were looking for, offered to go and call him. Within a few minutes about a dozen men had appeared.

They told us something of their troubles but said that they could not go into the whole story without all the old men being present. We arranged a meeting, at a more accessible place, for the next day. It was then nearly 5 p.m. and we still had to find our way back to Ladysmith. They assured us that there was a short-cut back to the main road. True, it involved crossing the Little Umfolozi, but that, they said, was no problem. They did not mention that there was not actually any road at all. One man came to lead us to the main road; he said that the quickest way would be for him to walk in front of the car. After a couple of hundred yards we decided it would be better for two of us to join him as the way was strewn with boulders and anthills hidden in the long grass. We came to the river and were faced with what looked like a vertical bank on the other side and a very stony river bed. But a tractor had once crossed it so why not a Volkswagen? With a little assistance from the three of us, the Volkswagen just made it, with only a slight scraping of the exhaust system. We thought that our troubles were over then, only to find that we had to cross a vast expanse of swamp – our guide seemed to know exactly at which blade of grass to turn. Finally we came to a track and our guide left us, telling us that it led straight to the main road. A hundred yards further on the car was marooned on top of a rock, but after that the road improved. We arrived at Nqutu five hours after leaving Babanango. We learned from the locals that the route we had taken used to be the ox-wagon route but was no longer passable.

I returned the next day and there was a gathering of sixty to seventy men sitting in a big circle, overlooking the land where Cetshwayo[1] had kept his cattle but which now belonged to White sugar magnates. The grandfather of one of the old men had been Cetshwayo's headman at this place. It was a very moving experience to be part of such a gathering. But it was also saddening to hear them speak, still with dignity, of their struggles and present misfortunes. I was only too aware of how little, if anything, I could do to help them. I somehow felt also a share in the guilt for what White men had done to these people. If any land is their land surely this is. Some of these men were born here at the time of the Boer War. They themselves are grandfathers or even great-grandfathers yet *their* great-grandfathers had settled on these farms before the time of Shaka, and long before the time of the sugar farmers. Now they have to beg a place from the White man. They are offered a place in a 'closer settlement'. As one old man said: 'I have four wives and too many children to count. I also have thirty cows. It is impossible for me to go to a place where there are no houses and no land.'

Later a delegation again went to Ladysmith and gave me the written account already quoted. They also told me that some

1. The last independent King of the Zulus, who reigned from 1872 to 1884.

more houses were to be destroyed by the police on a certain day and asked me to go there. I went, and at the first house I came to I inquired of a man outside whether any Government or police trucks had passed. He said that they had been expected but nothing had happened. So I turned back. I was later told by the people who had asked me to go that the houses were in fact demolished by the police on that day and this man had been told to misinform me. I was also told that a certain White man in the area had threatened to shoot me if I went there again!

I went to the Institute of Race Relations in Durban and explained the situation to the late Mrs M. Danks, the Regional Research Officer, who took the matter up with the Chief Bantu Affairs Commissioner, the local Bantu Affairs Commissioner, and the owners of the farms. Some of the people were eventually resettled on White farms; others went to the 'closer settlement' at Mpungamhlophe; some were still not properly settled when I last saw them. I went to Babanango again in September 1969, having been told that a deputation had been to Ladysmith to see me. But I was told by the local Africans that the man I really wanted to see was living in a tent in a completely inaccessible place. And if they say it is inaccessible it certainly must be! The ones I did see begged me not to mention that I had seen them nor to report anything they had said.

It is sometimes said that after the Bambatha Rebellion of 1906, the Zulus gave up and resigned themselves to working in the kitchens of the White man. But from my experience at Babanango I know that this is not true of all of them.

Mpungamhlophe, the 'closer settlement' to which some of these people went, is about twenty miles from Babanango, towards Dennydalton. The Bantu Affairs Department established the settlement by cutting off part of an existing tribal farm where the people continue to live in the traditional way, with their own land and cattle. It is called locally the 'location', as distinct from the farm, Mpungamhlophe.

The whole place had a general air of shabbiness with a number of overgrown, empty plots, many very poor, dilapidated houses, some half-built houses and no proper roads. Ragged, hungry-looking children surrounded the few taps that were installed in the 'streets' in 1965. There was no sign of any form of sanitation.

When I visited, in August 1969, there were about a thousand people living there. The first four families arrived in 1959. But most of them came between 1966 and 1968. Apparently all of them were from White farms in the Vryheid and Babanango districts, where they had had land and cattle. Seventy of the families came from one farm. It was not clear whether these, and some of the others, were simply evicted by the farmers or whether it was as a result of the enforcement of the labour-tenant law. The first arrivals were placed on one-acre plots, but the others had much smaller ones, probably half an acre, which they purchased for R80. They all provided their own transport and were not provided with tents, but had to erect temporary shelters to live in while they built their houses.

There was little sign of any development. There was a primary school with 620 pupils, including some from the farm. There were two shops, but the food was very expensive because of the cost of transport; for example, a bag of mealie meal cost R4.75 (the usual cost is R4 to R4.25). A doctor visited once a week but there was no permanent clinic. The scrub bush, of which there was plenty, did not make good firewood so they had to buy wood from people on the farms.

Some of the people previously worked on the farms where they were living, but many were, and still are, migrant workers. A few work on local farms, but there is no other work in the vicinity. Work-seekers have to go to Babanango, twenty miles away, and apply for contract work in Durban and other towns. The Bantu Administration Department has planted a lot of sisal near by but it appears to have failed.

As a result of my visits to Babanango, a number of people knew me and so spoke freely. They told me at length of the difficulties and hardships involved in moving and rebuilding, and complained that now they were hungry because they had no land, or cattle, or work. But, they continued: 'We can only sit, there is no one to hear us if we complain.' There was certainly plenty of evidence of their hunger and general need.

Mpungamhlophe is on the list of 'townships', given by the Deputy Minister of B.A.D., so we must not be misled when we hear that people from farms and other places are being settled in 'townships'.

Adjoining the 'location' there were four families in a cluster of tents. They had been evicted by a White farmer and left by the roadside. The Bantu Affairs Commissioner took pity on them, brought them to this place and left them the tents. They wanted a place where they could keep cattle, so they had not built houses. They had been in the tents for eight months and did not know how long they would stay or what their future would be.

Zululand

A. T. Bryant, writing of the Zululand of old, said:

This country, stretching from the Tugela to the Pongola, was typical African land. Here a vast expanse of treeless, grassy veld rolled away to the far horizons. There a whole domain of parklike scenery, chequered with sunny glades and shady woods enchanted the lover of sylvan beauty. Elsewhere, again, the landscape broke up into a wide expanse of broad valleys and precipitous ravines overshadowed by rocky hills and clad in forest or thorny bush. Temperate, healthy and moderately populated on its breezy, grassy highlands. ... This variegated piece of territory was parcelled out among a score of independent clans, each living for itself, ruled by its own chiefs and possessing its own recognized patch of country.[1]

Wars, land commissions and Land Acts have changed much of that. The natural beauty is still striking, except that many of the hills are now bare and eroded through overgrazing. Whenever I drive through Zululand I am struck by the incongruity of the presence of so many White-owned farms and sugar estates.

There are now, of course, a number of White towns in Zululand with their African labour force herded into nearby locations. And many of the Africans in the Reserve part are now gathered together in neat little Trust villages, the result of the Bantu Trust's 'betterment schemes', which have been put into effect over the past five years or so. The chief has to agree before the scheme is implemented and it entails grouping the people

1. *History of Zulu and Neighbouring Tribes* (reprinted by C. Struik, 1964), pp. 125–6.

together into residential areas and fencing off grazing and arable land. Water is usually provided in each village, but the people have to provide their own sanitation, which was previously no problem because they were so scattered. These schemes may be one way to make agricultural improvements. But such a set-up is completely contrary to the Zulu traditional way of life, which the authorities claim to be upholding. Traditionally the cattle kraal must be near the house, because of the important part it plays in rituals. In the Trust villages the people are crowded together, which they certainly do not like, and often their cattle and fields are a long way away.[1]

Such Trust villages have been established throughout Zululand – in the districts of Nqutu, Nkandla, Nongoma, Melmoth, Eshowe and others. I was particularly interested in the Nkandla district, because I had heard many reports of people from Weenen being moved there – a distance of about a hundred miles. Over the past five years the Bantu Trust has bought a number of farms adjoining the town of Nkandla and it is on these farms that the people from Weenen have been settled during the last three years, but especially during 1967–8, and some even more recently. They were told they had to leave the farms at Weenen and were shown the places at Nkandla. They agreed to go because, as they said later, it seemed to be either this or nothing. Two chiefs and their subjects were moved into a number of settlements which are quasi 'closer settlements', the difference being that they are allowed to keep five head of cattle. There is also a settlement of people from Dannhauser in Northern Natal. The general area is called Ngonisa; altogether there must be about five thousand people. They have half-acre plots for which they pay R1 a year; they also pay 50 cents a year per head of cattle. They were all moved by Government lorries and provided with tents but did not receive compensation for their houses or the farms.

1. Dr E. Cruz de Carvalho, who was for ten years the Director of the Angola Agricultural Census and Survey, in an unpublished work based on 3,000 case histories, strongly maintains that the reasons given for such 'betterment schemes' are false and serve to mask the harm done to the indigenous pastoralists. He concludes that the traditional African methods are preferable both for social and ecological reasons. He suggests that his conclusions should also be fundamentally applicable to South African conditions.

There are a number of schools which are probably adequate, though quite some distance from some of the settlements. There is an old-age home near by run by the Dutch Reformed Church, and a Government-run blind school called Vuleka ('be opened'). A vast amount of sisal has been planted by the Bantu Affairs Department providing some employment, mainly for women and girls, who earn R6 a month; some men are employed at R12 a month. But on 29 August 1969 most of them were told that there was no more work – presumably because of lack of rains. A factory to process the sisal was then being built. The only other source of employment is in the few shops and various institutions in Nkandla.

About thirteen miles from Nkandla there is a settlement of about twenty families from White farms at Weenen. It is almost two miles off the Nkandla–Kranskop road; the last part is just a track made by the lorries that brought the people at the end of June 1969. The settlement, which has no name, is on an exposed hillside covered with long grass and stones. There are no roads and no apparent order. When I visited it on 29 August 1969 the people were still living in tents while building their homes.

They had not agreed to move with the others from Weenen and so had had to provide their own transport. On arrival they found plots marked out and tents provided. I measured two of the plots and they were roughly 50 yards by 35 yards. They have no other land apart from grazing for five head of cattle for which they pay 50 cents a year per head. They did not receive any compensation, rations or building materials. The only water supply is a near-by stream; the nearest shop and hospital are at Nkandla. They have to walk two miles to catch the bus, then pay the fare of 50 cents return plus 25 cents for packages.

Most people removed from White farms are prepared to accept almost any kind of resettlement, however destitute it leaves them, as better than their former condition; but these families would rather have been left where they were. They said that they did not know what they would eat or how they would live. 'We have just been thrown away and have nothing.'

This is an example of what happens when people do not move 'voluntarily' at the appointed time. A report in the *Star* on 9 October 1969 stated that many more people were being moved from farms in the Weenen area to Zululand. The report also said that the local Bantu Commissioner refused pressmen permits to enter the area and that members of the Special Branch were on the road turning back would-be observers from the area. Therefore it was impossible to get any detailed information at the time.

Apart from these places there are also some new townships being developed near the bigger towns, for example Gezinsila, Sundumbili and Ngwelezana. These are ordinary townships, of no particular interest, except that Gezinsila is the only new township I have seen throughout the country which is near a town where most of the people work: it is only one mile from Eshowe. Most of the present two thousand or so people were previously living in shacks in the same area or in backyards in the town. Sundumbili is mainly for people who were living in the compound at the Mandeni Sugar Company near Tugela. Ngwelezana, near Empangeni, is very small at present but is expected to develop considerably as the township for Richard's Bay.

Mondlo

Mondlo, which according to the *Natal Mercury* report already quoted was to be one of the major 'Bantu towns' of Natal, is about twenty-three miles south of Vryheid and just within the Zululand Reserve area. The 'town' was started in 1963 when some 2,500 people were moved there from Besterspruit. Besterspruit was a settlement of African landowners and tenants on the outskirts of Vryheid. They were all removed at the beginning of 1963. Those who qualified to remain in Vryheid were moved just a couple of hundred yards to the location, where for some months they were housed in tents for which they paid R1 a month. They were later moved into wooden prefabricated huts, 13½ft by 9ft, for which they paid R1.50 a month, or a two-roomed one for which they paid R2.50.

The others were taken twenty-odd miles to Mondlo by Government lorries. There they were lent tents and told to build houses. There was no sanitation, no fuel, no building sand, no stores, no school (which eight months later was only 'nearly completed'), water was brought in by water-cart, milk and meat were unobtainable. Rations provided by the Government consisted of one pound of mealie meal per person per day for three days.[1] The water shortage continued and later the people dug for seepage from the surrounding hills within yards of pit latrines, which may have contributed to the typhoid outbreak which started a few months after their arrival. During the epidemic there were over sixty confirmed cases of typhoid, with at least one death. Kwashiorkor and pellagra also were common. At the first clinic forty children needed hospital treatment for malnutrition. Mass immunization campaigns against typhoid and diphtheria were carried out and a sanitation system was installed. The State Health Department gave every assurance that nothing similar would happen in future removals. There was occasion to remind them of this when typhoid broke out in the Limehill resettlement complex.

I went to Mondlo in August 1969, knowing that the initial mess had been cleared up, but wondering what sort of 'town' had been developed after six years. I found that many of the people had built good houses, and these, together with the schools, churches, stores and neat streets, gave a good general impression. But what development there had been was almost entirely due to the efforts of the people themselves and Church bodies. There were only about a dozen Government-built houses and these were for Bantu Administration Department workers. By August 1969, the Government clinic had reached foundation height. The present clinic is run by Hel-Wel, an organization sponsored by the Anglican diocese of Zululand.

The White superintendent has said that the people must all build proper houses according to one of eight plans approved by the Department. Many say they cannot possibly afford to build another house. He says if they do not, the Department will build them and they will have to pay rent. The landowners from Besterspruit were given a free plot but the others are buying their

1. *Blackspots. A Study of Apartheid in Action*, published by the Liberal Party of South Africa, pp. 19–26.

half-acre plots, which cost R80, at R8 a year. They also pay 86 cents a month for services. A few have been evicted for falling into arrears with their instalments. The Minister of B.A.D. said in the House of Assembly on 24 April 1964 that the Trust had bought this land at R9.82 an acre. The people are paying R160 an acre. A lawyer said, at the time of the removal, that the 'ownership' gives them no more rights than an occupier in a location.

At present there are about five thousand people in Mondlo. The superintendent says that another five thousand are expected to come but nothing can be done yet because of the water shortage. Everybody I spoke to complained about the shortage of water. On 27 and 28 August 1969, there was no water at all in the settlement; it had to be brought from Vryheid in Government tankers. After the typhoid epidemic, so-called 'aqua-privies' were installed; they are still not connected to the water supply.

There is still no sign of any form of employment being provided in the area; the nearest place where work is obtainable is Vryheid, about twenty-three miles away. Buses leave at 4 a.m. and return at about 7 p.m.; the return fare is 40 cents. This is particularly hard on the women. They go into Vryheid three or four times a week to do washing and other occasional work and the fare is at least half of what they earn. Other difficulties mentioned concerned the shortage of milk and the cost of fuel. Coal has to be brought from Utrecht about thirty-five miles away and costs 65 cents a bag; wood costs 30 cents a bag.

According to the statement of the Minister in the House of Assembly on 14 May 1968, Mondlo is planned for an eventual population of 22,400 but it is *not* intended to serve any border area. The area is notorious for its shortage of water; the surrounding district is completely rural. What is the sense of trying to establish a 'town' of 22,400 people in such a place?

Weenen Emergency Camp

Weenen is a small farming village about thirty-two miles south-east of Ladysmith. As has been mentioned, many people from this area were moved to Trust villages in Zululand. But those whose labour was needed in Weenen were put into an 'emergency camp', about three miles outside the village. I have visited this camp many times over the past eighteen months. My first reaction to it was that it made Limehill look like a holiday camp. The congestion, squalor and general appearance are certainly much worse; but the people do have the great advantage over those at Limehill of not having been moved away from a town and any source of employment.

People in such settlements are usually very chary of speaking to outsiders, especially White men. But not at Weenen. On every visit there I have been immediately surrounded by a sizable group of people who were most vociferous and bitter in their complaints.

My first visit there was in April 1968, when most of the people were still building. Some were able to stay at their old houses while they built but most of them were living in makeshift shacks. The camp was established by the Weenen Town Board in July 1967 for Africans living illegally in and around the urban area. Some were on white farms; others had owned the land where they were living. The latter were bought out but all had to provide their own transport to the camp and erect their own houses. Those from farms did not receive any compensation for their houses, nor will they be compensated for their present ones when they have to move on again, as the Government Gazette of 19 July 1968 says, in reference to this camp: '12 (5) No resident of the camp shall, either on the disestablishment of the camp or at any time, have any claim against the urban local authority for compensation in respect of any improvement made by him to any site; provided that such inhabitant may remove from the site materials which may be so removed without damaging the soil.' Nor have they any security of tenure, for the same Gazette says: 'The site permit may be cancelled on one month's notice if the holder is out of employment for one month; if he is employed outside the urban area for one month without the permission of the superintendent; if he is absent for more than one month without the written permission of the superintendent; or if his presence in the camp is undesirable in the sole and absolute discretion of the urban local authority; provided that the urban local authority shall not be obliged to furnish any reason for its decision.'

In April 1968, nine months after the first people were moved into the camp, there was no water, except from a furrow at least half a mile away; there was no sanitation; no temporary accommodation. The only sign of any official activity was a half-completed beer-hall.

The Government Gazette lays down that: 'No person shall in any way dig into or remove or disturb the surface of the soil, except in such areas as may be designated by the superintendent.' There was no superintendent to do the designating and the only way the people could obtain mud for building was to dig holes on their plots.

When I last visited, on 24 August 1969, the people were still complaining bitterly about their conditions and especially about the exorbitant rent, which was introduced in February 1968, of R2 a month, plus 50 cents for each grown-up child, parent or lodger. Some of the plots are only between 30 and 40ft square. At this rate the Town Board is making something like R750 a year per acre for a piece of scrub land. This rent is particularly excessive when it is remembered that in Weenen most men earn R8–R12 a month and most women R2–R5 a month. Some employees of the Town Board, which exacts this rent, said that they are paid R9 a month.

The Government Gazette states that communal toilets and washing facilities are to be provided. There was no sign of the washing facilities and the people said that there were only four toilets, which they were frightened of using since a child fell into one. I have seen the children relieving themselves on their doorsteps. There are now three taps within the settlement and one at the beer-hall. But they are all turned off at midday on Saturday until Monday morning.

Because of the beer-hall, which is another source of income for the Town Board, the people are not allowed to brew beer. One person was recently fined R50 for doing so and others were under threat of eviction. Yet the beer-hall, they complained, is closed when the men return from work and is out of beer by 11 a.m. on Saturday; then it closes for the weekend.

A 'hostel' was being built for nine men who work in the town; it was being constructed of wattle and daub, within a few feet of somebody's house, and measures about 25 ft by 12ft. There are no clinics or shops in the settlement. Indian traders deliver goods but neither they nor their lorries, even though driven by Africans, are allowed into the camp; so the goods, whatever the weather, have to be left by the roadside. The road, incidentally, has been slightly diverted so that it no longer passes directly in front of the camp. The Gazette states that no one except the local urban authority may trade in the settlement and that no orders may be solicited without the permission of the superintendent.

It is not clear what the 'emergency' was that led to the establishment of such a camp, which has been in existence for over two years and seems likely to remain. The people were told at one time that they were to be moved to Nkandla. But they have heard no more of that for some time and it is hardly likely that the Town Board would build a beer-hall and a hostel if a move were imminent.

Why don't the people themselves do something? Why don't they get together to make representations about such matters as rents? According to the Government Gazette they are not allowed to hold public meetings without the approval of the superintendent. Some of these regulations make the camp sound like a place of detention; for example, it is laid down that no one may enter or leave the camp other than by any entrance or exit provided by the urban local authority; no entertainment or meeting (if they could get permission for a meeting), except for weddings, funerals and church purposes, may continue after 11 p.m. without the approval of the superintendent; the superintendent or any duly appointed officer may 'at any reasonable time, having regard to the convenience of the residents, enter any dwelling or site in the camp for inspection purposes.'

There are now over eight hundred people living in these conditions and they have no indication of how long the 'emergency', whatever it may be, will last.

On my last visit I wished that I had had a tape-recorder with me to record the impassioned outburst of one old man about how all his life he had tried to live decently and bring up his children properly and now he was reduced to this. He was being trampled underfoot, he said, by White men who wanted to 'kill' him and his children and all his people. 'God alone knows what we suffer in this place. The tears from this place would make a river.' I don't know whether he was aware that the name 'Weenen' means 'a place of weeping'.

From Weenen I went on, through Ladysmith, to Newcastle. There was a curious sequel to this trip. Some time later the owner of the car which I had borrowed was approached by the police and told that they were making inquiries about a hit-and-run accident that had taken place near Ladysmith on 24 August – the day I passed through. They said that someone had taken the number of his car at the scene of the accident. He informed the police that I had the car at the time but they have never approached me about it. I certainly did not see any hit-and-run accident. But presumably somebody was interested enough in me to take down the number of the car I was driving.

Impendle

During my travels in Natal I heard a number of contradictory reports about the removal of a number of African farmers from the Upper Umkomaas area to Impendle, about fifty miles west of Pietermaritzburg. Some, supported by reports in the press quoting the B.A.D., said that the farmers were offered 'compensatory land equivalent in its agricultural and pastoral value to the land previously owned by them'. The people had been provided with transport to and fro before the move so that they could build new houses. This all sounded too good to be true – and so it was!

The farmers themselves told me that they had owned their farms for over sixty years, and were not happy to leave. Although they did all receive compensation, they did not all receive an equivalent area of land; some were given part of their compensation in cash. In the Upper Umkomaas valley where they came from there is rich, river-bottom soil (clay loam) which I am informed by farmers is excellent land. In general, according to one who has farmed in the district, the land in the Impendle district is much inferior.

Some of the farmers had had ten or more tenants, but were allowed to take only five families with them. The others were ordered to go and find their own place to live. By no means all the people were offered transport to and from Impendle while they built their houses. The others were just taken to the site and left with a tent.

The main worry of these people seemed to be whether they would have any security even at Impendle. They feared that having been moved from the farms where they had lived so long they might well be moved again. I tried to reassure them, but without much conviction. A Reserve could easily cease to be a Reserve when something valuable was discovered there. I knew that this had happened elsewhere, for example at Schmidt's Drift in the Northern Cape, so how could my assurances carry weight?

The landowners at Impendle were reasonably fortunate in that they owned enough land to qualify for compensatory land in a Reserve area, even if the quality may be much worse. Though their title deeds and length of residence count for nothing, at least they are not left without means of subsistence. The hardest hit are those farmers who own less than 20 morgen (about 40 acres), like many at Alcockspruit for example, since they lose their land and are forced to try to adopt a completely new way of life.

Alcockspruit

When I drove into one of the African farms at Alcockspruit, near Dannhauser in Northern Natal, on 27 August 1969, some people came rushing up, waving pieces of paper and demanding rather angrily where the lorries were. I hurriedly explained that I had nothing to do with the B.A.D. and knew nothing about any lorries. The pieces of paper were notices they had received telling them that they had to move on that day. The notices, in Afrikaans only, had been issued by the superintendent of Madadeni Township in Newcastle. Five families had been informed that they were to move on 27 August. The notices were dated 7 August, but, they said, they had only received them on 23 August. They had started dismantling their houses, kept their children home from school and were waiting for the lorries; by 3.30 p.m. there was still no sign of the lorries. What about those who had notices to leave on 28 August? Were they to prepare or were they to presume that everything had been postponed?

The land at Alcockspruit, comprising the farms Loch Lomond, Gardens and Craneville, was originally purchased by Africans in the 1880s. The title-deed, the people say, was signed by Queen Victoria and they presumed that they had every right to the land in perpetuity. There were sixty original buyers, each owning various amounts plus a share in the commonage of a couple of thousand acres; they took tenants on to their land at a rent of R6–R10 a year. Many of the owners and the tenants were able to earn their living from their land and cattle.

In 1964–5 the owners were told that it was a 'Black spot' and they would have to leave. The Bantu Affairs Commissioner told them that they would be resettled on an agricultural basis and that when the time came he would be there to see that everything – water, schools, etc. – was provided. Then another Bantu Affairs Commissioner came and told them that there was not enough land available so most of them would have to go to Madadeni Township – thirty-five miles away.

Those owning less than 20 morgen are given a free plot in the township as part of their compensation but they do not receive any title until they have bought the house; even then it is not clear what form of title they will have. Some with more than 20 morgen have been told that they will receive land but have not yet been shown it. But at least one with more than 20 morgen was told by the Bantu Affairs Commissioner that there just was not any land. (I heard of others in the same position but only spoke to this one.) Many would have more than 20 morgen if their share in the commonage were included; but apparently this is not done.

At the end of 1968, the Bantu Affairs Commissioner went to serve notices on eight families. He then asked how many more wanted to go and a number volunteered. They later explained that they had said they wanted to go because they knew they would have to go anyway and thought that they might get a better deal if they volunteered.

They started moving in January 1969. Only those who were qualified to be in the Newcastle district were allowed to go to Duckponds (Madadeni); the others had to return to where they were born and find their own place. They had also to be able to prove that they were married by Christian rites. (One family, at the time of my visit, had been consistently refused a place because they have a Sotho surname, even though their grandfather bought the property and the family had lived there ever since.) Some of those who moved first found the houses at Madadeni without doors and windows, and had to leave their crops behind. Some of them, once they had seen the accommodation at Madadeni, returned to the Alcockspruit district and managed to settle on other farms.

A senior spokesman for the B.A.D. in Pietermaritzburg could not give any figures for the number of families involved. But some indication is given by the fact that at the beginning of 1969 there were almost a thousand children in the school at Alcockspruit; in August there were only 220. Standards V and VI were closed, so some of the children in these standards had to go to Madadeni before their families were moved and find lodgings there; others had to change schools in the course of the year.

Some of those who have been moved have received their compensation but others had been waiting for over three months.

Many of the families at Alcockspruit had ten or eleven buildings and so find that they cannot fit into the four-roomed houses at Madadeni. In August there were at least a couple of houses in Madadeni with the furniture still standing outside.

On the adjoining farm there were people who had been settled there many years ago by the B.A.D.; they too have been moved. It is thought that all the land is to be bought by Iscor, the state-run iron and steel corporation.

The people, as usual, were resigned to their fate; many seemed just bewildered by the whole thing. They had never seen Madadeni and had no idea what to expect there. All they knew was that they would not have any land or cattle. A B.A.D. official told them that it would be good for them to have to find jobs as they had become lazy living off the land at Alcockspruit!

There is a similar situation, on a smaller scale, at Milton, about eight miles from Newcastle towards Utrecht. Here there is a farm owned by sixteen Africans which has been declared a 'Black spot'. Between them the owners have about seventy tenants, who each pay R20 a year. They claim that it is very good land and the tenants are able to earn a living from it.

The owners have recently received a letter concerning the expropriation of the land. Its market value as farm land is nothing compared to its present value now that Iscor has bought all the surrounding farms.

Newcastle

Newcastle district has two rapidly developing large townships, Madadeni (or Duckponds) and Osizweni (Mountain View). They are usually bracketed together in official lists of 'townships', but are in fact very diffcrent from one another.

Madadeni is eight miles from Newcastle and, as townships go, is rather a superior one. At present it has some two thousand people and it is envisaged that the eventual population will be 67,400 (Minister of B.A.D., 14 May 1968). There is a two-year waiting list for houses. The houses are mainly four-roomed with toilet and water outside, for which the rent is R4.23 a month. There are shops, schools and the usual township facilities. A Training College is being built there to replace St Chad's, the former Anglican college near Ladysmith. There is a large hospital for chest diseases, but while a General Hospital is being built the people still have to go to Newcastle for general medical treatment.

At present there is not enough work in Newcastle and many of the residents of Madadeni go to work in Johannesburg and the Gold Reef. Once Iscor is established in Newcastle the employment position should improve considerably. But it is doubtful whether, even then, it will be sufficient for the vast numbers who are to be housed at Madadeni and Osizweni.

The *Natal Mercury* of 14 December 1967 reported Mr T. F. Coertze, the Chief Bantu Affairs Commissioner for Natal, as saying that thirty-eight new towns and 'cities' were being planned for the Natal Bantu Homelands. 'Osizweni will become one of the "cities",' he said. He did not say when this would happen, but at present Osizweni is a sub-economic township with nothing like the same facilities as Madadeni. It has about 20,000 inhabitants and more are arriving all the time; it is 'planned' for 72,000. They are all either completely indigent or of a very low income group. 'Squatters' from White farms are usually settled here rather than at Madadeni; some choose it because the rent is lower.

About two-thirds of the houses are one-roomed, asbestos-under-iron structures, which measure 12 ft by 9 ft. The other one-third have two rooms of about the same size, one of brick, the other all corrugated iron. Whole families, up to fifteen people, live in them. Some have added shacks of corrugated iron, others have built mud huts, which is all illegal and adds to the slum appearance but at least provides more living space. Rows upon rows of these tiny 'houses' make a most depressing sight. The one-roomed dwellings are for indigent people who do not pay rent; others pay R1.85 for two-roomed 'houses'.

There are about three taps in each street; but this supply sometimes has to be supplemented by water tankers. There is no clinic, though it is said that one is to start.

Indian doctors are refused permission to practise there. The nearest hospital is at Newcastle, fifteen miles away. Kwashiorkor, pellagra and other forms of malnutrition are rife. For example, recently some 65 per cent of the African children in Newcastle hospital, which serves the whole of the Newcastle district and part of Utrecht, were suffering from malnutrition and of these 60 per cent were from this one settlement or 'city', Osizweni. Many of the bed-cards in the hospital gave the diagnosis simply as 'starvation'. There is no doubt many others cannot afford to go to the hospital because of the bus fare and the out-patient fee of 60 cents. The bus fare is 10 cents single in the morning and 13 cents single at midday. (R8,000 has been allocated by the B.A.D. to combat malnutrition but it had not yet been used, I was told in September 1969, because of the lack of personnel to administer it.)

There is a sub-section of Osizweni known as 'Umlazi'. Here a widow with no children may be put into a house with three or four orphans, who may also be spastics or cripples. They are all supported by the B.A.D., but the widow has to 'mother' them.

The people complain also that the houses are very cold and that they cannot afford to buy coal at 40 cents a bag.

It is interesting that when a White employer wants to register a servant from Osizweni, this is done through the office at Madadeni. So most of the Whites in Newcastle never have any occasion to see this 'eyesore' but they do see the more respectable township at Madadeni.

Many other people from White farms are settling themselves on African-owned land at Blaauwbosch, a few miles from Osizweni.

Ladysmith

In the Ladysmith area thousands of people have had the threat of removal hanging over them for many years. I remember when I was at Besters Mission about ten years ago, the Bantu Affairs Commissioner from Ladysmith used to visit us regularly and explain to us the advantages of cooperating with the Department in the removal of 'squatters' from the Mission farm. Neither we nor the people quite saw the 'advantages'. The people are still there and there is still the continual threat of removal. The fate of the people in the huge African-owned settlements of Roosboom, Driefontein, Watersmeet, Burford and other places has also been in the balance for at least as long. About ten years ago the Department started making new roads near Watersmeet and even started building a school, miles from existing houses; therefore it was thought that more people were to be moved into the area. But nothing more happened. Now it is thought that the whole complex will be moved.

There has been talk in Ladysmith for years of thousands of these people going to Pieters, seven or eight miles from Ladysmith. The Minister of B.A.D. said in the House of Assembly on 14 May 1968 that a township for 72,000 is planned for Pieters. By October 1969 there was still no sign of it; nor was there any sign of the township at Waayhoek, which, according to the same statement, is to have 19,200 people. Waayhoek is the name of a farm just a few miles from Limehill and about thirty miles from Ladysmith in the middle of the veld.

This kind of demoralizing uncertainty occurred over and over again among the communities I visited in all parts of the country. The frequent agonies and hardships of the removals themselves are made much worse by the Government's tacit assumption that Africans, like cattle, do not need to be consulted. They can be herded according to the Government's secret plans, and disposed of however the White man decides. This means that the Government see no need whatsoever to be even consistent in the application of their policy. People who have been moved once into a 'homeland' – a place where they are supposed to enjoy some at least of the rights denied them everywhere else – can be moved on again just as arbitrarily. Or, as in Besters Mission, the people are told they will be moved, but are not told when, and for years they live in suspense under the threat of removal.

Hobsland (*Vulandondo*)

This is a settlement about nine miles from Ladysmith to which a number of African landowners from Khumalosville, sixteen miles the other side of Ladysmith, were moved in 1963, with great hardship, despite the efforts of their legal representatives. The people bought the farm at Khumalosville in 1908 and divided it into two-acre plots; at the time of the removal ninety-one of these were owned by Africans. They were told in 1952 that the Government wanted to buy the farm but that they would be given a bigger place elsewhere. They were led to believe that they would be given four-acre plots at Hobsland and the rest of the farm as commonage. When they were eventually moved they were given compensation for land, improvements and 'inconvenience', a free half-acre plot at Hobsland, and the right to buy another half-acre for R110. The Government offered R42 an acre at Khumalosville and charged R220 an acre at Hobsland. The people refused to go for some time but were finally told in September 1963 that if they had not moved by 2 October they would be arrested. They were taken to Hobsland in Government lorries and given a tent and half a bag of mealie meal.[1]

When I applied for a church site in Hobsland in 1963, I was shown a detailed plan for residential sites, schools, churches, shopping centre etc. But these plans have never materialized. One drawback was that the surveyors had drawn up the plans in winter and had neglected to take into account the fact that a big portion of the area is completely flooded by the river every time it rains! I did not get the church site because all the remaining church sites, after the Dutch Reformed Church and a few others had been allocated theirs, were in the flooded area. There is still only a prefabricated school, which was blown down during a gale.

Some people were there before the removal in 1961 and others have come since. Most have built very good houses and it appears to be a well-settled community. In fact it is one of the more prosperous places in the area. But it can hardly be called a 'town'. There is also the possibility that they may have to move again as Hobsland may fall within the catchment area for the new dam at Ladysmith.

Estcourt

A new township is also being built about seven miles from Estcourt. In October 1969 it consisted of rows and rows of toilets!

A recent report says that, in this area, 100,000 Africans are to be moved from the Drakensburg watershed, the biggest operation yet attempted for the resettlement of Africans. A spokesman for the Natal Agricultural Union is quoted as saying: 'Farmers are absolutely determined to secure this removal, which is closely linked with the expansion of Loch Sloy, the projected African township near Estcourt. Loch Sloy is adjacent to the Drakensburg location No. 1, and these settlements are astride our vital watersheds – vital not only to Natal but to South Africa as a whole.'[2] The farmers may be determined to move this huge

1. *Blackspots. A Study of Apartheid in Action*, published by the Liberal Party of South Africa.

2. *Rand Daily Mail*, 4 July 1970.

group of people, but it is by no means clear yet where they are to be resettled.

Hammersdale

Hammersdale, about thirty miles west of Durban, is one of the more developed border industrial areas, having eleven factories, which employ five to six thousand Africans. The land for these industries was purchased in 1962 and the first factories were in operation in 1963; by 1965 they were all established. But the township to house the workers was not ready for occupation until the end of 1968. Part of the reason for the delay was the fact that the African landowners had to be expropriated. The township has now been established but there are still a number of landowners who are being expropriated. At the time of writing, the fate of these people was still to some extent sub-judice, since one of them was fighting the expropriation order in Court. They were also trying to arrange for a deputation to interview the Minister of B.A.D. These were the last stages in a long fight to hold on to the land which they have owned for many years; some was originally purchased in 1894. The area was declared a released area by the 1936 Land Act, so the people had every reason to feel secure in their ownership of the land. Five or six years ago the property owners were registered; a few years later they were told to hand in their title deeds in place of which they would be given occupational permits, which they did not receive; instead they were given a record of their title deeds. In 1963 when border industries were opened in the area thousands of African people flocked there to find work and became squatters on this African-owned land, since no housing had been provided by the Department.

The landowners immediately filed an objection to the expropriation order. Then they submitted a petition to the State President. In this, they acknowledged the need for a location, but pointed out that the Bantu Trust owned a long stretch of land along the railway line which was uninhabited, and which would be suitable for a township. There was also, four miles from Hammersdale, across the Umlazi river, 'many hundreds of acres of land (Trust land) entirely in the hands of the Authorities which the Authorities could use for the purpose of the location to house factory workers ...'

In support of their contention, they quoted a speech by the Minister of B.A.D. (House of Assembly, 14 October 1966) saying that more responsibility would be given to local authorities who should take over a large share of the authority and functions of the Bantu Trust and that the economic, social, cultural and educational development of the homelands relied to a great extent on activating and assisting the African authorities to participate in their own government and to lead their own people.

The local people in this case were only too willing to conduct their own affairs and to build a township. But they were not consulted when the Government decided to take over the land which they had inherited 'from their parents and as such hold as tokens of their parents, who had laboured hard to win these lands out of their meagre wages'.

The Government's response to their appeal was to reply saying that the Landowners' Association's objections 'could not be upheld'. They were also warned not to ignore the expropriation order and reminded that it was in the interest of 'the Bantu' to cooperate.

In 1968 the people tried again to have a local authority established in the area, so that they could seek permission to build the township themselves, and again petitioned the State President. As this attempt again led to nothing, the Landowners' Association brought a case in the Supreme Court to have the expropriation order declared null and void. The case was postponed *sine die* because the Association had not established its right to plead. A new case has now been brought by an individual landowner.

An official of the B.A.D. called a meeting of the people and told them that it was not fair that they should have so much land, while others had none at all. Therefore the Government must expropriate the land and give shares to all. No doubt the Government would not wish this argument to be pursued too far in South African conditions.

In 1968 the houses of both tenants and landowners were numbered for removal. At the end of 1968 the tenants were given notice to move. By this time Empumalanga township was ready for occupation and some of them went there. They were not paid any compensation for their houses nor were they provided with transport. Some of the landowners have now been paid their compensation and have moved.

Many are still in possession, but in some cases contractors are building roads on their property without reference to them. When I last saw some of the people involved, on 31 August 1969, they were pinning all their hopes on the pending court case. If that fails they will join the hundreds of thousands of people who, according to the Government, move 'voluntarily'.

Some of the 'squatters' went to Empumalanga township, which is, presumably, the township for the workers in the border industries at Hammersdale. At the time of my visit in August 1969, it had about two thousand houses but about a third of them were not occupied. It had tarred roads, which is most unusual for a new township, but there were no shops or a clinic. The rent for a four-roomed, township-type house is R6.10 a month and the bus-fare to the border industries is 16 cents return.

It is said that there is to be no more industrial development in this area for some time, as all efforts are to be concentrated first on Newcastle and then on Richard's Bay. But the township is planned for 61,200 people and there are thousands of others already living in the surrounding areas, so there does not seem to be much hope of the border industries fulfilling the employment needs of Africans in the area.

According to a report in the *Natal Mercury* of 4 April 1969, five thousand of the squatters from Hammersdale went to Fredsville, near Inchanga. They went there because they could not afford the rent in Empumalanga township and it was not much further away from the border industries.

I went in search of Fredsville and found that it was a well-established settlement of African landowners, each one having a 10-acre plot. But it had been rather disrupted by the great influx of squatters that had been going on since about 1966. It was extremely overcrowded, with many people living in shacks; it was also reputedly full of brothels and shebeens. When I asked local people the way to Fredsville, they asked me rather hopefully whether I was going to tell these people to move. They said it used to be a nice, peaceful place but now they were frightened to go anywhere at night-time because of the 'tsotsis'.

When I went there the houses of the squatters had already been numbered and they had been told that they had to move to the township of Hammersdale; most of them have since been moved. There was no question of the landowners being moved and I was told that some of the squatters with proper houses were being allowed to stay. It may indeed be necessary for some of the squatters to be moved because the place is turning into a slum. But it is hardly their fault. Their plight is yet another example of the whole social system in which they and we live, with its unjust wages, its forced migrant labour and its racial discrimination. At Fredsville they can get a place to live for R10 a year; in the township they have to pay R6.10 a month. They do not like living in shacks, they prefer the conditions in the townships, but they simply cannot afford the rents. And the landowners of Fredsville, although comparatively prosperous, welcome the extra income from the squatters.

Poll-Tax Farm

'There is some sort of transit camp or something out near Edendale.' So I was told in Pietermaritzburg. Edendale is the sprawling African township a few miles to the south-west of the city. At the fifth attempt I found the camp – a cluster of hovels on the side of a hill. There are about three hundred 'houses', almost all of them mud, wooden or corrugated iron shacks; in fact there is really only one properly built house in the whole settlement. The general appearance is even worse than the Weenen Emergency Camp. The inhabitants have no room to grow anything, as the plots are about half the size of those in an ordinary 'closer settlement'; two that I measured were roughly 35 yds by 20 yds; some are even smaller and a few a little bigger.

The first arrivals came in June 1967 from Ockert's Kraal, on the outskirts of Pietermaritzburg. There were about forty-five families, some of whom had freehold rights to the land on which they were living. But it was a 'Black spot', so they lost their rights. Their title deeds were taken away and they were promised compensation, for which they were still waiting in August 1969. Others came, and were still coming occasionally, from White farms in the Greytown and Pietermaritzburg districts; others were from African farms where some had owned land; yet others had been squatters. Those from Ockert's Kraal were given three months' notice, but most of the others were given only three weeks.

Most of them had to provide their own transport to the transit camp and none of them was provided with a tent or rations or any other assistance when they arrived. Some of those from White farms were transported by Government lorries, but these and other squatters did not receive any compensation for their houses. They were all told not to build proper houses because the place was only temporary. The latest arrivals were told that they would be there for about five years and would then be moved into a location. Some have already been there for two years. This place is not fit for anybody to live in for a week, let alone seven years. For living in this squalor they have to pay R1 a year rent. Children over sixteen are not allowed to stay with their parents: they must go to a hostel.

When they first arrived there was no water supply; a few days later a water tank was installed. Just a few months before my visit, in August 1969, a reservoir had been built and a few taps put in the 'streets'.

There is the usual attitude of resignation and helplessness but also some bitterness: 'There is nothing we can do except pray.' But also: 'It cannot go on for ever. The Whites will get what they deserve, if not now then in the hereafter.' Such remarks are also a sad reflection on the type of Christianity they have been taught – a Christianity which has been abused to lead people to accept present sufferings in the hope of a future reward. But they also remarked that the people who had taught them this were themselves living in comfort.

Natal has, therefore, the whole range of resettlement schemes from the comparatively well-planned and well-run township of Madadeni to emergency and transit camps, with agricultural and 'closer settlements' in between. Conditions do not seem to have

changed very much from the time of Mondlo and Khumalosville to the time of Limehill and Weenen. It has been estimated
that another two million African people still have to be resettled
in Natal; of these about 75 per cent will go into 'townships'. One
hopes that some at least will be of the Madadeni type rather than
the Mpungamhlophe type – not that even Madadeni is by any
means an ideal town. But many of the other 25 per cent will be
moved into 'closer settlements'.

We have also seen something of the abrupt and ruthless man-
ner in which the removals are carried out. Government officials
continually repeat that the removals are 'voluntary'; Mr M. C.
Botha, Minister of Bantu Administration and Development, said
in a radio interview that in *all* cases the Africans who were moved
were volunteers. 'On occasions we have to do a good deal of persuasion to get them to move – but they are volunteers.'[1]

The Bakubung people were released from prison on condition
that they moved. The people at Morajo, some of whom went to
prison rather than move, were eventually faced with an order
from the Supreme Court. At Solomondale it was made quite
clear in a letter from the Bantu Affairs Commissioner to the
owner of the property that if the squatters did not move they
would be prosecuted, and, in addition to any other penalties,
would be summarily ejected. At Syferkuil there was an official
letter which stated explicitly 'these people are being forcibly removed' (see page 134). I came across many cases where the people
protested, sought remedies through appeals to the authorities or
to the courts, and yet were evicted and their homes destroyed.

Moreover, the people are well aware that if they do not agree
to move when they are ordered to, they will later be removed to
even worse conditions. For example, at Barotha (Northern
Transvaal) those who moved when they were told to were allocated land for ploughing and grazing, whereas those who held
out against moving were eventually allocated only half a normal
residential plot for each family with no ploughing or grazing
land. In every settlement I visited throughout the country, every
person I spoke to, except for some who had been squatters or
labour tenants on White farms, said they had not wanted to

1. *Star*, 21 November 1969.

move. But – 'We had no choice,' 'There was nothing we could do.' They were told by 'G.G.' (Government officials) that they had to move, and so they moved.

There can be no pretence of voluntary moves in the case of the thousands 'endorsed out' of White urban areas every year. The people endorsed out because they have become 'unproductive' (through age, sickness or being widowed) are usually sent to one of the townships in the 'homeland'. But if a person is endorsed out because he or she is not qualified to live in the urban area under the Bantu (Urban Area) Act no. 25 of 1945 he is simply sent back to his 'homeland'. His reference book (pass) is stamped to show that he must leave the area by a certain date and he must make his own way back. If he has friends or relatives in the 'homeland' he will go to them, otherwise he must go to the local chief or Bantu Affairs Commissioner and ask for a place. He may then be assigned to any kind of place, a township or a 'closer settlement'. If he is found residing illegally in the White area, he is arrested and either fined or imprisoned. On release he will be escorted out of town by the police.

There are cases of such people being sent to the 'homeland' by the police after completing a prison sentence for being illegally in a White area. They go to the 'homeland' but find nowhere to stay and no hope of work, so they go straight back to the White town, only to be arrested and imprisoned again.

4. The Eastern Cape

The Eastern Cape Province is a vast area, encompassing a wide range of geographical and economic differences. It contains the busy industrial sea-ports of East London and Port Elizabeth, a number of fair-sized inland towns like Grahamstown and Kingwilliamstown, and sleepy rural hamlets dating back to the 1820 British settlers.

When the rains are good, which is not that often, the countryside is verdant and smiling. But the periodic droughts bring misery and suffering to many. As always, it is the poorest, the Africans, who suffer most. Around the sea-ports there is employment in the burgeoning industries, but in the rural areas and around the smaller towns the all-too-familiar spectre of unemployment, poverty, famine, malnutrition and stark starvation are to be found in the Black community.

Much as they desire apartheid, the Whites of Eastern Cape have a priceless economic asset in their impoverished Black neighbours, in terms of the vast labour pools of the adjoining Transkei, the most politically advanced and the only geographically consolidated of the Government's Bantustans, and the Ciskei, which exists as a scattered collection of seventeen separate pieces of land threading through the 'White' areas of the Eastern Cape. The Ciskei does not form a coherent whole, but, in the words of the Tomlinson Commission, is merely an administrative unit.

The Transkei itself is of course crucial to the whole argument about whether the South African strategy of apartheid can be justified in any way. As the one African Reserve in the whole country which had a situation and history which lent itself to some form of territorial identity, it was made the showpiece of Dr Verwoerd's new emphasis on 'separate development'. As a response to the shock to international confidence caused by Sharpville the separate development theory has served the Nationalist Government extremely well. But the Transkei today stands as evidence of what is meant by 'development' and 'self-government' in Nationalist practice.

The imposition of Bantu Authorities in the Transkei in the 1950s led, as happened in other parts of the country such as Sekhukhuniland, to widespread rebellion in 1960 and 1961 against the chiefs imposed or maintained in power by the Government. As the Secretary for Native Affairs told the Territorial Authority, 'Under the Bantu Authorities which you constitute you will be able to lead the people in a true sense. You will be able to tell them, not ask them, what to do.'

The rebellions were put down with considerable bloodshed and many were hanged in retribution. A state of emergency was declared in December 1960 which is still in force throughout the Transkei. Under Proclamation 400, the police and army have unlimited powers, and it is in these circumstances that 'self-government' was introduced in 1963. Even so the anti-apartheid party won an overwhelming majority in the first election, only to be submerged in the Assembly by a majority of Government-appointed chiefs. Since then the opposition has been systematically disrupted and crushed. Virtually all administration is in the hands of White South African officials and is rigorously enforced by the White police. All urban and administrative centres are in fact White enclaves within the Transkei in which apartheid is maintained without even a fiction of it being an African country.

Under its constitution, the Transkei Government has no say in its own defence, external affairs, internal security, postal and related matters, railways, immigration and frontier control, currency and banking, customs and excise. All legislation passed by the Transkei Assembly is subject to the assent of Pretoria.

After seven years of 'independence' and 'separate development' the Transkei is poorer than ever, and no less dependent on migrant labour. Out of a total population of some 1·4 million, 300,000 work as migrants in the Republic. Of the remainder, only 30,000 are in paid employment, and only 1,700 of them have jobs in industry.

The Tomlinson Commission in 1954 called for the redeployment of half the population of Transkei (then one million) in industry and in the urban centres, to relieve the extreme pressure on the land. Instead of this, the Government has swollen the population by its removals policy. The number of Xhosa 'repatriated' to the Transkei may be approaching a half million, according to estimates. Because of the state of emergency I was not able to visit any of these settlements or discuss conditions with the people, in spite of the fact that I have travelled through the Transkei during the last few years several times. Occasional reports reach the outside world of the desperate economic plight in the Transkei: queues of unemployed outside the labour bureaux; half the maize crop failed in 1969 and 1970; 20 per cent of the cattle died from drought in 1969; 40,000 infants died of malnutrition in 1967; an epidemic of tuberculosis affecting a fifth of the population in 1968 – it is impossible to verify these reports, but all the evidence supports the view that conditions are deteriorating. There is no sign of a change in the insignificant number of jobs available in the Transkei; the Government-owned Xhosa Development Corporation has a total share capital of only R7 million, and approved loans of no more than R94,000 to Africans in 1968.

The Ciskei is backward, impoverished, little short of a rural slum, with an average population density of more than eighty per square mile (according to the Tomlinson Commission), which is considerably in excess of its carrying capacity. In figures, there are about half a million Africans crowded into the Ciskei's 2,185,000 acres.

The territory is further handicapped by the Government's policy of removing Africans from the Western Cape. Many of them have been resettled in the Eastern Cape, at Mnxesha, Ilingi and Sada. The first Government plan was to remove all Africans who were living to the west of the 'Eiselen Line' (Kimberley/Humansdorp) near Port Elizabeth. The greater portion of the Cape Province lies to the west of this line, but later the line was drawn even further to the east and so the African inhabitants of Middelburg, Burgersdorp, Cradock and many other towns were doomed. This is known as the 'Kat-Fish Line'; it runs from Aliwal North, through Sterkstroom, to the Fish River. Beyond it, to the east, lies only a small corner of the Province, including the Reserves of the Ciskei.

The Government has in recent years become increasingly coy about furnishing statistics on the number of people being moved, so it is impossible to estimate how many new arrivals have been resettled in the Eastern Cape, particularly in the Ciskei.[1] The usual pattern that emerges is that the newcomers are unable to find work, so they soon return to the Western Cape towns or go to the Rand as contract labourers, leaving the women, the aged and the children behind them for long periods to exist as best they can.

I presume that the reason for the special camps for 'redundant' people in the Eastern Cape is that people endorsed out from the Western Cape usually have no ties at all with any of the Reserves. Whereas in the less old established cities in other parts of the country it is possible to trace some tenuous connection for most Africans with a 'homeland', the majority of people in the Western Cape, and all their forebears, were born there.

In the Eastern Cape, with the notable exception of the Roman Catholic Diocese of Queenstown, I received more cooperation than anywhere else. I met a number of people who were fully aware of what was going on, were concerned about it and were trying to do something at least to ameliorate the conditions. The Border branch of the South African Council of Churches is very active and is doing excellent work in some of the settlements. A number of people were able to give me a lot of information, which they asked me not to publish. This was still very helpful in that when I went into the various places I knew exactly what to look for. Nevertheless I stress that I am only using information which I found, or confirmed, for myself.

Mnxesha

Limehill has become symbolic of the plight of Natal's rural Africans. In the same way, Mnxesha has become a symbol for the Ciskei. As I travelled from Cape Town eastwards, the name kept

1. See Appendix 1.

recurring. Obviously conditions in this resettlement camp were more than usually atrocious.

When you have seen Morsgat, Weenen, Limehill, Stinkwater and so many others, it is difficult to be shocked or distressed by similar places. But one look at Mnxesha was sufficient to convince me that the reports I had heard had not been exaggerated and that here was grinding poverty, squalor and hardship equal to the worst places I had seen. There were the familiar, tiny one or two-room houses, many with a number of ragged, hungry-looking children or a bent old woman sitting outside. It was not quite true that I could no longer be shocked or disturbed. I was, in particular, by the sight of one tiny baby, a virtual skeleton, unable to move or even to cry and covered with flies. I have been through the children's wards in African hospitals throughout the country and over the past ten years have seen thousands of starving, dying children. But I doubt whether I have ever seen anything worse than this. I cut short my tour to take the child to hospital.

Mnxesha is about ten miles from Kingwilliamstown, on the road to Alice. From the main road you can see that there is some kind of settlement, but the worst parts are not visible. The first people were 'settled' there in December 1967 with the aim of eventually accommodating 1,800 families (about 10,000 people). But by July 1968 there were only about seventy families. The main influx took place between December 1968 and February 1969. This, I was told, was because once water had been laid on, the authorities in other areas pressed for the people to be sent to Mnxesha. The Minister of B.A.D. said in the House of Assembly on 4 March 1969 that 2,897 people, of whom 2,041 were children, had been moved there. Most of these had come from Middelburg (203 families), Burgersdorp (67 families) and Cape Town (39 families), with a few from a number of other towns. By May 1969, the official population figure was 3,400. My own estimate was much higher and seemed to be borne out by the numbers on the houses.

The first arrivals were put into wooden huts, with zinc roofs. The huts measured roughly 10 ft by 16 ft and 10 ft high, with no ceilings or floors. There are ninety-nine of these which are still in use. In one of them, chosen at random, there were three adults and four children; I was assured that some of the others contained more. These people are mainly pensioners and indigents who do not pay rent. Obviously such huts are extremely hot in summer and cold in winter and the earth floors become very damp, even wet, in the rainy season.

The bulk of the houses are two-roomed, cement-under-asbestos structures with no floors or ceilings. Some stand alone, others are semi-detached so that they appear to be four-roomed houses, but are in fact two-roomed ones. The rent for these is R3.42 a month, including rudimentary sanitation services. In one of them there were thirteen children whose mother was working in Cape Town. Many, if not all, of the houses are grossly overcrowded. Because of the number of widows and pensioners, the majority (53 per cent of the total in May 1969) of the householders are women. There are a few four-roomed houses for teachers and Government employees.

An official of the Information Office attached to the Chief of Bantu Affairs Commissioner's Office in Kingwilliamstown was was quoted in the *Daily Dispatch* of 16 January 1969 as saying:

Redundant people are being moved to Mnxesha. The township is the same as Ilingi near Lady Frere and Sada near Whittlesea. We house redundant people. The people would be of no particular age-group and could not render productive service in an urban area. Among such people were men who had lost their jobs and could not find new employment, old and infirm people and unmarried mothers. The Government would provide the children with one substantial meal a day and rations would be given to the old and infirm people. Able-bodied men would be able to enter into contracts for work on the mines, industries and other avenues of employment. The provision of employment in the new village is receiving the attention of the authorities.

How much attention they gave the matter we do not know, but they evidently decided against it. In the House of Assembly on 4 March 1969, the Minister of B.A.D. said that the Government was not contemplating establishing any industries in or near Mnxesha.

By May 1969, more people had arrived from Middelburg and

others were still coming. These, and many of the others, were victims of the Government policy of moving all Africans to the east of the Kat-Fish Line. Since this had been the intention for some time it seems that little or no development of African locations in towns west of this line had been made. So, at Middelburg, the Government had built a large new coloured township, but had for many years done nothing about the African location where many people were living in tin 'pondokkies'. Conditions were thus far from satisfactory, but they did at least have better facilities than they found at Mnxesha. At Middelburg there were two established schools, a clinic with a permanent staff, lighting in some of the streets and a satisfactory water and sewerage system. Rents were R1.75 a month for a two-roomed house, R4 a month for a three-roomed house and R2 a month for a 'private stand' – at the time of the removal this was increased to R6 a month, presumably to encourage people to 'agree' to move. Many people at Mnxesha were quite adamant that they had been employed, reasonably housed and very much wanted to stay at Middelburg. But, as one said: 'You can't say no to a White man.'

They said they were told by an official that at Mnxesha they would have proper houses with a bath and a stove; there would be shops and other facilities and special bachelor quarters with their own kitchens and cooks. Others claimed they were told that if they did not move dogs would be set on them. Some were told to settle their families in Mnxesha and return to work in Middelburg. Those who owned their houses at Middelburg were promised compensation at the time of the removal, but some said they had received it several months after the move. The highest compensation that I heard of was R240 for a four-roomed house; others received between R25.25 and R80.

By the time of my visit the health facilities had improved considerably; previously, I was told, they were virtually non-existent. A qualified nurse was appointed in May 1969 to run a free clinic, with a doctor visiting once a week. Until that time a nurse from Mount Coke had visited once a week. But the charge was 20 cents, so most people could not afford treatment. There was also a T.B. clinic once a week. Free medical treatment was available in Kingwilliamstown but the return bus-fare of 40 cents was prohibitive. There was (and still is) a free ambulance service. But the African superintendent has to drive four miles to the nearest telephone to call it and this telephone does not operate in the evenings or at weekends. The district surgeon ran a clinic about three miles away. He normally charged R1.50 for an adult and R1 for a child, which was well beyond the means of most.

The signs of malnutrition are obvious throughout the settlement and there have been many deaths. In May 1969 there were over ninety graves, of which over seventy were children's. The bulk of the population only arrived in December–February 1969.

There are now taps in the streets. These first appeared in February 1969. Until then water was brought in once a day Monday to Friday, twice on Saturday and not on Sunday. The people were told to boil the water before drinking it. Pit latrines are provided but they appear to be very shallow and are prone to overflowing.

Almost half of the men are migrant workers. The only employment in the area is on the building of houses in the settlement, for which men are paid R16.50 a month. Women are paid R6 a month for such work as planting grass in the settlement; this work is a form of poor-relief. In the beginning there was some employment in the settlement for one person from almost every house. But now there are many with no wage earner, who are provided with rations each month.

People complained that the rations were issued irregularly and that it appeared they were being cut down. Some said that the rations lasted them only two weeks: 'After that we have to pawn our clothes in order to buy food at the European store.' There are no shops in the settlement. The nearest one, which is White-owned, is about two miles away; there is another one and a Post Office about four miles away. The Border Council of Churches is subsidizing the sale of milk and soup powders. There is no fuel available in the area; I passed some children carrying wood four miles from the settlement. At first wood was being sold for 35 cents a bag and then for 25 cents. It is now being sold for 15 cents, the balance being paid by a relief organization. But even with this subsidy, wood was piling up with the distributor because the people could not afford it. A number of people have been fined R10 for trespassing while in search of fuel.

At Middelburg, and some of the other places from which they came, some of the people had been receiving maintenance grants of R5 a month for every child. But these grants are only applicable in urban 'Bantu areas', so they lost them on their removal to Mnxesha, which is a rural township. The Bantu Affairs Department in Zwelitsha had said that they would apply to Pretoria to make the grants applicable to Mnxesha.

A lower primary school was opened on 14 March 1969. Before that, the children had to walk about three and a half miles to school and often arrived exhausted, which was not surprising considering their undernourished state.

No matter how bad a settlement is there are usually some people, who have come from White farms, who prefer it; this is true even at Mnxesha. In general, the people from the towns did not want to move, but some said that, despite all the hardship, they were 'happy' because they felt that they had some security and were free from continual harassment about reference books. For example, at Middelburg many had to report every month to have their book stamped and they never knew when it would be the last time.

The sufferings of the people at Mnxesha are exemplified in the case of Mrs E.M. She arrived at Mnxesha from Burgersdorp in December 1968, with her six children. By May 1969 two of the children had died; two others, aged thirteeen and six years, had 'gross pellagra' according to a doctor; another younger child was in hospital with malnutrition. She is a widow and was supporting herself in Burgersdorp by doing domestic work; now she has no employment. She is only thirty-seven years old and so does not receive a pension. As Mnxesha is a rural area she cannot get a child maintenance allowance. Since she went to Mnxesha she has had no source of income apart from the few cents which she manages to earn by collecting wood from miles away and selling it in the settlement. She has taken her children to the nurse several times but because she did not have the 20 cents they were not attended to. She was receiving Government rations, which were obviously inadequate.

The Discarded People

About one and a half miles from Mnxesha there is a growing settlement for pensioners and their families, called Emadakeni. In May 1969 there were sixteen mud huts, measuring about 10 ft by 15 ft; the roofs were also mud with a layer of tarpaulin in between. There were no windows, only two small openings. These huts housed more 'redundant' people from town locations. They did not pay any rent for the mud houses, which were certainly inferior to the normal farm house. There were no toilets provided and there was no sign of any having been built by the occupants of the sixteen huts. There was a water tank which was filled by a tanker. Some were building their own houses, for which they had been given doors and windows, a few yards away. Some of the people in the wooden huts at Mnxesha had been given plots at Emadakeni and told to build their own houses. A dozen or so wooden houses had recently been erected on this site.

Zwelitsha

There are two big townships in the area, Zwelitsha and Mdantsane. Zwelitsha, which is three and a half miles from Kingwilliamstown, was started in 1949 and planned as a town in itself for 'landless Natives and full-time industrial workers from the over-populated Ciskeian Reserves'.[1] (Further evidence that the land shortage and over-population in the Reserves was recognized as long ago as 1949.) But for some reason the building was halted in 1958, after 993 houses had been built. Building recommenced in 1963 and since then the population has more than doubled with people endorsed out from towns in the Western Cape.

The township is on Bantu Trust property and so is classified as a rural township. This means, according to local informants, that the residents are not allowed to seek work in near-by Kingwilliamstown; the labour-force required there is drawn from the municipal location and the coloured population. There is a large factory just opposite the township, the Good Hope Textile

1. Prof. W. D. Hammond Tooke, *The Tribes of the King William's Town District*.

Company. According to Professor Hammond Tooke,[1] the township was sited adjacent to the factory in order to ensure employment for the residents. I was told that the factory employs between three and four thousand people, but that many of these come from the rural areas of the Ciskei and the Transkei. My informants said that the wages were very low (starting at R3.15 a week), because the people from the rural areas were willing to accept anything. Every day there was a queue of about a hundred people from these areas looking for jobs. Therefore, they said, most of the men from Zwelitsha did not work there. Many of them return to the towns from which they were endorsed out, leaving their families at Zwelitsha. They become 'single' men living in a hostel, which satisfies the authorities because they are no longer residents of the urban area.

The rents are between R3.90 and R5 a month. If the residents fall into arrears with the rent, a policeman goes round and locks up the houses. They go to court and, if they cannot pay, are evicted. Many of them then look for a place in one of the rural Trust villages. For example, one such village about seven miles away, was planned for four hundred people; there are now about two thousand. On some plots there are four or five sub-tenants. I was told by a person who had at one time worked for the B.A.D. that the authorities turn a blind eye to this and to the development of slums which must inevitably follow.

Mdantsane

Mdantsane is a large township about ten miles from the town of East London. It is by little more than a legal fiction that its residents conform with the requirements of being outside a White urban area. The township is in a Reserve area but is almost surrounded by the East London municipal area.

In May 1969, the population was officially 58,000. Unofficial but well-informed estimates put the figures as high as 120,000. All the people from Duncan Village, a shanty location near East London, are to be moved to this township. So far, about half of them (37,000) have already been moved. The residents from

1. ibid.

West Bank municipal location in East London have also been moved in. The others have come mainly from towns in the Western Cape, from which they have been endorsed out in furtherance of the Government aim of moving all Africans from the Western Cape, looking for employment. So many people have flocked in that it has not been necessary to compel people to go there. Many people have been evicted for non-payment of rent; they then move in with friends or relatives in the township, causing great overcrowding.

The people at Mdantsane find some employment in the industries of East London, which is conveniently situated as a 'border area', with the advantages that this carries for industrialists. Some factory owners in East London say that a year ago they had an average of ten people a week looking for jobs; now they have forty a day.

There are the usual township facilities, but Dr J. H. Moolman, M.P., in the 'No Confidence' Debate in 1969, pointed out the deficiencies of the place. He said that there were thirty-two schools but more than half of them had no staff; there was not a single public telephone; there was no resident doctor or hospital and no pharmacy; there was no form of entertainment.[1] And of course there is the usual problem of increased rents (R6.75 and R8), and bus-fares (12–15 cents a day).

Mount Coke

At Mount Coke there is a big Methodist hospital and very little else. All around there are the usual Trust villages. But just a little way from the hospital there is a strange-looking settlement. It consists of about forty wooden huts, similar to those at Mnxesha, all huddled together. I was told that the African superintendent lived about three miles away at the Reformatory of which he was the principal and that I should go to see him to find out about the place. I went but he, very politely, explained that he had strict instructions not to give any information about the settlement. So I had to return and find out what I could for myself.

1. Hansard, No. 1, col. 144 et seq., 1969.

It appears that this settlement started off about five years ago as a transit camp. At first people stayed a year or two and then moved on. But for the last two years only a few people have moved on – to Sada. It now seems to have become a settlement for pensioners, some of whom have been there since the establishment of the settlement and presumably will stay there. In May 1969, about twenty-five of the huts were occupied, all by old-age pensioners or disabled people. There were also a number of small children; most of them are the illegitimate offspring of the inhabitants' children who either cannot afford to support them or cannot have their children with them in an urban area. The old people whose children could assist them were able to get a house in Zwelitsha.

These old or disabled people are mainly 'rejects' from farms in the Karoo who were evicted when the 'five labour-tenants law' was enforced; there are also a few 'redundants' from urban location. The Secretary of the Farmers' Union denied that these people had been evicted from farms. However, one family was found living in an old motor-car and another in a cave, after having left a farm, and other people said that they were evicted, put on a train to Kingwilliamstown and then brought by lorry to the settlement.

They receive a pension of R5.05 every two months and rations every three months. The rations are in the form of a coupon, valued between R3 and R6, to buy food at the local store. They also receive skimmed milk when it is available and Pronutro (though they were not receiving the latter when I visited). Fruit from a Government farm, which is rejected at the market, is sometimes dumped there. About a ton of rotting pineapples was once dumped (so that the statistics can show that seventy-five people were given one ton of fruit in a year).

They do not pay rent for the huts and between them they have two taps. The people complained about the lack of food and general poverty but the general attitude was that experience has shown that it is no use complaining. One old person commented: 'Death is a release from such a place.' They said that they had been better off on the farms. Those at Sada said they had been better off here, which does not say much for Sada.

Malnutrition is widespread in the surrounding Trust villages. Some of the staff at the Methodist hospital said that this was due to a great extent to the ignorance and wilful neglect of the people, despite all the Government was doing for them. The hospital is 90 per cent Government subsidized.

Komga/Mooiplaas

There are also a number of Trust villages in the Komga-Mooiplaas area. Most of them have been established for some time and are of the usual pattern, which means that while the residents have a little land and a few cattle they are basically dependent on the income of migrant workers. When there are a number of Trust villages in an area you can generally assume that there will also be at least one 'closer settlement' for the 'left-overs'. In this area there is one called Sotho Township, seven miles from Mooiplaas. At the time of my visit, May 1969, there were about 150 houses. These people had been coming in, in ones and twos, over the past twelve years, mainly from White farms in the Queenstown, Kingwilliamstown and East London districts. An occasional one still joined them.

As a variation on the 'closer settlement' theme, they pay R1.50 a year for their 50 yd by 50 yd plots, instead of the usual R1. They have no land for grazing or ploughing. There is no employment in the area, except for a few White farms. The men work in East London and further afield; many of the women also have started going to East London to work. The bus-fare to East London is R1.30 return.

All of these people had to provide their own transport to the settlement and erect their own temporary shelters while they built their houses, which, in general, they have done very well. It is a common feature of such settlements that the people themselves make such efforts to build decent houses and to overcome the hardships imposed upon them that a casual observer might look upon them as prosperous rural villages. He might not realize that they have had to build this from nothing; he might not notice that there are no shops or other facilities;

that they have no land nor cattle; that, most importantly, there are no men, because they are all migrant workers.

At Sotho Township a doctor visits once a week; the nearest hospital is in East London, thirty-six miles away. There is a dam and one borehole.

The nearby White farmers have complained that there is a lot of stock-theft and the Bantu Affairs Commissioner has assured them that these people will be moved again.

Queenstown

My main intention in going to Queenstown was to visit the notorious settlements of Sada and Ilingi, which were established to house people endorsed out of the Western Cape. On my arrival in Queenstown, I was virtually arrested and subjected to interrogation and a small dose of brain-washing – not by the police but by the clergy! I arrived a little tired and rather dusty and was immediately hauled off to the Roman Catholic Bishop, my request for the opportunity at least to be able to have a wash being brusquely dismissed. The Bishop, untimely aroused from his siesta, at first seemed just as bewildered by the whole affair as I was. But he soon warmed to his theme and argued that it was not fair to do any report or survey of Ilingi and Sada at that time because these places were still being developed. Actually, thousands of people had been living there for six years. He said that the Government was doing its best to rehabilitate the residents and that they were better housed than they had been on White farms. Some of the 'better houses' consist of one room, for ten or more people, about one-quarter of the size of the room in which the Bishop was speaking. I was eventually released, after having been warned that I would not be able to get into Ilingi anyway and that I was not to involve any of the local clergy in helping me. Before I had had time to leave the town, which I was in a hurry to do, the Vicar General was sent, in an enormous Mercedes, to repeat the warning that anything I did, I did on my own authority and at my own risk and that I did not have the Bishop's blessing – which I had not asked for in the first place.

Ilingi

Despite the Bishop's prediction, there was no difficulty at all about getting into Ilingi. I drove straight into the settlement and at every house I went to, or in any group I met in the streets, I found people only too willing to talk about their conditions.

Ilingi is about thirteen miles east of Queenstown, in a beautiful but bleak setting and far away from the public eye. It was started about three years ago and when I was there, in May 1969, there were about a thousand houses, stretching along the side of a valley completely exposed to the wind, the sun and the snow. The majority of the houses consisted of two rooms, one built of corrugated iron and the other of brick, each about 10 ft square; these were the more recently built ones. The first arrivals were housed in wooden huts, similar to those at Mnxesha, and later ones in one-roomed corrugated iron huts. These wooden and corrugated-iron structures were still in use. Rent for the one room was R1.50 a month and for two rooms, R2.40. Pensioners did not pay rent. A batch of two-roomed concrete houses, with iron or asbestos roofs, was being built.

The people of Ilingi have been evicted from farms or endorsed out of locations in Uitenhage, Colesburg, Cradock, Cathcart, Molteno, and the Western Cape generally. The population is increasing all the time as more and more people from the Western Cape towns become 'redundant' or unwanted. Some of the people claim that they had been in employment in the towns from which they were endorsed out. They then leave their families in Ilingi and return to work. There are also about forty former political prisoners, mainly ex-members of the banned African National Congress, from Port Elizabeth, who have been virtually exiled to this settlement.

The first thing that everyone I spoke to complained about was the complete lack of fuel. There were no trees in the area and all fuel had to be brought in. A lorry-load cost R12 and was the most economical way of buying it, but few could afford to buy in such bulk. I was shown some sticks, about a foot long, for which they had paid one cent each. But this was only the beginning of their complaints. They said they had been cold throughout the winter, had insufficient room and were hungry. Most of the people I spoke to had come from farms and so complained of having no land or cattle. They said that on the farms 'saphila ngenyama' – 'we lived on meat'. The signs of hunger and malnutrition were obvious. When a local missionary asked what he could do for them at Christmas, they replied, 'Bring us food.' Ilingi and Mpungamhlophe are the only two places I can remember where people came to me begging for food and clothes.

Some of the people said that they preferred to be there in that at least they were free from harassment, but they too agreed with the complaints of the others. Another complaint was that they no longer received rations, but one member of the family had to work in the settlement for R5 a month, if they were in need of relief. I had heard elsewhere that if there was no man or woman capable of working and the family was destitute, one of the children was forced to leave school and work in the settlement. I put this to a group of young people and they agreed that it was the case. The work they are given involves weeding and picking up stones, which appears to be intended just to give them something to do. While there is doubtless a lot to be said for providing employment rather than simply handing out rations, it still seems hard on women and children to have to work for a whole month for R5. It is hardly their fault that they or their husbands or fathers are not employed elsewhere; there is no employment for them.

About three hundred men are employed as drain-diggers and general labourers at R16.50 a month; about thirty-six as bricklayers at R24 a month, and seven as tractor drivers at R24 a month. The others have to apply for labour contracts as migrant workers in the industrial areas of the Republic. They are not allowed to seek work in Queenstown. Some of these people were endorsed out to Ilingi because they had lost their employment in the White urban area; now they have even less chance of ever finding a job.

Just prior to my visit a second primary school was opened; previously there had been one school with nearly a thousand pupils and nine teachers. A clinic was started at the end of 1968;

a nurse and a midwife are on call and a doctor visits once a week. Many people said that, at the beginning, hospital cases had to wait until there was a lorry-load. It was not clear whether this was still the case. There was a small shop, but it was a couple of miles from other sections of the settlement; people in some parts of the settlement said that there was no shop, presumably considering that the place where the shop is was not part of the same settlement. The nearest urban centre was Queenstown, to where the bus-fare was forty cents return. A Post Office had recently been opened, and there was a police station.

There were a number of pensioners in the settlement who were no longer able to work on farms, or were 'non-productive' in the urban areas. They were receiving a pension of R6 every two months. It appeared that they were the only ones receiving rations, which are much the same as those at Mnxesha.

I was told that there had been plans for a dam, but they seem to have fallen through. There were a few taps in the streets – one for about every forty houses. It was recently announced that a handicraft centre is to be built at a cost of R65,000, and also sports facilities, but there was no indication as to when these will be completed; nor was there any sign of industries being established in the area.

Sada

The conditions at Queenstown's other infamous settlement, Sada, have been known for some time. Before visiting there, too, I had to listen to a long lecture from the local Roman Catholic priest on the mores of the 'natives' and all the Government was doing to help them. I then went into Sada and found it to be a slightly larger edition of Ilingi – the same tiny houses, the same evidence of poverty and overcrowding. I went into Sada to visit the new Roman Catholic church, a large edifice standing rather incongruously among the shacks. But the superintendent had no qualms about letting me look around. He saw nothing wrong with the situation and obviously thought that he was doing a good job for the 'native', as I suppose he is according to his lights.

Sada is three miles from Whittlesea and twenty-four from Queenstown, in the midst of a rural area. The housing covers roughly two square miles. When I was there, about one thousand four hundred houses were occupied and a further three hundred were to be completed and occupied within the next three months. These people are mainly 'squatters' from White farms, but some also come from locations in the Western Cape, and even from the Orange Free State. There are a number of pensioners, widows and unmarried mothers. The population consists mainly of families with no income, though there are also a number of families of migrant workers.

The house-types are even more varied than at Ilingi. The first houses, erected about five years ago, were one-roomed wooden huts with mud floors, no ceilings and a small window at each end; they are still in use. Then a number of one-roomed asbestos huts with corrugated-iron roofs were put up; some of them are still in use. Then followed an attempt to mould walls from local earth. They cracked and were washed away; there are none still standing. After this, one-roomed corrugated-iron huts were used. Later one room of concrete or brick was added to these huts. The most recent houses are built of concrete or brick with either two or four rooms. But some of them have an outside door in each room so that a separate 'unit' can be accommodated in every room.

Very few of the people can afford to buy a stove, so many of them have to cook in the open; they usually build a mud wall as a shield against the wind. But on the day I was there it was raining and, in a number of the houses which we visited, the people were huddled around a brazier or an open fire in the middle of a room full of smoke. The thorn trees and dung from the surrounding countryside had by then been almost completely used up, so the people had either to buy wood or travel long distances to collect it. Farmers near by sell wood at R9 a load; three sticks, each a foot long, cost five cents.

People are said to go to Sada 'voluntarily' but, as we saw in the official statement about Mnxesha, Sada is one of the places for 'redundant' people. Some of its residents claim that they were led to believe that they were coming to a much better place;

95

for others the choice was either Sada or nowhere; some, from White farms, do prefer it. My guide, a Roman Catholic missionary, explained that 'the native' liked to live in such places with his own people and did not want to mix with Whites. He asked one woman, living in a four-roomed house, whether she preferred this place, and beamed with approval when she said she did. But he was rather taken aback when, asked why she preferred it, she replied, 'Because we are near to the White people.' I also noticed that he always phrased his question: 'You like it here, don't you?' To which almost any African would give an affirmative answer, realizing, quite rightly in this case, that it would be pointless to say anything else anyway.

Families entering or leaving the settlement require a permit from the magistrate at Whittlesea, who is also the Bantu Affairs Commissioner. Police patrol the settlement at night to prevent people from entering and settling illegally. The people who might try to enter are those who have been evicted from White farms and have nowhere at all to go; it is not a question of leaving their homes in order to settle at Sada. It shows how desperate the plight of some people must be if they will try to settle illegally at Sada.

Many of the men are migrant workers and many are unemployed. About 120 are employed in the brickyard, and others on building houses and roads. The standard wage for those employed by the Bantu Affairs Department as labourers is R16.50 a month. Some seven hundred women are employed by the superintendent, in cleaning and weeding the settlement, for R5 a month. This wage, as at Ilingi, is in lieu of rations. A few work on the local White farms. When extra labour is needed by the Government forestry department, a few fortunate ones are employed at R10 a week, plus food. The brick factory was started by the superintendent primarily to make bricks for building at Sada. It can produce far more than are needed at Sada but, since the nearest railhead is at Queenstown, twenty-four miles away, there does not seem much possibility of these being marketed. This would also seem to preclude the establishment of any other industry in the area. But, again, as at Ilingi,

Mnxesha and many other settlements, many of these people were sent here because they were unemployed, and the intention seems to be either to keep them thus or to make them full-time migrant workers.

The Moravian Mission has started a sewing centre, which will be able to train some women and help them to gain an income. Having failed, after repeated attempts, to obtain a site for this purpose in Sada, the Moravians decided to build the centre on their own church site. The Department of B.A.D. recently announced that it is to build a handicraft centre at a cost of R65,000; the building was being erected when I was there. As with the proposed centre at Ilingi, it is not clear whether this is to provide employment for the residents or is to be a training institution.

At the time of my visit about 45 per cent of the people were living on Government rations. They were given monthly vouchers, valued at R1.70 for an adult and R1.40 for a child, by the superintendent and exchanged them at a shop in Whittlesea. There was then no shop at Sada, though the building had been completed and the prospective shopkeeper was there – living in the house which had been built for the nurse who had not yet arrived. People were attending the clinic at Shiloh, two miles away, where there was a doctor in attendance once a week. The superintendent called an ambulance to take urgent cases to the hospital in Queenstown.

There were the obvious signs of malnutrition everywhere. This was due partly to the poverty of the people and partly to their lack of education in nutrition and diet. Milk was available but it was not used very much. Some people spent what little money they had on more bulky but less nutritious foods; others could not afford it anyway. A soup kitchen was provided by the superintendent but only about half of those eligible made use of it. This may seem surprising in view of the high incidence of malnutrition. But many of the people, having spent their lives on farms, are not aware of the nutritive value of the soup. Also, they object to having to drink the soup on the spot; they would prefer to take it home and share it with the rest of the family. Another consideration is the apathy engendered by poverty and the whole social system. The plight of these people also illustrates one of the many contradictions in the practical application of the Government's policy. Officially the policy is to uphold the traditional African way of life. Yet what could be more untraditional than herding thousands of people together in a place like Sada? If people are to adapt to and survive in such an environment, they must firstly have employment and secondly be educated in the use of modern food products.

Water was pumped from the river into two concrete tanks, each containing 20,000 gallons, near the camp and from there it was piped into the settlement, where there were taps every hundred yards or so. This seemed adequate for everyday purposes, but it was not sufficient to allow the use of hoses for watering gardens. Most of the people attempted to grow a few mealies, pumpkins and other vegetables on their tiny plots; some kept a few chickens. They could have their plots ploughed for R1.

Two lower primary and one higher primary school had recently been opened. Previously the children had to go to Whittlesea or Shiloh, both about three miles away. The secondary school had been completed but it could not be used because the sewerage was not ready. The higher primary school had 340 pupils and six teachers; the total school-going population was about 1,200.

Herschel

It was with some relief that I left the diocese of Queenstown and headed for Herschel, hoping to meet some clergy who would be more cooperative, though knowing that the Herschel Reserve is one of the poorest in the country and has more than its share of resettlement problems.

The whole of the magisterial district of Herschel, apart from the two villages of Herschel and Sterkspruit and a few Mission stations, is an African Reserve, which is obvious enough when you drive through it. It is approximately 514 square miles in area and has an estimated population of 75,000. A lot of the area is mountainous and most of the rest is badly eroded, so there is not much left for cultivation. What is left is not very fertile, since the whole region is very dry. According to the Tomlinson Report, the Herschel area is one of the most badly eroded in the whole country, yet at the time of its study had a population density as high as a hundred per square mile.

The people used to be spread out over the land, in particular on the mountain sides. But now they are grouped close together in Trust villages. The replanning of the area began in 1961–2. There are about twenty-one major residential areas and several smaller ones. The resettlement went smoothly, with a couple of exceptions. In one place, Jozana, the people repeatedly cut the fences as soon as they were erected. Their view was that once the land was fenced it was no longer theirs. Eventually police were sent to guard the fences and one man was allegedly shot by them when the people attacked the police. Nothing further happened about the matter and after that the people gave way and 'agreed' to move. In another place, the people were very much opposed to moving but the headman was in favour. They tried to persuade him to join them in opposing the resettlement. But he would not agree, so they burnt his house down.

The old people objected to moving because, apart from the great inconvenience and expense involved, they did not like to move away from the graves of their ancestors. This complaint is common to all resettlement areas. It has additional weight as an *ad hominem* argument, when it is remembered that the authorities who are implementing these schemes claim to be upholding the traditional way of life, in which the ancestors and their graves figure prominently. The younger ones felt that, while the official reasons were to prevent soil erosion and make communication easier, the real reason was so that there could be greater control. Most of the new settlements are near the road.

The grazing and arable land is allocated by the headmen and councillors: the amount of arable land per family varies from nothing to six acres. The people complain that the headmen and councillors keep the biggest and best portions for themselves and that they have much less land than they had before. This is particularly true of the old and widows. In some villages the land is divided only into grazing camps, with no arable land available. Young men setting up home are given only a residential site, as are those who are endorsed out of towns. People also complain that the compensation they received for their houses was most unsatisfactory, for example R5 for a rondavel and R12 for a four-roomed house. Many had to borrow money to build their new houses. Sometimes, they say, the arable land is too far away to be of any practical use. The area is supervised by agricultural demonstrators and people are fined R10 if they plough without permission or if their cattle stray on to the arable lands. Cattle-culling, always a very sore point, was due to start shortly. There is a school and a water supply in each village. The people are expected to make their own pit latrines, which very often they do not do. There is a Mission doctor, a district surgeon and two Government-subsidized hospitals in the area.

A number of dams have been built but nobody has heard of any irrigation schemes. There is a very large dam near Sterkspruit, the main purpose of which, although it is within the Reserve, seems to be to provide boating facilities for the White people of Lady Grey!

There is virtually no work in the whole area. Herschel Reserve is merely a labour-pool for contract and seasonal workers, since only headmen and councillors can possibly make a living from the land. As in other Reserves, White farmers come from miles away to collect labourers for the harvesting season. In Kuruman and Taung they come from the Western Transvaal, in Sekhukhuneland they come from Brits, and in Herschel they come from as far as Bethal and Standerton, a distance of about three hundred miles. I saw hundreds of people waiting in the village of Herschel for the lorries to arrive. As in other areas, some of them go along just for the adventure, but for most of them it is their only hope for food to see them through the winter. In some cases at least, they have to pay R5 for being transported to the farm and back and then 70 cents for every bag of mealies they bring back. In one case the people claimed that throughout their stay they received only black coffee and mealie porridge; most of them returned suffering from pellagra. They complained also of being beaten with sjamboks. Often men and women are housed in one barn – with the result that many of the younger women return pregnant. They also claimed that many people who go to Bethal do not return. I heard of one case in particular where a schoolboy went off on one of the lorries early in 1968; after six months he wrote to his parents asking them to find out where he was as he wanted to return home. They were unable to do so and, by May 1969, he still had not returned and nobody knew where he was.

Many of the men work on the diamond mines on the South-West African coast, or in Cape Town, Johannesburg and other cities, returning home only once a year. The local clergy say that this has caused many broken marriages and other problems. Many men, on returning home and finding their wives pregnant, dismiss them. The women then return to their parents, who already find difficulty in supporting themselves.

All forms of malnutrition are obviously a problem throughout the Reserve. The doctor at the Anglican Mission runs a kwashiorkor home, where malnourished children are admitted and their parents can stay with them. The parents are shown that the children can be cured without medicine at all but just by a proper diet. But one doctor can hardly hope to be able to spread her teaching to the many thousands of parents of hungry children.

Orange Fountain

Near the White village of Herschel there is a settlement that must surely be unique in the whole country. Unique, not in its conditions, but in the curious fact that it houses most of the sheep shearers in South Africa.

From the road you look down on rows and rows of tin huts on a flat open plain. There is absolutely nothing else for some distance around. There are some 200 huts, of which about 150 are occupied, each with its own smaller tin hut which is the latrine. The place is called, for some unaccountable reason, Orange Fountain. The huts are made completely of corrugated iron, with a row of small windows high up at the back; they measure about 10 ft by 10 ft and have no floors or ceilings or insulation of any kind. The residents are allowed to build additions, which must be the same shape as the huts and approved by the local magistrate, who is also the Bantu Affairs Commissioner. They have to obtain his approval before erecting any structure, even a chicken run. (But when I was there, in May 1969, none of the residents had built any additions.)

All the householders have the one thing in common, that they are sheep shearers, but they come from many different places. They were living on farms or in locations in Middelburg, Burgersdorp, Bethulie and Colesberg. The ones who were living on farms were told by Bantu Affairs Department officials, and those in the locations by municipal officials, that they had to move. Some of those from Burgersdorp say that they objected to going. They were then taken to the police station and told that if they did not move they would be sent to prison and then moved anyway. Their passes were confiscated and returned to them when they reached Herschel, with the registration stamp changed to Sterkspruit. Some of the men from Bethulie say that their families were moved while they were away working. There seems to have been some arrangement between the agents of the Sheep Shearers' Companies and the B.A.D. to put all the sheep shearers in one place, so that they could be more easily collected when needed. Officials told the people that they had to move, but the agents of the Sheep Shearers' Companies provided the transport. The families were first moved into the remnants of houses of people who had been resettled in Trust villages at Pelindaba, Sterkspruit and Qoboshane in the Herschel Reserve. That was in May 1967; six months later they were moved into the tin huts at Orange Fountain. Again they were transported by the Sheep Shearers' Companies.

There is one hut per family, which in some cases that I saw numbered eleven. The rent, for what is no more than a tool-shed, is R1.50 a month. The people complain of the coldness and dampness of the huts; they say that during the winter some children literally died of the cold. Some of them sleep during the day when there is warmth from the sun and huddle around a fire at night. Those with many children try to get friends to give some of the children a place to sleep. They explain, with some embarrassment, that they sometimes try to house all the children somewhere else for the night so that husband and wife can be alone. Sometimes whole families have to vacate their huts when it rains, as the water comes up through the ground; they move into the empty ones on drier land. Many say that they brought furniture with them, having been told that they were being moved into proper houses, but had had to sell it after arrival because there was no room in the huts. The cooking, of course, has to be done outside. They are unable to collect wood in the vicinity, as people usually can in rural areas, so they have to buy all their fuel. Coal costs R1 a bag and wood 50 cents a bag. Some claimed that fuel cost them R3–R4 a month.

There is a dam and a pump a couple of hundred yards away; but there are no outlets within the settlement – there is nothing in the settlement apart from tin huts. Some of the people are trying to grow vegetables on plots that are only about 50 ft square. Two doctors visit near by. They charge R1 per visit, plus 75 cents for an injection; though one doctor claims that he would not turn anybody away if he genuinely had no money. The district surgeon also visits. The children attend school in a near-by village where, the parents said, they have to pay 20 cents a term school fees.

The men work from about July to November or sometimes until January. They are paid 4 or 5 cents per sheep, or 1 cent if only the hindquarters are to be sheared; an expert can shear up to a hundred sheep in a day. They are also provided with food while they are away. But they are not guaranteed employment for the whole time they are away; sometimes they cannot work for three or four weeks at a time because the farmer is not ready for them or because of the weather. While the men are away, their families can buy food on credit at the local store to the value of R8 a month. Their rent is also paid through the Sheep Shearers' Companies. Some claim that after six months' work they were left with only R6 after their rent and accounts have been deducted. The usual amount seems to be about R20; a few of the real experts, if they have been paid the top rate and been fortunate enough to have been employed for the whole season, would have considerably more. They also buy on credit during the off-season; so their wages just about cover their expenses.

When they return from shearing, they can take other contract work, if they can get it, for a short period, provided they are back in time for the shearing season. Those who had previously been living on farms had had cattle, which they have had to sell, and usually their wives worked on the farm; they themselves, when they returned from shearing, either worked on the farms or in the near-by town. Those from urban locations say that they were always able to find temporary work locally during the off-season. So they were once reasonably prosperous people. Now they have to work simply to keep themselves and their families alive in a tin hut. Is it any wonder that they turn to drink, as the local clergy and others said they do?

Certainly on the Sunday when I visited the place, a number were 'under the weather', but they were sober enough to speak with feeling of the inhuman conditions in which they are now forced to live – eleven people in a tin hut, 10 ft square. Some spoke of returning, illegally, to their old homes; others were just resigned to their position; others were blissfully unaware in their drunken stupor.

The local Minister's Fraternal provides some relief. But it is a situation that calls for far more than material aid. The settlement is administered by the B.A.D. and it is significant that the residents of Orange Fountain come from the same places as the people at Mnxesha. Obviously, although they were not 're-dundant' or 'non-productive', in terms of general policy they were not wanted in those places, so they were dumped here, which is very convenient both for the B.A.D. and the Sheep Shearers' Companies. They are out of the Western Cape, which is the most important thing for the B.A.D., and the Sheep Shearers' Companies no longer have to collect them from their various homes. It does not seem to matter that the people have lost their decent homes, their cattle and their supplementary sources of income and simply exist in order to get enough money to continue existing. When I visited them, they had been living in these conditions for eighteen months and there was no sign of any attempt being made to improve them.

Lady Grey

Nineteen miles from Orange Fountain, at Lady Grey, there is a similar-looking settlement, with the same tin huts packed even more closely together. When I went into the settlement the first thing people asked me was whether I had a permit, as, they said, not even an African is allowed in without permission from the location office. They were therefore rather nervous throughout our conversations.

The settlement consists of about 250 huts; they are in two groups, separated by a large *donga*.[1] The larger part has about 120 plots. Most of these plots measure about 25 ft by 50 ft; on each of which there are two tin huts and two latrines. In some cases both huts are rented by the one family. But in many cases there are two separate families, which means that their plot is one quarter of the size of a normal township plot and one thirty-sixth of a 50 yd by 50 yd 'closer settlement' plot. The rent is R1.90 per month per hut; it has recently been reduced from R2. A few of the people were using three huts, two on one plot and one on half of another, and so were paying R5.70 a month. If a visitor, and this includes a son or daughter who works elsewhere, stays more than three days, an extra 20 cents is charged.

These people were previously living in the town of Lady Grey. They were told to move in February 1967; some said that they were given only two weeks' notice. They were called to the municipal office and told that they had to move because they were living in a White area. At least two of the families, and probably many others, had title deeds to the property on which they lived. The property of one of them had been valued at £890 by the municipality in 1966; it had been given the same valuation by officials from Port Elizabeth in 1963; the owner was paying R20 a year in rates. She had not yet received or been promised compensation, but it seemed that her land and five-roomed house had not yet been expropriated, since she was letting it to a Coloured family. But another person who had title deeds demolished her house in order to take the zinc and fittings

1. A gully or ravine caused by soil erosion.

with her. Some of the others had been tenants on land owned by Coloureds.

There are a few taps in the settlement, the water being pumped from the dam which serves the old location adjoining this settlement. There are no shops, clinic or schools, the nearest being in the old location or in the town of Lady Grey. No fuel can be collected in the vicinity; wood has to be bought at 50 cents a bag and coal at 73 cents.

Some of the residents are migrant workers, but many of them work in Lady Grey – at the garages, hotel or shops, or as domestics. The garage workers are paid R5.50 a week; garden workers R6 a month; domestics less than that – in some places in the area, at least until recently, domestic servants living out were paid R2 a month; others up to R10 a month.

On the other side of the *donga* there are about forty similar houses, housing people who had to move from the location because their homes had been condemned, plus a few who went of their own accord.

Some of these people were moved from very good houses, as could be seen from the quality and amount of furniture crammed into the tin huts. Now they are cramped, sometimes wet and cold, at other times sweltering hot, and are paying an exorbitant rent for a tin hut and a tiny portion of land. But they are out of the White area and one more town has been 'cleared'.

5. The Northern Cape

When I visited the Northern Cape I had hoped to be able to get some up-to-date information about the people at Mammuthla, but, owing to lack of cooperation locally, it proved impossible. In 1966 Bishop Crowther of Kimberley and Kuruman raised an outcry about the conditions of people being moved into the Mammuthla Reserve. Some five hundred people were moved about fifty miles northwards from old diamond diggings at Holpan into the Mammuthla Reserve, where they were left virtually destitute; no tents, no rations, an insufficient water-supply and no work. The Bishop established a relief fund, but he himself, being an American citizen, was unable to enter the area.[1] Later Bishop Crowther was deported, presumably because of these and other activities on behalf of the Africans, and there does not seem to be anyone of the same calibre in the area. The Mammuthla Reserve is quite a big place, so it was impossible, unaided, to find five hundred people and I could find no one willing to guide me. In an area the size of the Northern Cape, how many more people may be suffering a similar fate?

In the Northern Cape there are three major African Reserves: Vryburg (Ganyesa), Taung and Kuruman. Any towns that there are in these areas, for example Kuruman and Shishen, are White even though they are completely surrounded by Reserve area – such 'White spots' obviously do not suffer the same fate as 'Black spots'. The mines too are all White-owned, although some of them are geographically within the Reserve area. It seems that the idea of segregation can be compromised when its complete implementation would mean serious financial loss to

1. *Survey of Race Relations* (Institute of Race Relations, Johannesburg, 1966).

Whites. There has so far been no question of these towns and mines forming part of the Bantustan.

These three Reserves form part of the Tswana Territorial Authority, which is the oddest of the proposed Bantustans. It is made up of several areas, some of them hundreds of miles apart. There are a number of smaller Reserves which are due to be 'consolidated' into the major Reserve. The chief of these areas is the Kuruman Reserve, which extends to close to the border with Botswana. This is very dry country, and when you drive the ninety miles from Vryburg to Kuruman along the straight road over the flat semi-desert, you think you must have arrived at the end of the earth.

Round Kuruman a number of White-owned farms have been bought by the Bantu Trust – no doubt to the farmers' relief. The general idea seems to be to move as many as possible of the Tswana close to the Botswana border. There are resettlement areas a hundred miles north of Kuruman, and the terrain gets drier as you move north in these parts.

The smaller Reserves that are being consolidated are scheduled 'native areas' in terms of the 1913 Land Act, which means that the people have been living there since at least 1913. In fact these places were generally settled in the 1880s and after 1913 the people had every reason to expect that they would stay there.

Within the major Reserves most of the people have been re-settled into Trust villages of the usual pattern. In the Moro-kweng area, about a hundred miles north-east of Kuruman, a number of the villages have irrigated land. In the Taung district there is a big irrigation scheme, known as the Vaal-Hartz scheme, which covers an area some forty miles by twelve miles. Some of this belongs to White farmers, but some Trust villages also benefit, for example Rooivaal, just outside the town of Taung.

The main sources of employment for all the Northern Cape Reserves are the diamond mines at Kimberley, the diamond diggings on the banks of the River Vaal, and the asbestos mines in the Shishen and Postmasberg areas and in the Kuruman district. But many of the Reserve people also find work as seasonal labourers on White farms in the Western Transvaal. They usually go from May until July or August. In 1968, 22,000 people went from the Taung magisterial district alone. On the White farms they are housed in barns and paid with mealie meal or mealies. Many return with gross pellagra and also with venereal disease: at Batlharos Mission Hospital near Kuruman the number of in-patients increases by about one-third when the people return from the farms. Children who have been neglected during their parents' absence account for some of these, the others are cases of pellagra and venereal disease among the returning farm-workers.

These problems, reports Dr Mackenzie, the superintendent of the hospital, result in widespread malnutrition and all too often actual starvation, and in these conditions other diseases such as pulmonary tuberculosis and syphilis can only flourish.

The Kuruman Reserve is almost all desert or semi-desert. There are no border industries and virtually no means of subsistence in most parts. Except for a few areas with irrigation works, it is impossible to grow green vegetables, with the result that everyone, including professional people like priests and teachers, suffers from scurvy. It is not a matter of not knowing what to eat but simply of not being able to get it. TB and kwashiorkor are very prevalent; the kwashiorkor is obvious and, as for TB, the hospital's annual report in 1968 stated: 'this disease flourishes as never before,' and the 1969 Report said, 'the more one looks for TB here the more one finds it.' There is an outbreak of diphtheria every year, yet no immunization is carried out. Every year Batlharos hospital has to provide emergency wards for diphtheria cases.

This hospital originally served only its own immediate vicinity. But since the Reserve in which it is located has been made into the dumping ground for thousands more people, it now finds itself serving a population of over 100,000 people, spread over an area the size of Belgium. It has 310 beds, and two doctors, Dr Mackenzie and his wife – or had until they returned to England at the end of 1969. Dr Mackenzie pointed to the system of migrant labour, leaving many thousands of destitute families of old people, wives and children in the

Reserve, as the main cause of the appalling number of cases of malnutrition and starvation.

Dr Rachel Mackenzie, who is in charge of paediatric work at the hospital, said, 'So many of the children are starving, I don't know what to do about the baby clinic other than immunize the local children and hand out the milk, and, if possible, contraceptives to the mothers of the starving.' She writes of a 'despondency verging on despair among the Tswana people' and points to the names being given to Tswana children. Translations of some of them are: 'Woman in the ruins', 'I am done for', 'What shall we do', and 'I have suffered'.

Batlharos Hospital used to be a Mission hospital, but now, while it is still managed by the Anglican Church, it is financed by the Government. The list of requirements urgently needed by the hospital was severely pruned by the authorities, however, on the grounds that a large hospital for Africans was recently built at Mafeking – two hundred miles away. In the event though, this new hospital, Bophelong, has not brought any relief, because its admissions have been almost exclusively mental patients. This did not deter Mr I. S. Klopper, the Commissioner-General for the Tswanas, when addressing Tswanas at Dobsonville near Johannesburg, from encouraging them to return voluntarily to their 'homeland', where among the attractions is the new Bophelong hospital – one of the 'biggest in the world'.[1]

Batlharos hospital manages to cram in many more patients than the number of beds it is meant to hold. There are often four hundred or more patients. But, as the annual report for 1968 says: 'numbers ... are misleading, as due to over-crowding many cases which should have been admitted had to be treated as out patients.' Often, I was told, the only norm the doctors can apply when deciding whether or not to admit a patient is: Will he die if we don't admit him? In the 1969 annual report the overwhelming scale of the need is illustrated:

During the winter of 1968 the number of in-patients rose to 400 and the widespread starvation and very real suffering witnessed then

1. *Rand Daily Mail*, 24 October 1969.

in and around the hospital can only be described as a disgrace to the country ... the children's ward, originally built for forty cases, housed last winter over 160 at one time, all of whom were seriously ill and would certainly have died if they had not been admitted.

I myself saw death certificates at the hospital where the cause of death was given quite simply as starvation.

Into this area, rife with scurvy, beri-beri, pellagra, malnutrition of all kinds, TB and starvation, thousands more people are still to be moved for the sake of tidying up the map of apartheid.

Schmidt's Drift

One of the smaller Reserves that has already been 'consolidated' with the Kuruman Reserve is Schmidt's Drift. This was a scheduled 'native area' in terms of the 1913 Land Act, about forty miles west of Kimberley, where the Batlhapeng tribe settled in the 1880s. The most reliable estimate of the number of members of the tribe seems to be between six and seven thousand. For many years they lived in the traditional way spread out over the whole Reserve, raising cattle and growing a few crops – the Vaal river runs through the Reserve, so there were some arable parts. In the early 1960s the Reserve was replanned according to a Bantu Trust 'betterment scheme' and the people resettled in prescribed residential areas. They received compensation for their houses and, in general, used this to build very neat houses on the new sites. The Bantu Trust drilled a number of boreholes and erected a lot of fencing. But a few years after this the people were told that they were to be moved to a completely different area, so all this effort seems to have been a waste of time and money. The boreholes and fencing are still there but the houses have been completely flattened. The actual village of Schmidt's Drift was a 'White spot' in the Reserve. There is still a trading store, police station and Post Office there but it now looks like a tiny ghost town. There were also other shops scattered throughout the Reserve, and, perhaps most important of all, the District Surgeon visited twice a week.

The people to whom I spoke at the new Schmidt's Drift told me that the explanation which was given to them for the removal was that there were diamonds on the land and De Beer's Consolidated had the mineral rights. They said that they sometimes went out at night looking for diamonds, claiming that they could see them reflected in the moonlight! The area is certainly well dotted with small diggings, some of them obviously very old. Most of the men were working on the mines at Kimberley or Douglas (about thirty miles away) and so could return home at least weekly. The people did not want to move, they said, but 'we had no choice'.

They were threatened with removal for some time and were eventually moved in February 1968. They were removed by Government lorries to a place about twenty-five miles north of Kuruman, which had been purchased from White farmers; this place is now called Schmidt's Drift, though it is also known as Ga Sehunero, meaning 'the home of Sehunero', who is the present chief. They were able to take what they could salvage from their homes and their cattle were also transported by Government lorries. About a hundred lorries, I was told, were used for the removal. The journey, on open lorries, took about five hours; the distance is between 130 and 140 miles. They received satisfactory compensation for their houses and improvements and the new place is about the same size. But the ground is too dry to grow any crops or vegetables; livestock scratch about to find blades of grass. The place is infinitely remote, like a lost, dead land.

They were settled in nine 'Wyke' or villages, several miles apart. They found tents, boreholes and roads bulldozed through the arid landscape. I tried to drive to one of the boreholes but soon became stuck in the sand. The residential areas in particular are inches deep in sand. When I first visited in June 1969, some people had built proper houses but many were still in the shacks. The men who were working in Kimberley and Douglas were unable to return home to build lest they lost their jobs or were endorsed out, so the building was left chiefly to the women. One blind man was living in a construction made of old sacking. At that time he was not receiving a pension; I do not know whether he received one before he died a couple of months later. When asked what they thought of the place people simply shrugged their shoulders and said : 'What can we say?'

The chief was given an old farm house, but by far the best house in the area is that of the local representative of the Territorial Authority.

There is a lot of TB in the area and many people had been receiving treatment twice weekly from the District Surgeon at the old Schmidt's Drift. At the beginning there was a lot of sickness. It is said locally that one woman lost all seven of her children from pneumonia and malnutrition. The authorities at Batlharos hospital were not informed of the arrival of all these people. But some of them eventually found their way to the hospital – some travelling the thirty miles on foot – and the hospital started a fortnightly clinic in a room in 'Wyk 5', which is four or five miles from some of the other villages. According to the doctor's report in the Mission's annual report for 1969, this was one of their worst clinics.

There is a twice-weekly bus service to Kuruman which costs R1 return. In cases of emergency on other days people either have to walk or hire a donkey cart or truck; the hire of a donkey cart costs about R5 and a truck R10 to R15.

I heard reports of another large-scale removal of people from Groenwater, another scheduled 'native area' ten miles from Postmasberg, which had taken place in 1964. But I was unable to find anyone who could show me the place where they had been settled. The conditions, from hearsay in the area, seem to have been much the same as the Schmidt's Drift move. According to a report in the Natal *Daily News* of 13 November 1964, two thousand people were involved in this removal and they were moved 150 miles. Mr H. P. Kloppers, a senior official of the B.A.D., according to this report, said that the removal was successfully completed with the full cooperation of the people themselves. He is quoted as saying:

These operations quite naturally disrupt the lives of the people to some extent, but we do our best to make it as trouble-free as possible for them. There used to be some resistance to moving in the early days of consolidation but these days we are getting the full cooperation of the Africans when they realize that they are not being deprived of their land, but are in fact being given better facilities.

Do the people really 'cooperate' or are they by now so cowed that they can do nothing else? Nobody in his right mind could possibly want to go to Kuruman. Certainly the people in outlying Reserves who are due for resettlement are far from looking forward to going there. But when their turn comes no doubt they too will 'cooperate fully' and realize that they are getting 'better facilities'. 'Cooperation' must be another of those words like 'voluntary', which have a special interpretation in the B.A.D.

Gatlhose–Maremane

Three or four small Reserves in the Postmasburg area are to be moved to Kuruman. There is also a fairly large one thirty-five miles from Kuruman. This is the Gatlhose-Maremane Reserve which, from the map, appears to be about two hundred square miles in extent. Again it is a scheduled 'native area'. It consists of at least seventeen separate villages, with a population of at least ten thousand people; there may be twenty thousand or even more. The first people settled here in the 1880s and there was another sizable influx between 1906 and 1910. All of these are now to be moved again, even though only five years ago they were all regrouped into Trust villages, which normally only happens in areas which have been finally set aside as Bantustans.

Being regrouped into Trust villages meant of course that they had to rebuild their houses, for which, they claimed, they received no compensation. They keep cattle and goats but the land is too rocky for cultivation. Boreholes were sunk in each village, but there was the usual problem of people being moved closer together and no sanitation being provided. The people were recently given the order to build latrines but few have done so. They argued that they could not see the point in doing so when they have already been told that they are going to be moved elsewhere.

In 1965, just a year after being regrouped into Trust villages, they were told that they would have to move to the other side of Kuruman. Most of the people are Batlharos. But one village, Bojelakgomo, also has Zulus and Xhosas. Only the Batlharos are to go to Kuruman; the others have been told that they will have to go to their own ethnic areas. But they have not been moved yet.

Although they are not able to cultivate the land, the people are at present relatively prosperous and well settled. Most of the houses are very neat and they have schools, shops and churches. Three years ago a new community school was built, the people contributing on a rand-for-rand basis, even though they had already been told that they were to move. Most of the men work on the iron-ore and manganese mines near Postmasburg, which is twenty to thirty miles away, or at Shishen, which is about ten miles away. Some manage to return home daily though they usually commute weekly or fortnightly. Some of the privately owned mines pay wages of R100 a month and more. On at least one of them, if an African takes over a White man's job he is paid the same rate.

I was told by the people that they expected to be moved to somewhere in the Mashowreng River area on the border of Kuruman and Vryburg, which is about a hundred miles away. There is a train as far as Hotazel, which is forty to fifty miles from the area to which they expect to be moved. Even a fairly detailed map shows a completely blank area around the Mashowreng river and the river itself is usually dry.

Di Takwaneng

Fifteen miles from Vryburg there is another group threatened with removal to Kuruman. These are members of the Matlhopi tribe, which settled at Di Takwaneng in 1889. On official maps it is marked as a scheduled 'native area' or Reserve. But the chief says that they have title deeds, so it is not really a Reserve but a tribally owned farm, which is now a 'Black spot'.

They were first told in 1960 that they would have to move, but so far the chief has refused. The official reason for the move, presumably, is that it is simply part of the plan of 'consolidation'. But it is rumoured among the people there that some precious metal has been discovered on the property. Apart from objecting to the whole idea of being forced to move from their homes, they object in particular to being sent to Kuruman, as they say they are Vryburg people. The chief said that they had been shown a place at Kuruman where the only water-supply was from a windmill, whereas at Di Takwaneng there is plenty of water from a spring. They grow kaffir-corn, wheat and vegetables, and keep cattle. They have a Standard VI school and a clinic.

When I visited the area for the second time in December 1970 they were still expecting to move but did not know when. The Bantu Commissioner was expected to hold a meeting the next day to give them some definite information. They had engaged a lawyer to represent them but they did not seem very hopeful of the result of his intervention. The chief asked me to tell the lawyer what a beautiful place Di Takwaneng is, as he was under the impression that the lawyer was not allowed to visit the area. Some of the people thought that the chief should now give in, otherwise they may end up with nothing. As one of them said: 'We know that by hook or by crook we will be moved.'

The local storekeeper moved in 1960 and the authorities have refused to grant a trading licence to anyone else, so they have to go to Vryburg for their shopping. Also there is no public transport. It is such things, and the fear of what else might happen, that make some people think that they may as well 'agree' to go.

Pampierstad and Mothibistad

Within the Reserve area there are also two new townships: Pampierstad and Mothibistad.

Pampierstad is about seven miles from Hartswater in the Taung district. Already it is a sizable township with about two thousand families and nobody seems to know where they have come from. I was told that the people at Barkly West were supposed to move into Pampierstad but that the Whites complained of losing their labour force and so the plan was shelved. The Hartswater location has been moved here and Warrenton is scheduled to move also.

In general appearance Pampierstad is the same as any new township with row upon row of identical little houses. Water, sanitation, schools and other normal township facilities are adequately provided. There are African-owned shops in the township but they can hardly hope to compete with the large White-owned store about half a mile away. The proximity of White-owned stores to the African Reserves hardly seems consistent with the Government spokesmen's encouragement of African traders to leave the urban areas and go to the 'homelands' where they can work among their own people and be free from White competition.

While the residents of Pampierstad are more fortunate than those in many other settlements in that they have houses and other basic facilities, there is still a great deal of poverty owing to the lack of employment in the vicinity. The only work available locally is on White farms, which is very poorly paid, and on the building of houses within the township. There is no industry and there are no signs of border industries being established. Many have no employment other than the seasonal harvesting on White farms in the Western Transvaal. A local clergyman remarked that the main source of income seemed to be theft from the near-by White farms. He also pointed out that a clear indication of their poverty was the fact that the people stole and ate donkey, which was contrary to Tswana custom (only the Basotho eat donkey).

Mothibistad is the new township for the people from Kuruman location, which was moved in 1964. Most of the people went to Mothibistad but those who could not afford the increased rent and bus-fares went to tribal or Trust villages. The old location was within walking distance of the town of Kuruman and the rent was R1 a year for a plot on which they built their own houses. The new township is seven miles from town and the return bus-fare is 16 cents. The rent is R2.99 for a two-roomed and R4.33 for a four-roomed house. In June 1969 there were about six hundred houses and it was still being extended.

Mafeking

Mafeking is the capital of the far-flung Tswanastan but the town itself is White. The Chief Minister and the Cabinet Ministers live in a row of special houses in the township on the outskirts of the town. This township, Montshiwa, started five or six years ago and is still being developed. In June 1969 it had between five and six thousand people; it is planned for twenty-five thousand. Most of the people rent the houses, but it is possible for them to buy a plot for R44 and build their own house; or they can buy a two-roomed house for R270 or a four-roomed one for R490 – this includes the purchase of the plot. But these houses are shells; I was told that to make a four-roomed house really decent with guttering, floors, ceiling, etc. the total cost would be about R1,000.

A small 'Black spot', Mosita, about forty miles from Mafeking, where there were about five hundred people, was removed in June/July 1968 to a place about forty miles closer to the Botswana border – which is in keeping with the general trend. I could find nobody who has seen the place and was told that it is inaccessible in the rainy season, which is when I wanted to go there. According to the local agricultural officer who supervised the move everything was provided and there was no cause for complaint. But 'everything' seemed to have consisted of tents.

6. Central Transvaal

For the purposes of my tour and of this report, I divided the Transvaal, which is the second largest of the four provinces and has the largest area of African Reserves, into four sections: the Central, Northern, Eastern and Western. This leaves out the Southern portion, consisting largely of the Witwatersrand – Johannesburg, the gold reef and the surrounding industrial towns – where there are neither Reserves nor 'Black spots' to be cleared.

However, resettlement concerns the Africans living in the Witwatersrand very closely. The Johannesburg townships alone, known simply as Soweto (Southwestern Townships), have about 700,000 people. They have been moved from old locations on the edge of Johannesburg to the sprawling barrack-like Soweto fifteen miles away, with a difficult and expensive journey to work every day.

Every year thousands of Africans are 'endorsed out' of Johannesburg alone and sent to the 'homelands' because they do not qualify, or at least cannot prove that they do qualify, for residence in an urban township. The following extract from a Johannesburg parish newsletter is typical of many cases. It says:

Alexandra (one of the old locations near Johannesburg) is a depressing place, and more so now that people are being moved and houses knocked down. . . . Three of our families have either been removed or have disappeared without a trace. One writes: 'I left Alexandra very bad – the police pull me out of the rooms – I never take my dresses and I have nothing to ware.'

We pointed out to the authorities the problems involved in moving Sarah Cele away from a hospital since she has developed cancer secondaries. She has now disappeared without trace.

And their new home – a paradise in the country? Two recent

letters speak for themselves: 'But this place at Hammanskraal is know good to us since we came there. We all ill and starving – everything is up and shops are very far to us. Alexandra is ten times better' and 'This place is a bad place. I never saw an old age home like this – bad food not cooked we starving in this place.'

Hundreds of thousands of Africans on the Witwatersrand face the bleak prospect of being sent to settlements in the 'homelands' with all that it implies – the menfolk having to return to live in workers' hostels leaving the families destitute in the settlements. The fear of arrest and removal causes acute stress, on top of all the hardships and crushing alienation of African existence in South Africa.

One of the Reserves which is expecting a massive influx of people from the industrial town of the Transvaal is the Hammanskraal district, to the north of Pretoria. The present population of the district is approximately 230,000; the planned population is 750,000. It is strongly rumoured locally that Mamelodi and Atteridgeville, the large African townships of Pretoria, will be moved into the Hammanskraal Reserve, forming a vast complex of townships linked to Boekenhoutfontein, a settlement which was started some ten years ago.

It was exceptionally difficult to obtain detailed information about what was going on in this area. People whom one would have expected to know the situation – clergy, welfare workers, newspaper people and political party workers – had only the vaguest idea. They knew that a lot of resettlement had been taking place for some time and that a lot more was planned, but they had no detailed knowledge. Possibly it is too vast and complex for people to grasp.

As you drive around the area, you continually come across small settlements, often miles from anywhere. These have been established since about 1958. Some of them are ordinary Trust villages, where the people have some land and cattle, while others are just residential sites for people from White farms or for those who have been endorsed out of the cities. Most of them have a school, a borehole and a shop; little else.

The Central Transvaal covers a relatively small geographical area but has a very large rural African population. However, it does contain the most developed border industry area in the country, at Rosslyn, located twelve miles north-west of Pretoria, which has seventy factories providing employment for the inhabitants of the townships at Ga Rankuwa and Mabopane in the Hammanskraal Reserve.

Stinkwater and Klipgat

Various forms of resettlement have been taking place in the Central Transvaal in recent years. But one case in particular attracted a great deal of public attention during the course of 1968. The outcry about the lack of preparation and atrocious conditions at Limehill had hardly died down when a similar situation developed at Stinkwater and Klipgat, two 'closer settlements' in the Hammanskraal area, about thirty-five miles north of Pretoria.

As at Limehill, the position of the people at Stinkwater and Klipgat became known only because some of the White people living at Hammanskraal and Pretoria started to look into the conditions. It is significant that at first White people living only a couple of miles away from Stinkwater were totally unaware of what was going on in their neighbourhood. I am not casting blame on these individuals for their ignorance, but pointing to the lack of any communication between Black and White. The White public began to hear about the existence and plight of the people at Klipgat and Stinkwater only through domestic servants whose families had been moved – or who had to move themselves.

Some four hundred families had been living at Eersterus Township, about ten miles west of Pretoria, and near Silverton where many of them were employed, for many years. The land on which they were living was bought from the owners by a private concern, and the people, most of whom had been tenants, were given notice to vacate the property. They did not move for two years, so the new owner requested the Pretoria City Council to move them. The owner of the property said later that he had presumed that houses and other facilities would be provided at the place to which these four hundred families would be moved.

Instead they were taken and dumped at Stinkwater and Klipgat in the middle of an extremely cold winter. Each family was lent one tent for three months, after which they were expected to have built their own houses. There was no sanitation or other facilities, apart from one water point for two thousand people. One of the main complaints was that whereas at Eersterus they were within easy reach of their places of employment either at Silverton or Pretoria, they were now thirty-five miles away and had to leave home at 4 a.m., returning at 9 p.m. One man claimed that he had to pay R12 a month for bus-fares, which was almost one-third of what he earned.

On 14 June 1968, the *Pretoria News* reported Mr J. S. de Wet, the Deputy Secretary of B.A.D., as saying that the people at Klipgat and Stinkwater were better off than they were at Eersterus. He also pointed out that they could reduce their travelling expenses by staying in a hostel in Pretoria. What does it matter if a couple of hundred more men are separated from their families?

The same news-item reported also that the Dean of Pretoria, the Very Reverend Mark Nye, had launched an appeal for food and clothing. The Dean was quoted as saying: 'The river water is foul-tasting and the families complain that it is causing serious diarrhoea. Cattle drink from the same water holes and river – so it is hardly surprising that there is an outbreak of illness. . . . The thing that worries me is that Africans are moved to these areas before any facilities are provided. Why don't the authorities construct the facilities like clinics, schools and water supplies, before the move? This seems only logical, but they do not.'

The *Pretoria News* of 27 June 1968 carried a report of an official guided tour of Klipgat and Stinkwater. It said that at Klipgat: 'What the Pressmen saw was a primitive area of thick bush-veld where the new residents made do with shacks of rusted corrugated iron and mud huts. No sanitation facilities are provided and the shortage of schooling and medical clinics in the "homeland" is chronic.' And at Stinkwater: 'The area consists of marked-out plots of dense thorn-bush on which the families have erected tin shacks. The tents provided by the Department are still standing – some occupied, some not.' There was an

Moving out - 1

Moving in - 1

Moving in - 2

Home - 2

Home - 3

accompanying photograph of a woman standing in the open veld, surrounded by what looks like a pile of rubble, with the caption: 'Here stands a woman surrounded by her possessions with the order to "build your own house". The tent provided has not been erected.' One of the officials said: 'I must emphasize that we do not build houses for them, but they are given the land and told to build their own houses. They do not own the land but pay rent at R1 a year.' But an official also said: 'Many Bantu ask to be resettled here. They like the area and the traditional way of life.' And again: 'These people ... are now settled legally and permanently. As you can see they're happy.' Without land for ploughing or cattle, being forced to live in tents – what element of traditional life has not been stripped away?

Stinkwater was in the news again early in 1969 with reports of a chronic water shortage. The *Pretoria News* of 4 February 1969 carried photographs of women and children scooping water from a hole in a dry river bed. The report said: 'The water crisis became serious last week when water points dried up completely leaving thousands of families without water for several days. Dirty water – scooped from the sands of the river bed where cattle gather – has led to serious outbreaks of enteritis and diarrhoea amongst the children. Parents are desperate with worry but cannot foresee any relief. ... An African man told a reporter that his wife spends all day at the river bed trying to scoop enough water for her five children to wash and drink.'

Post of 16 February 1969 carried a similar report. It also quoted the Bantu Affairs Commissioner of Hammanskraal as denying that there was a water shortage: 'He claimed that people dug for water in the river beds "because they prefer the taste of this water" to that supplied by Government borehole pumps and emergency tankers.' But the report continued that the people claimed they were being illegally charged R4 a year for tanker and pump water and it was because they could not afford this that they dug in the river beds.

A spokesman for the B.A.D. came up with another explanation. He was reported in the *Pretoria News* of 18 February 1969 as saying that if there was a water shortage it was because the people were too lazy to walk for it. 'They want water provided on their doorsteps,' he said. On 4 March 1969, the Deputy Minister of B.A.D. said in the House of Assembly, in answer to a question from Brigadier H. J. Bronkhorst, 'The average distances which the Bantu (at Stinkwater) have to transport water to their homes depend on which residential area they reside in and vary from an average of approximately 800 yards to three-quarters of a mile.' Most Europeans' houses have a minimum of six taps, yet these people are called 'lazy' if they complain at having to walk three-quarters of a mile. They would have had cause for complaint even if the boreholes had always supplied an adequate amount of good drinking water which, according to the newspaper reports and the people I spoke to later, they did not. But even when the boreholes have water some of the people do not trust it. They may have inherited this distrust from White farmers, who claimed that borehole water in this area causes arthritis.

Stinkwater still had problems almost a year after the removal. These are summed up in a report in the *Star* of 13 March 1969, which pointed out that the people of Stinkwater had been an urbanized community and were finding it very difficult to adapt to life in a rural settlement. While their tribal neighbours had built mud, thatched-roof houses, the people from Eersterus had erected rickety shacks, made from rusted corrugated iron. There was still no sanitation and just one borehole. Children were attending school under a tree. 'But gravely threatening the whole fabric of family life at Stinkwater is the fact that more and more working men are forced to stay in the "kitchens" or hostels in Pretoria during the week.' The report concludes that many of the inhabitants, men, women and teenage boys and girls, seem to find 'escape from boredom and drabness at Stinkwater' in heavy drinking.

When I visited Stinkwater almost a year after the removal, many people were still living in shacks. There were still the same complaints about the distance from work and the expense of getting there and the water supply. Whatever the reason, people were still getting water from the river.

One of the leading figures in organizing relief and helping people to build houses at Stinkwater was the Reverend Rob van der Hart. He has since been forced to leave the country on the expiry of his residence permit. With him went a lot of first-hand knowledge of the conditions at Stinkwater; but he is still remembered by the people whom he helped so greatly in this and in many other ways.

According to the Deputy Minister of B.A.D. answering questions put by Mrs Helen Suzman,[1] 228 families from Eersterus were settled on one of the Trust-owned portions of Stinkwater and it was planned to settle 700 families. There are no preparations for this influx. He also said that some of the families who moved to Stinkwater would have to be removed from there. 'The non-Tswana families will be removed to the different homelands where they fit in ethnically.' So they will have to go through much the same process all over again. But the homelands are well away from the prying eyes of observers, so perhaps we will not hear about their fate next time.

At Klipgat, too, people were still living in shacks in March 1969. There was no sign of extra schooling facilities being provided: the children were attending classes in twelve tents at a school in Nooitgedacht, one and a half miles away. The people admitted they were very frightened of answering my questions: one woman suddenly broke off in the middle of a conversation and went away when some others called out to her to be careful of what she said.

Boekenhoutfontein (Mabopane)

From Klipgat I went to Boekenhoutfontein. On the way I gave a lift to a young African who, it transpired, worked for the Special Branch of the Police. His job, he explained to me, was to catch communists. A 'communist', according to his definition, is 'anyone who is against Government policy'. He assured me that there were a lot of such communists among school-teachers. On our arrival at Boekenhoutfontein he demonstrated his powers of deduction by announcing that he knew that I was a priest because I had driven straight into the township and only priests could enter without a permit. He had to call at the police station

1. Hansard, No. 7, col. 2720, 18 March 1969.

and said he would like a lift with me on the way back. Somehow I took the wrong turning and missed him.

Boekenhoutfontein is about twenty miles north-west of Pretoria and eleven miles from Rosslyn. It was started in 1960 and at present has some three thousand houses – houses of all odd shapes and sizes. The people came from Lady Selborne Township, near Pretoria, where they had freehold rights, Walmansthal Mission, White farms and other places. At first they were put into one-roomed prefabricated 'houses' roughly 12 ft square, and had to build their own kitchens. The B.A.D. later added another room of brick and many people have added lean-to rooms of corrugated iron which they brought with them from their old houses. The rent for these patchwork structures is R1.76 a month. There are about two hundred rent-free ones for pensioners and other indigent people. Some have also built their own excellent houses, which emphasize the bizarreness of most of the others.

Many find employment at Rosslyn, but others continue to work in Johannesburg or Pretoria, where they were working before they moved. There are subsidized bus services to Rosslyn and to Pretoria. In many cases both man and wife are migrant labourers, especially those who came from Walmansthal, where many of the women were able to go to Pretoria two or three times a week to do washing and other occasional work. Many who were living and working on farms are now full-time migrant workers. The local clergy say that owing to lack of parental control there is a lot of fighting and drinking among the youth.

There are now primary and secondary schools. When the people first moved in there was a primary-school building to accommodate four hundred children but it was found that there were over a thousand. So the authorities decided to use the primary school building as a secondary school and housed the thousand primary school children in a mass of tents.

Everybody I spoke to complained that the rents were too high and that they did not have enough room. One woman complained that, owing to ethnic grouping, difficulties concerning qualifications for residence in towns and registration for work and other laws, it would soon be impossible to marry anyone outside one's own township. (This is not such an outlandish complaint as it may at first appear. In a debate in Durban, Mr Con Botha, the Nationalist Member of the Provincial Council for Newcastle, said that if Africans were forbidden by law to live in the same area 'they were foolish to get married'. It was the people, not the laws, that were at fault.[1]) The same woman said to me, 'the time will come when we will have to fight with bare fists against guns'.

According to the Minister of B.A.D. in the House of Assembly on 4 May 1965, Boekenhoutfontein was originally planned for six thousand families. But since then the concept has changed. There has been a statement from an authoritative source[2] and a number of reports in the press that Boekenhoutfontein would be developed into a city for 300,000 people, described as 'the first fully fledged African city'.[3] In 1969, however, it did not even have the normal facilities of an ordinary township – there was no water supply to houses, only taps in the streets, and so on. Parts of Lady Selborne Township, from which many of these people were moved, had degenerated into a slum. Boekenhoutfontein seems to be rapidly following the same pattern.

Ga Rankuwa

If a prominent visitor were to ask the B.A.D. to be shown a new township he would probably be taken to the model township of Ga Rankuwa. It is situated about twenty miles north-west of Pretoria on the edge of the African Reserve. In March 1969 there were about six thousand houses which could be rented for R5.62 a month or purchased for R585 and upwards. There are a number of primary schools, a secondary school, churches, a crèche and a clinic. Other developments are planned.

Ga Rankuwa is one of the townships that genuinely serves a border industry area. Rosslyn is only about six miles away and the railway passes the township. The township was sited here in

1. *Star*, 26 September 1969.
2. Professor Moolman at the Congress of the Association of Geography Education in Potchefstroom on 9 July 1969.
3. *Star*, 16 July 1969.

order to serve the industries at Rosslyn, which still remain within easy reach of the city of Pretoria. So, while it is technically a border industry area, there was no question of the firms concerned moving away from the White cities in order to be near African Reserves and to provide employment for the population of the Reserves. Many of the residents in fact come from the cities.

But an official tour would probably not include a drive down the dirt road alongside Ga Rankuwa. Here, just a little further into the Reserve, there are a couple of hundred families living in utter squalor. They are mainly people who could not afford the rent in Ga Rankuwa and their 'houses' are mainly extremely dilapidated tin shacks. The general appearance is similar to that of the old Edenvale location, which was commonly known as Transvaal's dirtiest location and has now been demolished. There is no water in the vicinity and the people say that they often have to buy it at 40 cents for a 44-gallon drum.

Mogogokela

Mogogokela, which is about fifteen miles from Hammanskraal, just a couple of miles from Stinkwater, is fairly typical of settlements in the area, and one of the biggest. It is a Trust farm with about a thousand families. (When I was there, in April 1969, it was said that the B.A.D. was about to conduct a census because they had no idea how many people were there.) One part is an old-established settlement where people have land and cattle: the other part is a 'closer settlement'.

The people started moving into this part in 1965 from Walmansthal, Boekenhoutkloof and White farms; the latest arrivals were in 1968. They were transported by Government lorries and brought the building materials from their old houses; with these they built temporary shacks to live in while they were building houses, since they were not provided with tents. Some have now built very good houses, but there is a fair smattering of shacks and a general impression of overcrowding.

Having recovered from the actual move, they are now concerned mainly about work and water. There is, of course, no work available near by: there is nothing in the vicinity except bush. Some are migrant workers in Johannesburg and return home only occasionally. Others commute daily by bus or bicycle to Hammanskraal. But the hardest hit are those who work in Pretoria. Many of them previously lived at Walmansthal and could commute daily fairly easily. Now three bus-loads of workers go to Pretoria, about fifty miles away, every morning. The first bus leaves at 2.30 a.m.; they return between 5 p.m. and 8 p.m. A subsidized weekly return ticket costs R1.20.

For the whole 'closer settlement' there is one borehole operated by a windpump. When this runs dry, as it often does, water is brought in by lorries from the Apies River and sold at 40 cents for a 44-gallon drum. People showed me the drums of water that they had bought the day before. Having seen the Apies River, I was not keen on drinking it. Fortunately I was offered some orange squash to mix with it, which disguised the colour and the taste.

There is one Standard VI school, built with the help of contributions from the people, but no clinic or visiting doctor. A nurse visits once a week, charging 20 cents per patient. The nearest hospital is the Jubilee Mission hospital at Hammanskraal, fifteen miles away. Local missionaries say that there were a tremendous number of deaths from malnutrition and cold in 1966–7 when the people were still in temporary shacks. It was not possible to obtain accurate figures, since most deaths are not registered and the graveyard is so full that I gave up the attempt to count the more recent graves at about two hundred. The local people said that from September–October 1966 to January–February 1967, there were at least five to six babies dying every week. The authorities may consider that 'normal': I suppose it is normal if the mother herself is starving and the whole family is living under a piece of corrugated iron.

The Bantu Affairs Commissioner has told the people that they will at some time be separated into their various ethnic groups and moved again. I came across a number of cases where people had been removed, to clear them out of 'White areas', but still had no permanent home. The Government's ethnic dogma insists that they must be moved again until they are all pigeonholed, labelled and controlled. The threat of further moves hung over, for example, the people at Elandsdoring (cf. page 142) and Ledig (cf. page 155).

Temba

At Hammanskraal there is a small township, Temba, into which the people from the surrounding area were moved in 1965–6. They were joined by people from Walmansthal and White farms and by some who were endorsed out of White urban areas. When the first people arrived they had to build their own houses. But later the B.A.D. built houses; these are mainly two-roomed township-type houses, but there are some with four rooms. The water supply still sometimes gives cause for concern. The *Pretoria News* report on the water shortage at Stinkwater, on 4 February 1969, also says: 'Temba African village near Hammanskraal will be faced with an equally critical situation if the rains do not come within the next week. At present the families are restricted to half a bucket each per day, as the water pumps dwindled to a mere trickle.'

Near by there are two tribal villages, Marokolong and Ramotse, the former having four hundred families and the latter five hundred. They were told ten years ago that they would have to move because they were living on 'Black spots', but they still do not know when or where they will have to go. The residents of Newkraal, a village adjoining the main road at Hammanskraal, were told in 1947 that they would have to move, and they are still waiting.

Syferkuil Farm

About twenty miles from Hammenskraal there is a railway station, a mill and a few stores. This is Radium. Five miles off the main road from there, there is a settlement of people who were moved from three Lutheran Missions at Walmansthal, Middelfontein and Heidelberg. The settlement is called Syferkuil.

These people are more fortunate than most others who have been moved from Mission farms. They are able to keep some cattle and do some cultivation, though in general they have less land than before. Their rent varies according to whether they have land and cattle – R1 a year for a residential plot only; R3 for some land but not cattle; and R6 for those with land and up to five head of cattle. Usually 'squatters' from Mission farms are simply put into 'closer settlements' with no land or cattle, as happened with the people from Maria Ratschitz Mission who were moved to Limehill.

The total area of Syferkuil farm is 9,275 acres divided into Sections A, B and C. The people from Middelfontein Mission were moved into section A in August 1965. There are 206 families there now, but residential plots have been set aside for several hundred more. The people from Heidelberg Mission were settled on Section B, also in 1965. There are seventy-four families, but again considerably more plots are marked out. Section C is where fifty-eight families from Walmansthal Mission were settled in October 1967, and there is provision for more people to follow again.

The local agricultural officer said that the plan was that all the men should return from the cities and support their families on the farm. But it is clear that the farm even now cannot support all the families living there, and it does not seem possible that it ever could if all of the 803 plots set aside are occupied.

Many of the men in fact work in Johannesburg, and can only return to Syferkuil once or twice a year. Others, working in Pretoria, can get home once or twice a month, but it costs them R1.56 on the train and 36 cents on the bus from Radium station. There is a lot of unemployment among the young men, since they are no longer allowed to register for work in Pretoria, but can only be recruited through a labour bureau.

According to local clergy there is a great deal of liquor selling and fighting which did not happen on the Missions. Many of the children suffer from open sores, a usual sign of malnutrition. There is no clinic, but a doctor visits the area.

The people complain that the residential sites are very exposed to windstorms, which are quite common in the area. In one storm early in 1969, thirty strongly built houses in sections B and C had their roofs blown off.

Soon after the people were moved in, two primary schools were built. The nearest secondary school is at Rathlane, sixteen miles away, which means that the parents have to pay for their children to board with local residents there. The real difficulty, though, is that in this district instruction at schools is in Tswana, whereas the people from the Missions are primarily Spedi speaking. The primary schools at Syferkuil have started using Spedi as the medium, but they now fall under the Tswana section of the Department of Bantu Education and Culture and it is expected that they will be forced to change to Tswana.

I was able to find out something of the history and conditions of two of the Missions from which these people came, Walmansthal and Middelfontein.

Walmansthal is a Lutheran Mission, twenty-two miles north of Pretoria. It was founded in 1869 on a large farm; nobody could even estimate the acreage, but it stretched almost to Hammanskraal and was the biggest farm owned by the Lutheran Church. The houses were spread over this vast area, as many still are. There was a secondary school on the Mission.

In the 1930s most of the farm was sold to the tenants. These people later took on sub-tenants themselves, sometimes as many as ten. The Mission retained part of the farm, on which it had eighty-four tenant families. They paid similar rents to those they have to pay now at Syferkuil, but they had more land.

Walmansthal was declared a White area on 1 June 1963. After that a census was taken and the landowners and their tenants had to apply for a residential permit to stay there. Almost every weekend after that there were many arrests of people who did not have a permit. Many men were simply ordered to leave, and not deported to any specific place. This explains the smattering of Walmansthal people in almost every settlement in the area.

On 12 September 1967 the Chief Bantu Affairs Commissioner, Mr Nel, called a meeting of the Mission tenants and announced that the whole community would be moved, starting with the eighty-four tenant families. Later, he said, the rest of the people would be moved to different places 'according to their ethnic group'.

The removal started on 2 October 1967 and was completed on 19 October. Fifty-eight families agreed to go to Syferkuil, faced with the alternative of being split up and sent to various townships. The remaining twenty-six families decided to go elsewhere, mostly because they had relatives with whom they could live. Those who went to Syferkuil received compensation for their houses, and have been able to build new houses (and in general better ones) with the money. The others received no compensation.

The Church officials tried to negotiate with the Bantu Affairs Department but failed to prevent the move. Perhaps their intervention helped to ensure that the people were resettled on an agricultural basis rather than in a 'closer settlement'. At Syferkuil they were provided with tents and a ration of mealie meal and beans for about two weeks.

In addition to the Mission tenants, there were about six hundred landowners at Walmansthal, each of whom had an average of about four tenants. These people, or the bulk of them, have not been moved yet, but they will be. The Botswana among them have been told that they will be moved to Boekenhoutfontein; the Bapedi and Mandebele have not been told where they will go. Those who are tenants will be lucky if they are allocated any place, even in a township. The landowners themselves have been told that they cannot be compensated with land; they will receive only cash.

Middelfontein Mission, between Naboomspruit and Nylstroom, is another Lutheran Mission settled for a hundred years. It was founded in 1868. The farm was 9,250 acres, roughly the same size as all three sections of Syferkuil. About 150 families lived there, originally free of rent. After the First World War a rent of £2 a year was introduced; this was increased to £3 after the Second World War. In addition they paid 2s. 6d. a year per head of cattle and 6d. a head for goats. As at Walmansthal, they had far more land than they now have at Syferkuil. There was a school for five hundred children.

The Bantu Commissioner informed them that the Mission was a 'Black spot' and they were given notice to move. Some of the men were taken to see Syferkuil, and complained that there was only one borehole. The Commissioner promised to remedy this.

When they moved to Syferkuil, married sons were given their own plots; hence the 206 families there. They were transported together with what they could salvage from their old homes, by Government lorries. The promised boreholes were provided, and there was a shop and a school as well as the tents they had to live in at first.

Government officials and spokesmen invariably reiterate that all removals from 'Black spots' are voluntary. I have already shown what 'voluntary' means in a number of examples in this report. But concerning the arrangements for the removals from the three Missions to Syferkuil I actually saw a letter (I cannot reveal how or where I saw it) from the Bantu Administration Agricultural Department to a local official. It said:

> *Cooperation and Initiative.*
> *Remains to be seen as these people are being*
> *forcibly removed to this farm . . .*

My look at the letter was of necessity surreptitious, but I can swear that these were the exact words. It also said: 'The carrying capacity has not been previously assessed. . . .' The aim was allegedly that the farm should support all the families, but nobody had bothered to assess its capacity to do so.

According to the same letter 'The present inhabitants of the farm (i.e. before the removals) will be moved elsewhere to fit in with their ethnic group.' In fact they were moved to a near-by farm, Swartbloom, where there are eighty-four families and 197 plots. Conditions there are much the same as at Syferkuil, except that the people are clamouring for a school.

Botsabelo Mission

While on the subject of Lutheran Missions we should mention Botsabelo Mission near Middelburg. This is the oldest Lutheran Mission in South Africa. The name means a 'place of refuge'. It was so named because a Minister, Bishop Alexander Merensky, and his Christian followers fled there 110 years ago from the anti-Christian Chief Sekhukhuni and built a fortress to defend themselves.

There are now at least 150 families scattered over a 12,600-acre farm. The men are mostly working in the cities but the women and children farm the land. This Mission has been declared a 'Black spot' and the people have been under threat of removal for many years. They have been told that they would definitely be moved to Motetema Township at Groblersdal by 1971.

The local Lutheran Minister says that the removal to a township will mean a complete rearrangement of their lives, but he says that they are now reconciled to the idea. However, on 28 June 1970 the *Post* reported that the people had told the authorities that they would be willing to move if they were offered land with sufficient water and grazing for their cattle, building materials for new homes, a new training institute to replace the one at Botsabelo which has good buildings and a first-class reputation, a high school and higher primary school; and the recognition of the Lutheran Church in their new community. Of these demands, it is said that the training institute will be rebuilt for them at Motetema. But they will get no land.

These people's ancestors escaped from the pagan chief, but they can no longer escape from the Christian Government.

Groblersdal

There are so many resettlement villages in the Groblersdal area and they are in such out-of-the-way places that it is impossible for an outsider even to find all of them. In two days, with the help of a guide, I visited six of them; I heard of at least six others by name and vaguely of more. I cannot give the exact geographical location even of those places I did visit. On one occasion we had to go miles around to find a way across a flooded river. We drove on tiny, faint tracks and most of the time I had no idea where we were.

Klipplaatdrift

Between Groblersdal and Bronkhorstspruit there is a small settlement called Klipplaatdrift. From the road you can see a few one-roomed asbestos houses, which gives you the clue that it is a resettlement village. (My guide thought it was part of a road-camp.) But it is not an ordinary resettlement village. It is a village solely for old-age pensioners. They were moved there over the past few years from locations in Springs, Witbank and Johannesburg. They said that they were told by the Bantu Commissioner that it was not fair to them that they should receive a pension from the Government and then pay most of it back in rent; so he said he would give them a place where they would not have to pay rent. They were brought by Government lorries and given a one-roomed mud-and-thatch house, to which some have now made additions, and an outside latrine. There were thirty-nine families when I visited; it was planned to have fifty. The one-roomed asbestos houses were being erected for the new arrivals.

There was a store near by and water available from a borehole a little distance away – though the distance probably seemed great to an old woman. There was no clinic; a doctor visited once a week. The bus-fare to Groblersdal was R1.5o return, but the inhabitants went there only if they had business with the Bantu Affairs Commissioner.

Most of these old people were looking after their grandchildren, but some lived alone. Their only income is a pension of R6–R6.50 every two months. One old man was previously receiving a war disability pension of R10 a month, but since moving to Klipplaatdrift he had received only the usual old-age pension. They said that at Springs and other locations voluntary organizations gave them blankets and sometimes food; here they get no help. They were a most pathetic sight – all without exception said that they were starving. They were most anxious to talk about their conditions and did so at length. They felt, with plenty of justification, that they had simply been abandoned.

These are some of the 'unproductive' or 'redundant' Bantu or 'surplus appendages', which B.A.D. officials refer to. They are no longer capable of working for the Whites in a White area so there is no place for them there. This is what it means for an old person to be endorsed out of Soweto or the other city locations and sent to the 'homelands' which they have never even seen before. I am sure that most of these people had no more idea of exactly where they were than I had. They are just waiting to die.

Pieterskraal

Seven miles from Klipplaatdrift there is a settlement, Pieterskraal, of about two hundred families. I went there on a Saturday afternoon so there were a number of gatherings of men. At first I was greeted with suspicion and I realized I was dressed like a typical Government official in a safari suit, and my Volkswagen was also typical of many officials' cars. But when I had convinced them that I had not come to tell them to move again, they spoke freely enough.

Most of the people settled at Pieterskraal between 1964 and 1968. They came from White farms in the Witbank, Middelburg and Stoffelburg districts. A few came from an African-owned farm. The latter were transported by Government lorries and provided with tents on arrival. Those from White farms had to provide their own transport, were not given tents or any temporary accommodation and did not receive any compensation. Some of them left the farms of their own accord, because they were tired of conditions there, which is not surprising since they had to work for four months without wages to pay for their ploughing and grazing rights and then received a small wage for the other eight months. They were not inclined to say how much this 'small wage' was, but in other areas it varies from R1 to R5 a month. Others worked on the farm for six months and then elsewhere for six months. But the farmers told them that if they wanted to live on their farms they would have to work for the whole year. Others, especially in the Bronkhorstspruit district, were given notice by B.A.D. officials. The notice varied from seven days to one month. In some cases the houses of those who did not move by the expiry date of the notice were burnt down by the police. At Pieterskraal they pay R1 a year for their half-acre plot and for grazing for seven cattle. There is no land for ploughing.

There is a primary school and a clinic; also, surprisingly for a 'closer settlement', there are taps in the streets. There is a small shop which the people said is a shop in name only – just before my visit it had had no mealie meal for three months. It is very difficult to get supplies from Groblersdal; the people must walk the seven miles to Klipplaatdrift and take the bus from there.

The main complaint of the people is that they have no work and no land to plough. Most of the men work in Johannesburg and Pretoria. But the youth have great difficulty in getting any job. (It is not permitted for people from the rural areas to go and seek work in the cities; they can only enter into a labour contract, for a year at the most, through their local labour bureau.)

Maduma

Leaving Pieterskraal I drove for miles along tiny tracks through numerous villages and then suddenly came upon a huge complex of buildings, which was the Roman Catholic Mission at Steilpadfontein. It seemed strange to find such a centre of 'civilization', with electricity and a neon-lighted cross, in such a setting.

A few miles from the Mission there was another settlement called Maduma. Five years ago the people in the immediate vicinity were moved into demarcated residential sites; then others came from White farms in the Nylstroom and Tuinplaas districts and a few were still coming. They had no land nor cattle; just the half-acre residential plot, for which they paid R1 a year. (R2 a year per acre is not a bad return for all these places. I remember having great difficulty in persuading very wealthy White farmers to increase the rent they paid for land leased from a Mission from 50 cents to R1 a year per acre.) They did not receive any compensation; they had to provide their own transport and their own temporary accommodation to live in while they built. Each family had to pay R10 to the local chieftainess.

Others came from an African-owned farm. They received cash compensation for their houses, were transported by Government lorries and were housed in tents, as was the school. They have two acres of arable land and grazing for four head of cattle, for which they pay R3 a year.

Vlakplaas

One of the older settlements in the area is Vlakplaas. About three hundred families settled there between 1957 and 1968 from White farms in the Naboomspruit and Nylstroom districts. Most of them were given notice by the farmers. None were provided with transport or temporary accommodation; nor did they receive compensation.

When they first arrived there was one water pump and a school, no toilets, no shops and no clinic. The water is now adequate in summer but runs short in winter. There is now one shop in the settlement and one at the station two miles away. A Mission nurse and a Government nurse both visit once a week.

Those who arrived first have six acres of arable land and grazing for cattle, for which they pay R3 a year. But the later arrivals are allowed no land or cattle.

Uitvlugte

A few miles on from Vlakplaas there is an extremely neat little settlement called Uitvlugte, where there are about a hundred families. They started arriving in 1964, from White farms, and more are still arriving occasionally. They have no land or cattle, and have to find work in the towns or on White farms.

The first arrivals found nothing provided. Now there is a water pump, a shop and an unregistered Standard II school which the residents took three years to build; in the meantime the children went to school in a near-by village.

Waterval No. 3

One of the biggest settlements is Waterval No. 3, which is ten miles north of Denilton. When I first went in I could find only women and they were too frightened to say anything. They even professed not to know the name of the place or of the place they came from. But I eventually found the men, many of whom were gathered for their Sunday drink.

This settlement started five years ago and must have something like a thousand families, who came from White farms in the Bronkhorstspruit and Middelburg districts. They had been living there on the usual terms – four months without wages and eight months paid. Sometimes a son worked on the farm and the father went to a town as a migrant worker. Some were given the option of staying on the farms provided that they worked full-time. But they were no longer to have their own ploughing and grazing land. Instead they were to be paid R6 each month and given fifteen bags of mealies at the end of the season.

They moved at their own expense and on arrival found two water pumps; no houses – not even a temporary shelter – no school, no clinic. Each family had to pay R1.25 to the local chief.

Now there are two shops and one café. The people themselves built a school, which they completed in 1966. A clinic was started in 1967 and a doctor and a nurse visit it once a week.

Apart from those who had already worked in the towns, very few have become migrant workers, simply because they cannot get the necessary contracts. It is particularly the young men who are unemployed.

The people complain mainly of being far from town with no work and no land or cattle, and they now say that they were better off on the farms in spite of having to work for four months for nothing. Some of these people received only three days' notice from B.A.D. officials to quit their former homes; others received three weeks' or longer, but in every case it meant that their cattle had to be sold off in a hurry to White farmers or butchers at low prices.

Mission clinics and the people themselves say the malnutrition in the whole area was exceptionally bad in 1969, partly owing to the drought.

Motetema and Marble Hall

In addition to all these resettlement villages in the Groblersdal area there are also three townships. The Deputy Minister of B.A.D. listed four in the House of Assembly on 4 May 1965. It was only after many inquiries and much searching that I discovered that two of his names referred to one and the same place.

The three places are: Motetema, which is the township attached to the White town of Groblersdal; Marble Hall (also known as Leeuwfontein), which is similarly attached to the White place of the same name; and Elandsdoring, which is by contrast a mixture of transit camp, 'closer settlement' and township; all of which adds up to a slum.

The old location for Groblersdal was a mile and a half from the town. It was a municipal location in which the people rented a plot and built their own houses. They were told in 1967 that they would have to move and were moved in March 1968. They were promised compensation but in March 1969 it still had not been paid.

As usual, the new township is much farther from town – eight miles away. The bus-fare is 16 cents return or R2 a monthly ticket. The rent for a four-roomed house is R4.50 a month; in addition they have to pay 50 cents a month for lodgers.

There is no clinic nor does a doctor or nurse visit the township. For all medical treatment they have to go to Groblersdal. There is a lower primary and a higher primary school and a secondary school is being built. There are no recreation facilities; in the old location they at least had a soccer field. In March 1969 the shops were just being built.

Most of the people work in Groblersdal, where factory workers earn about R5 a week, garage attendants R6 to R7 a week and domestic servants R6 to R10 a month. The people admit that the houses are better than at the old location, but on these wages they simply cannot cope with the increased bus-fares and rent.

The residents of Leeuwfontein were moved from the old location, which was two miles from Marble Hall, to the new one, seven miles away, in December 1968. There are about a hundred

houses, mainly four-roomed with toilet and water outside, for
which the rent is R4.50 a month. There are a few five-roomed
ones, with water and toilet inside, for teachers, policemen, etc.
According to the Deputy Minister's statement, it was planned
for nine hundred families, but many of the people from the old
location found the rent too high and went instead to the Trust
villages. There are still some left in the old location who do not
qualify for the new townships because of pass irregularities or
because they are not married according to Christian rites. Some
have been told that their marriages can be legalized immediately
for a sum of R20.

Elandsdoring

Elandsdoring is a sprawling mess of eight or nine hundred
houses of many shapes and sizes, one and a half miles from
Denilton.

The people started coming in 1965. The bulk of them moved
in 1966 and a few have been trickling in since then. They come
mainly from farms but also from locations in Witbank, Nelspruit and Middelburg. Some moved because the rent in the
locations was too high; others were evicted for not paying their
rent. They were told to go to Elandsdoring, but no transport
was provided. On the farms they were given notice by the B.A.D.
officials. Some, who had not moved when the notice expired,
were arrested by the B.A.D.'s police, fined between R5 and R10
and ordered to leave immediately.

There are a few four-roomed houses but these are only for
officials. The first arrivals were given two-roomed houses on a
50 yd by 50 yd plot. Each room is roughly 12 ft square; one is
built of brick and the other entirely of corrugated iron. They
can buy the house and plot for R390 or the plot alone for R40.

They were told that they could bring their parents and grown-
up children with them; but now they have to pay an extra 50
cents a month for every child over sixteen and for parents or
lodgers. They were also told that the iron construction was only
temporary and that the B.A.D. would build another room later.
Now they have been told that they have to build themselves; but

they are still paying the same amount. The corrugated-iron rooms are hardly habitable: they are like an oven in summer and a refrigerator in winter. The brick room is only of single brick and so lets the rain in. Some use the iron room as a kitchen, but others with big families cannot afford this luxury and have to cook outside. They are not allowed to collect firewood from the neighbouring Trust area and have to buy coal at 50 cents a bag.

The latest arrivals do not get even this much. They are given only a plot and have to build their own house and toilet. In March 1969 many were still living in shacks made of old corrugated iron.

Elandsdoring has no clinic or visiting doctor. There is a hospital about three miles away and the charge is 25 cents a visit. There is one small shop, a primary and secondary school. When the people first arrived there was just one water pump, now there are some taps in the streets.

Before the people came they were told that there would be a border industry. But there is still no sign of it. Many of the men work in Johannesburg, Witbank, Springs and Middelburg, where they were working previously; but now they are all full-time migrant workers. Some work in the local hospital and are paid R8 a month; others work for the B.A.D., also for R8 a month. There is a lot of unemployment among the youth because of pass difficulties. An African man can only seek work in the area in which he is registered. The residents of Elandsdoring are now registered at Groblersdal, where there is very little opportunity of employment, so all they can do is wait for a labour contract permitting them to work in another town.

Last year the residents were told that Elandsdoring is supposed to be for Basotho, whereas the present residents are mainly Zulu, so they will have to move again. But they have not yet been told when or to where. It cannot be to anywhere much worse than Elandsdoring.

Tafelkop

Tafelkop is a huge settlement about twelve miles from Grob-lersdal, towards Lukau. The residential sites stretch for about two miles; so there must be at least a thousand families. It looks like a well-established, peaceful, orderly settlement. But it has a history of extreme suffering and hardship, which many of the people I spoke to remembered bitterly.

At least six or seven hundred of these families came from a tribally owned farm at Maleuskop, between Groblersdal and Middelburg. Their forefathers settled there before 1860. A hundred years later they were told that it was a 'Black spot' and they had no right to live there. They were shown two or three farms and eventually accepted Tafelkop; they had to accept something. They moved in June–July 1962. They were transported by Government lorries, taking what building materials they could salvage with them. When they arrived at Tafelkop they were given tents on half-acre plots. There was no water supply, no school, no shop, no clinic. For the first few days the water was brought in by tractors and then by tankers. It continued to be brought in by tankers until 1964.

There was unrest and complaint, especially about the lack of water, from the beginning. They soon decided that they had had enough and would return to Maleuskop. The Bantu Commissioner, together with an African assistant/interpreter named Scott, went along to try to pacify them. They were met by an angry crowd which stoned the car. The Bantu Commissioner managed to escape but poor Scott was stoned and beaten to death. A number of people were arrested, but they were eventually discharged.

Only a few people started building houses – most stayed in tents for a year. Then, when the tents were taken away, they built only temporary shacks because they said they were going to return to Maleuskop. Some of them eventually built houses in 1965–6; a few have still not built.

In 1965 about a hundred families, having suffered these hardships for three years, gathered their belongings and started trekking back to Maleuskop. But they were intercepted by the police and sent back. Following this, ten of the leaders and their families were banished from the village. The chief's son, who was one of them, was banished to a place near Glen Cowie and the others to a place near Nebo. They were told that they were not allowed even to visit the village.

In 1964 the people were allocated two-acre, bush-covered plots for ploughing. They refused them at first, saying that they had had much more land at Maleuskop. But in 1966 they cleared off the bush and in 1967 did their first ploughing.

The school was opened in 1964; the boreholes were drilled in 1964; the land was allocated in 1964. But the people moved in 1962. They had lived at Maleuskop for a hundred years. Would their living there for another two years have been such a great threat to White civilization?

In August–September 1963 many of the cattle died, some say as many as two-thirds. More died in August–September 1964. It was ascribed to a poison weed (makgou) which is widespread in the area but to which the local cattle were immune. By 1965 what was left of their cattle had become immune.

At the beginning at least three or four people died every week. These people had lived together long enough as a community to know, without any knowledge of statistics, when an excessive number of people were dying. They considered this very excessive. A clergyman said, 'If you saw the cemetery you would think that all these people had been living here for a hundred years, not seven or less.' Another missionary said that at the beginning people were literally starving to death. One missionary who did a lot of relief work and who published a report of the conditions at Tafelkop in a news-sheet overseas to solicit more funds lost his residential permit.

There is a Roman Catholic Mission clinic three miles away and a Dutch Reformed Church clinic visits. One of the churches wanted to build a clinic in the settlement but the people refused to cooperate saying that it was the Government's job.

When they first came there was plenty of bush, which they could use for fuel; in fact there was very little but bush. They are now at the stage of cutting down green trees, which will soon be exhausted.

A couple of hundred families have since moved in from White farms by arrangement with the chief. Some moved on again when they found that if they stayed they had to have the chief's name stamped in their reference books. Some are still coming but they are given only a residential site.

A chief from Brakfontein, near Maleuskop, moved at the same time to a village next to Tafelkop. The people of Tafelkop say that the other village has better conditions so far as the allocation of land is concerned because the chief was more cooperative with the authorities.

7. Western Transvaal

All but one of the major resettlement schemes in the Western Transvaal are centred round the town of Rustenburg, some sixty miles west of Pretoria. Rustenburg is one of the principal citrus-growing areas of South Africa, and has important uranium and platinum mines. Around this town lie three of the worst settlements in the country: Morsgat, Rietspruit and Ledig.

The other settlement, De Hoop, is near Lichtenburg, further west and not far from the borders of Cape Province and Botswana. De Hoop seems to be planned to absorb the 'surplus' Africans from all the small towns within a radius of about a hundred miles, including Potchefstroom, Ventersdorp and Delareyville.

Morsgat

Morsgat is about sixty-five miles north-west of Rustenburg. A year after it was established it did not appear on any official list of townships. The Department of B.A.D. changed the name, according to press reports in October 1969, to Modikwe. The Minister, Mr Botha, explained that the old name, meaning mess-hole, like the names of Stinkwater and Limehill, was 'unfortunate'.[1]

When I first visited the settlement, in March 1969, I almost had to hack my way through the bush even to see the tents; certainly one could have driven past on the road a few yards away without noticing them. The whole area was thick bush and in between there were hundreds of tents. It was impossible to judge how many there were because of the density of the bush, but the local inhabitants said there were about five hundred families and

1. *Star*, 21 November 1969.

the last plot occupied was numbered 543. It was almost un-
believable that so many people could be living in such conditions. At that time there were no buildings of any kind, just the
tents, and a few shelters which looked like piles of old corrugated
iron but where in fact people were living or storing their belongings. They said that they had been told not to build because the
Bantu Affairs Department was not sure what the plans were;
whether the Department was going to build houses or whether
the people were to be moved to another township; or whether
they were to build their own houses. An indication of the
Department's confusion was the fact that the plots were between
25 and 30 yds square, which is between a township-size plot and
a 'closer settlement' plot.

The first people arrived on 3 December 1968. When I visited,
there was no shop of any sort, no clinic, no toilets, and the school
was housed in four square tents. (Whenever I see such schools I
am reminded of the strict requirements enforced by the B.A.D.
for Church schools. Every year you have to fill in forms stating
the number of pupils, the area of the classrooms and of window
space. At Amakhasi Mission we were forbidden to use one class-
room because it did not meet the Department's specification; at
the same time, two miles away at Limehill, there were twenty to
thirty pupils being taught in a tent at the Government school.)
There was a borehole about half a mile away which was operated
by a hand-pump which a couple of people had to push around
in a circle.

All the people I spoke to had come from slate quarries at
Mazista, Duradek and Chachalaza, where they had been living,
some in quite decent houses, within a couple of hundred yards
of their work-place. Now they were forty and more miles from
their work and the bus-fare was R1.20, or R1.80 return, so that
men could return to their families only once a fortnight or once
a month. Some of the people, from Duradak, claimed that they
were given no notice at all; the lorries simply arrived one morning and took them to Morsgat. None of the people received any
compensation.

I visited the settlement a number of times in the following
months and each time it was more and more depressing. The

only improvements were the building of a school and the attach-
ment of a proper pump to the borehole. More and more people
built crude shacks, many of which were even worse than the
tents. The complaints about sickness of various kinds increased.
On the first three or four occasions people spoke freely, but on
my last visit they seemed to be evasive. This, I presumed, was
due to the presence of two big cars with Whites in them, one of
whom was watching the proceedings through binoculars. I also
learned later, from outsiders, that a number of the people had
been interviewed by the police. One man was interviewed five
times about my visits. The only reason I had spoken to this particular man was because I needed petrol and he owned a truck.
All we discussed in fact was the unenviable prospect of being
stranded between Morsgat and Swartruggens.

In August, September and October 1969 the *Rand Daily Mail*
investigated the conditions at Morsgat and the following extracts are from the report they published on 25 October:

For ten months more than 100 families have been living in tents
at the side of a dirt road some 28 miles outside Swartruggens. . . .
They have been resettled on land earmarked for the Tswanastan.

They have camped through most of one summer and all of one
winter. In February and March this year 9·3 in. of rain fell in the
Rustenburg district, while the average minimum temperature for
July was 3·4 degrees C.

There are well over 300 families at present camping on the makeshift site. They have no prepared sanitary facilities. There is no
health clinic (the nearest is at Swartruggens, the bus fare R1.10
return; average wage for breadwinners R3–R4 a week). The single
water tank supplying the entire community has a layer of green slime
floating on the surface; the families have complained of severe
stomach disorders.

The *Rand Daily Mail* began investigating this tent settlement
three months ago. When the B.A.D. was later approached for official
information, a spokesman said the request would be considered.
Asked 16 days later whether any information was available yet, the
spokesman said 'No. Not at all'. . . .

Fenced on three sides, with the fourth abutting on the road to
Swartruggens, Morsgat is made up of between 60 and 70 acres of
brown bushveld, now bursting into green after the rains. From the

road there don't appear to be enough tents to house as many as 1,200 to 1,500 people; at first glance indeed Morsgat might be the temporary quarters of one of those nomadic road repair gangs, with half a dozen asbestos prefab huts in one corner and a few trucks standing by to heighten the image. But there are too many women and children walking around and too few men.

Besides there are in fact enough tents for a small tent-town; the view from the road is deceptive. Uncleared bush and thorn trees obscure more tents behind, and more shacks; severely regular shacks, grotesquely malformed shacks, some neat and prim as a spinster's Sunday hat, most untidy heaps of sheet metal blown together in a high wind and now too tired to drift apart. There is no order to the placing of the tents and shacks; here they cluster together for company, there they stand stubbornly apart separated by clumps of uncleared bush. . . .

When the . . . families arrived . . . some were unloaded beside their plots and found their tents lying there. . . . Some had to wait for tents, like the woman from Swartruggens location. . . . 'I spent the night in the open because there was no tent. They brought it the next day'. . . .

They had called for this woman at dawn one morning towards the middle of May . . . to load the couple's belongings in the truck. The men were polite and helpful. . . . The couple could take all movables, they said, but they could not take 'cattle, goats, pigs, sheep or donkeys'. . . . Three head of cattle were left behind with friends. . . .

In another case the truck called at Mazista in the morning and four families and their belongings had been packed in. . . . 'It was very uncomfortable, I was pregnant and stood all the way in a crouched position.' It was a hot day and the journey in the open truck seemed to have taken far longer than it probably did – 'about four hours'. . . .

In spite of the heat and the discomfort, this woman says she was luckier than others she knew. . . . People who, with their belongings, had been drenched in a downpour during the journey and who had had to pitch their tents after dark in the rain . . .

No sanitary pits had been dug before the families arrived last December. There are still none. 'We started to dig pits,' says a resident, 'but they told us to stop. They promised us lavatories, but we haven't seen them yet. Now we use the veld!' Families living on the perimeter of the settlement obviously suffer most from this practice. 'The stink is terrible after the rains,' says an elderly woman. Until two months ago there was some sanitary relief in the form of a dozen black pigs who kept human waste under some control. But their presence was illegal and so they were slaughtered on official instructions. . . .

At Morsgat most of the families are still living in tents eight, nine, ten months after being moved. When we visited the settlement two weeks ago there was not a single brick house (though, significantly, building started after our inquiries). The only brick structure was the school, completed around mid-year. There were half a dozen asbestos prefabs; there were a few tidy mud huts and a few neat corrugated-iron structures. But then, as now, the vast majority were still living in their tents, many families beginning to look on them as permanent quarters. . . . It is not as if they like the tents. . . . They say the tents are flooded in heavy rains and choked with dust when the wind blows; and they are cold in winter. . . .

While a few people are genuinely confused about whether or not the authorities said they could build their own quarters, it is generally accepted that they can in fact build, as indeed some already have. . . .

However ... it is said that bricks must be obtained from official sources. . . . 'We were told to build, but only if we bought bricks from them.' 'Them', is of course, 'G G', the Government, the authorities. . . . The sum of R80 is generally mentioned as the price of the bricks needed for a house. Sometimes the people laugh when they repeat this figure. They feel it is a huge joke that they are expected to produce R80 for the bricks, let alone more money for other materials such as windows, roofing and doors. To ask if anyone has saved enough money for a house is to invite ridicule.

An elderly woman, however, does not laugh. ... 'At a meeting they told us the bricks cost R80. One of the people who worked with builders said this was too much and he was told he was a communist.' She is clearly angry about this. 'We can barely afford food,' she storms.

Asked why he could not afford a house, a Chachalaza quarry worker looks around at his companions in bewilderment. When the question is seriously repeated it becomes clear to him that he is being addressed by a fool. But he takes the trouble to explain, all the same, speaking slowly and pausing frequently to allow his words to sink in. He earns R4 a week, he says. He has a wife and three small children. His wife used to work seasonally on farms surrounding Chachalaza, but now at Morsgat there is no work for her. So the family wage remains only R4. Is that understood? Well, the return bus fare from Chachalaza to Morsgat is R1.80 and because it is so high, he visits his family at Morsgat only once every two weeks, at the weekend. That means he has R6.20 left ... with which to keep himself and the four other members of his family alive for two weeks. He feels he is becoming far too serious now so he bursts out laughing. Food, he says, with a wide grin, that's the trouble. He pats his stomach. Food.

'They can build a nice little house for about R1,000,' says the White works foreman of Morsgat. . . .

The nearest clinic accessible to the people of Morsgat is at Swartruggens. The return bus fare is R1.10; in emergencies a taxi will do the trip for R5.

Families complain of starvation, malnutrition, skin diseases, and stomach troubles. ... 'Many people have terrible sores, especially the children.' A senior official at one of the quarries bears this out, 'I never believed a human skin could carry so many sores,' he says of Morsgat children he has seen. He does not go into Morsgat – White people must have a permit – but the children of some of his workers have been brought to him at the quarry. 'It was terrible; horrible to see,' he says, grimacing. . . .

Last summmer there was a widespread outbreak of stomach disorders, the worst symptom being 'Isisusegazi' – running stomach with the sufferer passing blood. The people blame these disorders largely on the water. . . .

Like most rural African settlements Morsgat is desperately poor. There is a small elite earning more than R10 a week, but most breadwinners earn R3.50 to R4 a week, the labouring wage at the quarries. ... The man from Chachalaza who earns R4 a week and visits his family is in a predicament shared by most people at Morsgat. When his family lived together as one unit, close to his work, they did not live in anything approaching reasonable comfort, but they managed to get along without what they considered undue hardship. Separated, they are finding it a hard life transformed into a nightmarish existence. The man even harbours some sort of guilt about the money he spends on bus-fares. 'I have to go to Morsgat every two weeks,' he explains, 'I am worried about my children.'

Ten of the 23 family heads who were moved from Chachalaza refuse to go back. They refuse to be separated from their families.

Even workers who earn comparatively generous wages complain that just staying alive is a battle. It was always a battle, but now they are feeling less equal to it. . . .

The removals have forced a new social pattern on to the families. Where before they had something approximating an integrated family life, they are now separated. Morsgat is in fact mostly a settlement of women and children, who receive short visits – at weekends – from their menfolk. . . .

Poor, often non-existent facilities; unhealthy and degrading living conditions; additional costs eroding wages that are already far too low; the enforced break-up of families. These are the morale shattering hardships responsible for a comment that is heard again and again in Morsgat: 'We have been thrown away.'

The main feeling is not so much of bitterness and frustration as of hopeless resignation, as shown in this snatch of conversation with a worker from Mazista. . . .

'What is it like living in Morsgat?'

'It's not so bad.'

'Not bad to live in a tent for nine months. Summer and winter?'

A short laugh, a shrug of the shoulders: 'You get nothing by complaining – it's their country.'

Almost as corrosive is the fear of authority. Men and women move away, refusing to speak; they don't want to be seen speaking to strangers. Once before, says somebody, strangers had been, and there was trouble. 'GG' wanted to know who the strangers had been, what questions they had asked, who they had been speaking to; people who said they were police came. White people in plain clothes, and they questioned families.

No, we have nothing to say; everything is fine! A woman talks for a minute or two, then moves away nervously.

Another woman nods. Yes, she will speak, but only inside her tent where she can't be seen. Halfway through the interview a pair of urchins run past screaming 'Pickup! Pickup!' The woman says 'please don't go outside yet; wait until they have gone.' When they have gone she changes her mind and refuses to continue. 'Please go,' she begs.

Not only the simple, uneducated rustics are afraid, but teachers too. There are six teachers at the school, which caters for higher and lower primary. Three of them, maintained by the community, went without wages for eight months. But they don't want to talk about it. They don't even want to say how many pupils there are.

'Once bitten, twice shy,' says one cryptically. Another murmurs something about trouble, about being woken in the night . . . shrugs shoulders, turns away. . . .

A man who says he is a headman smiles and doesn't seem to be scared. Yes he'll speak; what information is required?

But at that moment an open van arrives in a cloud of dust; inside are half a dozen local 'policemen' with sticks and a White official.

The official jumps out and wants to know who is asking questions and why. .... The official is Mr G. C. Vermeulen ... he is the superintendent and lives three miles away at Tulani. He says he doesn't know why newspapers should be interested in Morsgat. 'It's a lovely place,' he says.

Rietspruit

In some ways Rietspruit has an even more depressing air than Morsgat. This is a 'closer settlement' situated about twenty-three miles north of Rustenburg. I was told that it is planned to settle 1,300 families there. At the time of my first visit there were 207 families who had come from White farms in the Pretoria and Rustenburg districts. Some moved voluntarily in order to be near relatives who had already been moved. But others were given notice by the Bantu Affairs Commissioner. I saw one of the notices and my informant said that most of the others had received similar notices. This particular man said that he did not mind moving because he was 'tired of working for Dutch farmers'. He thought that most of the others felt the same. This was a widespread attitude towards farmers, regardless of their nationality. Others said that they had been quite happy. But they went on to explain that having been given notice by the B.A.D. there was nothing they could do about it and so there was no point in complaining.

Many of the men and some of the women were still working on the farms where they had been living; others used to commute daily to Koster, where also some of the women were employed as domestic servants. They had land for ploughing and cattle. None of the people I spoke to had received any compensation and they said that nobody had. They had to sell their cattle as they are not allowed any livestock at Rietspruit. They were transported by Government lorries and took what they could salvage from their old homes. On arrival they were given tents but no building materials at all; these have to be purchased at Rustenburg with the money they receive from the sale of their cattle. Most of the men now work in Rustenburg or Koster and because of the distance they can return home only weekly or, in the case of Koster, which is about sixty miles away, fortnightly or monthly. The bus-fare to Rustenburg is 80 cents return; to reach Koster they have to take a bus to Derryvale, which costs 85 cents, and then walk or cycle a few miles. Those women I spoke to said that their husbands were earning R4–R6 a week in Rustenburg.

The first people arrived on 4 April 1967 and when I first visited the latest arrivals had been there a few months so all had built some kind of rough shelter. No sanitation was provided and very few had built their own latrines. There was one borehole, about a mile from some parts of the settlement, serving all the people – whenever I went there, there was a fairly long queue. There were no shops at all; hawkers visit the area and there are shops in a village about two miles away. There was no clinic or resident nurse; a Government health inspector visits once a week and deals with cases of malnutrition. The school was temporarily housed in tin huts; two years after the start of the removal the school building was at window height. A few one-roomed houses had been provided for old people; some were brick under asbestos, others were all corrugated iron.

It was when I visited Rietspruit again a couple of months later that it struck me as being more depressing even than Morsgat. Some of the roughly built shacks had started to fall apart; more people had arrived, some of whom were still in tents, others in temporary shacks. One shack was made entirely of old plastic fertilizer bags. The settlement, bad as it was before, had deteriorated even further. At the end of 1969 it was very strongly rumoured locally that all these people were to be moved again because of shortage of water at Rietspruit.

Ledig

The residential area at Ledig, about twenty-five miles north-west of Rustenberg, is in two sections about two miles apart. The first section consists mainly of very neat mud-and-thatch houses, but in the second section there are about two hundred tin shacks. When I visited there, in September 1969, there was still no sign of anybody building a proper house. Another striking feature of the second section is that there always seems to be a big crowd of people flocking around the two boreholes on the opposite side of the road, waiting their turn at the tap.

Virtually all of these people came from a tribally owned farm near Boons, about twenty-five miles south of Rustenburg. They had lived there for about 130 years and bought the farm on which they were already residing in 1894. The land was expropriated in 1965 because it was a 'Black spot' and part of the tribe, under Chieftainess Catherine Monnakgotla, moved to Ledig in 1966; these are the ones in the comparatively habitable part of Ledig.

But about 180 families refused to move. In November 1967, eighty-eight of them appeared before the Bantu Commissioner's court in Rustenburg and were sentenced to a fine of R100 or three months' imprisonment; their appeal was dismissed but the sentences were suspended provided that they moved by 1 September 1968. This group had been opposed to the chieftainess for some time, preferring Chief Lukas Monnakgotla, the late chief's brother, who was the tribe's nominee for the regency but was rejected by the B.A.D.[1]

They did not move by the prescribed date. Sixty of them appeared before the Bantu Affairs Commissioner on charges of ignoring the Supreme Court's order to leave, another ninety-eight appeared on 19 September. The sentences (R100 or 100 days) of some were suspended on condition that they did not plant crops or keep cattle and that they moved by 31 December. Their animals were impounded; they got them back in November, after paying R2.90 per head. Those who went to prison were released on 11 November, after doing forced labour on White farms.

The next date fixed for the move was 13 January, but they did not go and were arrested in a dawn raid. On 17 January, forty-four men were released on condition that ten families would be ready to move on 20 January. The chief had to be among those ready to move on that day. Others were released on 21 January

1. *Post*, 16 February 1969.

provided that from then on at least fifteen families a day were ready to move to Ledig. They were offered State-employed help to demolish their houses, free transport for themselves and their belongings (excepting bricks), and, on arrival at Ledig, at least one tent and 45 lb. of mealie meal. All cattle had to be sold and an auction was arranged for 28 January. Everyone was removed by the end of January. Thus another 'Black spot' was 'voluntarily' cleared.

I gathered both from the people at Ledig and outsiders that those who moved with Chieftainess Catherine were quite well settled but that the later arrivals are being victimized. Local missionaries said that the people in the second section were desperately poor and in great need of help. I first visited the place in March 1969 and then on a number of occasions until September; every time it looked more and more like a slum.

The people from Boons were members of the Bakubung tribe, which is part of the Tswana 'nation'. But at Ledig there are also a number of other people who are Zulu, Swazi, Xhosa or Ndebele; these have either been endorsed out of the cities or come from local White farms. They will presumably at some stage be moved on again to their respective 'homelands'.

I spoke to a number of other chiefs in the area, who, while not willing to commit themselves on conditions in their own areas, expressed concern over the situation at Ledig.

A few people in Rustenburg have tried to provide some aid for people in these three places but obviously they have not been able to make any appreciable difference to the conditions of the thousands of people suffering in these hell-holes.

De Hoop

The other major resettlement site in the Western Transvaal, De Hoop, twenty-two miles north-west of Lichtenburg, is quite decent compared to the other three. This township is officially planned for five thousand families. When I went there in March 1969 it had about 1,500 families, who had been arriving steadily since 1965. Many of them were evicted from their locations for non-payment of rent; others were simply 'surplus' or 'non-productive'. There are rumours in the locality that De Hoop will eventually be swelled by people from as far away as Thaba 'Nchu, another fragment of Tswana 'homeland' in the Orange Free State, almost three hundred miles away. This rumour was lent some substance by a report in one of the Afrikaans newspapers, and it would be consistent with the trend to remove all African areas to the most remote edges of the country.

The first arrivals were put into one-roomed all-corrugated-iron huts measuring only about 10 ft square (like those at Herschel, Witsieshoek and elsewhere). Later another room of about the same size was added. The rent for these was R1.68 a month. Some four-roomed houses had been built and others were being erected. I was told that fifty or sixty people were then in jail for non-payment of rent. (Having been evicted from one location for not being able to pay the rent it is difficult to see how they were expected to find the money in De Hoop.) I heard of a man who refused to pay because he claimed that the White men had no right to make him pay to live on 'the land of my fathers'.

Lichtenburg has its own location, so most of the men from De Hoop have to seek work elsewhere, often in the places from which they have been moved – Potchefstroom, Klerksdorp, and Johannesburg.

There is a provincial hospital at Sheila, about three miles away, and it has an annexe at Gelukspan, some twenty miles further. Two resident doctors at Sheila serve both hospitals and a number of clinics for Africans.

Sheila hospital was opened at the end of 1968, and Gelukspan had previously been run by the Dutch Reformed Church. Non-White hospitals at Lichtenburg, Delareyville and Ventersdorp closed when Sheila opened. This has meant that many people now have to travel seventy miles to a hospital – and even then may be transferred to Gelukspan, yet further away. The hospital insists that every patient must have a letter from a doctor before being admitted. It may take many hours and involve much extra travelling for Africans in these parts to find a doctor and there have been a number of cases of people dying in the process of trying to get admitted to this hospital.

It was impossible to obtain figures relating to malnutrition, though I heard from an unofficial but well-informed source that 70–80 per cent of the children were affected.

Local clergy and others said that there were many broken homes and family problems due to numbers of men, who had previously worked near home, having to take employment in Johannesburg and being able to return only once or twice a year. There was also, they said, a growing crime rate, especially assault, due to lack of parental control.

A number of people have been arrested for being 'squatters' on old diamond diggings and farms near Lichtenburg; this applies particularly to young people who work in the town but live with their parents in these 'Black spots'. They were born there and their parents live there but they are told they must go to the 'homeland' – De Hoop. Others who go from De Hoop to Lichtenburg to look for work stay with friends there and are then arrested.

The location at Lichtenburg is only eight years old, but, it is said, all the people are to be moved to De Hoop and hostels will be built for those who work in Lichtenburg.

At De Hoop, apart from the rows and rows of tiny houses, there are also primary and secondary schools, shops, churches and the usual basic facilities of an urban location. But the whole set-up looks rather bizarre in the middle of nowhere. It is obviously destined to be not a city but a giant dormitory for the 'superfluous appendages' of migrant workers.

Zeerust

A new township is being developed at Welbedacht, a few miles outside Zeerust, which lies close to the Botswana border. The old location at Zeerust has been moved, which meant that people had to leave decent houses, built and added to over the years, for the usual little township boxes.

The Reserve outside Zeerust is the home of the Bafurutse tribe, a section of the Botswana. This tribe became famous in

South Africa for its heroic resistance to Government measures to further apartheid policies. The conflict first came into the open in the mid 1950s when Dr Verwoerd (then Minister for Native Affairs) summoned the Bafurutse chief, Abram Moiloa, to Rustenburg to sign his agreement to the Bantu Authorities Act. The chief refused to sign and later declared, 'They just want us chiefs to sign a document which says "Destroy me, baas!" Let them destroy us without our signatures!'

The conflict turned to violence when the Government took steps to extend the hated pass ('reference book') system to women in the Reserve.[1] A deputation of women anxious to discuss the meaning of the passes with the authorities at Lichtenburg led to the police shooting and killing four people. When the Government started issuing the passes to the Reserve, in April 1957, the Bafurutse women almost universally refused to take them.

The chief was deposed, and the people responded with a boycott of the Government school and the White trader in the Reserve. The Government removed the teachers, threatened the 1,200 pupils that they would not be allowed to attend any school thereafter, closed the Post Office at the Royal village and stopped the bus service. As an official of the Native Affairs Department said, 'The sins of the fathers shall be visited on the heads of the children, even unto the third and fourth generation.'

The Government then mounted a campaign of intimidation against the people. A mobile para-military police force with armoured cars was moved into the district. They forced some of the sub-chiefs to collaborate, and press-ganged some of the men in each village to form gangs of 'bodyguards' for the chiefs. They systematically arrested and assaulted anyone alleged to have spoken against the Government or to have incited the people against the passes. Police detachments roved the Reserve

1. The 'reference book' contains permits to work, to reside in a given area, and certifies payment of taxes and fees. Without valid permits the holder of the pass is automatically endorsed out of a White area, or arrested, and he must carry the pass at all times. Formerly it was necessary only for men to have reference books, and the extension of this degrading system to women was the cause of widespread opposition throughout the country in the late 1950s, leading up to the massacre at Sharpville on 20 March 1960.

at night, hauling people out of their houses and beating them up. Thousands of people fled to Botswana (then the British Protectorate of Bechuanaland) or to other parts of South Africa. Others took to sleeping out of doors, in hiding. Normal life in the Reserve came to an end, and the fields went untended.

Some five hundred people were arrested in six months, and countless numbers were assaulted. But the people refused to accept the passes, and held public burnings of those few which had been issued at the beginning. There was bitter strife between the people and the chiefs' bodyguards in those villages where the chiefs were trying to carry out Government orders. Many houses were burnt down, and people lived in daily – or nightly – terror. Some of the incidents were particularly serious, such as an unprovoked shooting by the police at the village of Gopane, when four people were killed as they ran from the police.

The tribe scraped together all the money they had to pay for legal defence, fines and other costs of the struggle. An emergency was proclaimed. The Government were set back a long time in their plans, but in the end they silenced the resistance; a number of people were deported to Natal and others were jailed. On 8 August 1959 the Reserve, after two and a half years of upheaval, was proclaimed a Regional Authority. The head of the Authority appointed was the junior chief of the district – usurping the position of the traditional tribal authorities; the Authority now administers a crushed and resentful people.

There were two villages, Braklaagte and Leeuwfontein, which constituted 'Black spots', lying outside the main body of the Reserve. The Government's plans to move the people of these two villages underlay the original conflict over the Bantu Authorities Act. I do not know what happened to Braklaagte, but when I was in the district I heard that the people of Leeuwfontein were still holding out against moving, in 1969. I tried to visit the village, but I found the road leading to it was guarded by police trucks, and I turned back rather than jeopardize the rest of my tour by creating an incident with the police in such a sensitive area.

The history of the Bafurutse resistance is known because an Anglican priest, Charles Hooper, served as Missionary in the

Reserve at the time of the troubles and faithfully recorded what he witnessed in his book *Brief Authority*. One hears of similar episodes in other parts of the country though there may be no such thorough chronicle of the events.

8. Eastern Transvaal

Most of the resettlement of Africans in the Eastern Transvaal is concentrated in the Bushbuckridge–Pilgrim's Rest area, an area noted for its superb climate and great scenic beauty – Blyde River Canyon, Kowyn's Pass, the Long Tom Pass, the Echo Caves, the Mac Mac Falls. It is a very popular tourist area in its own right, besides being on a pleasant route to the Kruger National Park. The Transvaal Provincial authorities have recognized its appeal and are developing facilities for White tourists.

A luxurious resort for Whites is being developed near the Blyde River Canyon, twenty-five miles from Pilgrim's Rest. At a cost of about R5 million, it will provide cottages, a restaurant, tennis courts, a swimming pool and other recreations. It will have all the amenities so notably lacking at a place a few miles back on the Pilgrim's Rest road, which a notice board at the roadside describes as 'Dientje Bantoedorp'.

Dientje

From the roadside you can see only a row of neat mud-and-thatch houses much like African houses throughout the country. They belong to people who arrived there in 1960 and so have had time to settle themselves. But when you go in you soon see that not all the inhabitants are so fortunate.

In April 1969 there were about 120 families in this settlement, which cannot possibly be called a town. They came from three farms, Frankfort, Thanda Creek and Uitspan, in the Pilgrim's Rest area. Frankfort farm was owned by a mining company which leased residential, grazing and arable land to Africans.

They went to Dientje in three batches; the first group in 1960, the second in 1965 and the third in November 1968, when the company wanted to increase the rent to R34 per annum per family. A group came from Thanda Creek, which was an old Crown Land farm, in July 1968. In November 1968 a group came from Uitspan, which was also an old Crown Land farm where people had lived for generations and had had land for ploughing and grazing. But the Government, they said, sold the land to a White farmer who said he did not want Africans on it.

Those who were moved in July and November 1968 were given four weeks' notice by the farmer and then transported by Government lorries to Dientje. They have no land for plough-ing but there is a commonage where they can keep cattle. On arrival they were shown a 50-yd square plot, nothing else. They did not receive any compensation nor were they provided with emergency rations. They were not given a tent to live in or to store their belongings in while they built some kind of shelter. They brought with them what materials could be salvaged from their old homes and erected temporary shelters with the old corrugated iron or pieces of wood. No sanitation was provided throughout the 'town'. Some, though by no means all, have now dug their own pit latrines on their plots.

In April 1969 about twenty-five families were still living in shacks made of old corrugated iron. They had been living in these conditions for nearly six months. This was not due to their laziness or because they liked living in such places. One said that he would like to offer me some tea but was too embarrassed to take me into such a place. But they were explicitly told by the Bantu Affairs Commissioner not to build proper houses. He told them that as this was a township all houses had to be built according to approved plans. He told them that he would come again with copies of the plans and they could choose the one they wanted to build. That was six months previous to my visit and they had heard no more from him. They did not know how long they would have to continue living in these conditions, of which some of the men, at home on holiday from Johannes-burg, were most articulate in their criticism. But, as usual, they ended by saying to me: 'But what can we do about it? We just have to make the best of it.'

The area is barren and the women have to go to the mountains at least a mile away to collect wood for fuel. There is no work available in the immediate vicinity. The nearest would be at Pilgrim's Rest, twenty-five miles away, but that is only a tiny village and moreover has its own location from which employers can draw labour. There is not one proper township house built by the B.A.D. in the whole settlement, though some of the people have been there for nine years. The only amenities in the 'town' are one borehole and one small shop. They have to go to Pilgrim's Rest for their major shopping and for official business; this costs them 60 cents return bus-fare. There is a Dutch Reformed Church (N.G.K.) hospital about seven miles away but no clinic on the spot.

It is said that many more people are to be moved into Dientje in the near future – according to a statement by the Minister of B.A.D. in the House of Assembly on 4 May 1965, Dientje is 'planned' for six hundred families. At the time of my visit another borehole was being drilled but there was no sign of any development of the normal township amenities. There was certainly no indication that any attempt was being made to establish any industry in the area.

Dientje is officially described as a township. Yet the facilities, or lack of them, are those of a 'closer settlement'; no houses provided, no sanitation, no running water, no clinic. But the people have cattle, which is not a feature of either a township or a closer settlement. It is not an agricultural settlement because they do not have land for ploughing. It simply combines some of the worst features of various types of settlement.

The people who go to enjoy the luxury of the Blyde River Canyon Recreation Resort will probably never even be aware of the existence of Dientje. If they were, one doubts whether they would be particularly perturbed. Such contrasts are part of the South African way of life, in which Black poverty and squalor are one price of White wealth and luxury.

Elandsfontein

Adjoining Dientje and immediately opposite the Recreation Resort there is a large agricultural settlement, called Elandsfontein. This is definitely an agricultural settlement, though it appears on the Minister's list of townships.[1] It consists of eight residential villages, each with its own arable and grazing land. Most of the present inhabitants have always lived there but were previously scattered over the whole farm, which is about seven miles long. They were under two chiefs and rented the farm from Whites at R4 per annum per family.

In about 1960 the farm was bought by the Bantu Trust. Part of it was taken for the building of a road and the Recreation Resort. The rest of it was re-planned on the usual Trust farm lines, which meant that the people who were scattered over the farm had to demolish their houses, move to the allocated residential sites and build new houses. Only those with very good houses, I was told, received any compensation; the others were not given any assistance whatsoever. Most were able to build their houses on the allocated site before they moved. But those who had to move from the part that was needed for the road were not given the opportunity of doing so and had to live in temporary shacks made from the salvage of their old houses while they built. If they refused to move their houses were bulldozed down.

Other people came in 1968, from Frankfort and other White farms, who had been evicted or had left of their own accord because they were tired of conditions there and applied to the Bantu Affairs Commissioner and the chief for a site. So there is now less land for more people. Each family has a residential plot, two acres of arable land and a share in the common grazing. They pay R3 per annum for each additional head of cattle. Everybody I spoke to complained, sometimes at very great length, that they had less land than before and were unable to support themselves on it.

There are two primary schools and a number of shops owned by the local inhabitants. There are boreholes for each village. A

1. Hansard, 4 May 1965.

private doctor visits once a week, but there is no clinic and the hospital is eight miles from the nearest village and thirteen from the farthest.

A few people are employed in a small brickyard, which is situated on what used to be part of the farm. A few have found temporary employment, at R3 a week, on the building of the Recreation Resort; but the contractors have also brought their own workers. The people complain of lack of employment and say that the need is now more urgent as they do not get so much return from the farm.

From the Recreation Resort, Elandsfontein may look like a peaceful, well-ordered, tribal farm. But the people who live there know and feel differently. While they do not have enough land to make even a subsistence livelihood, they look across the road to the 90 square miles of playground for their White brothers.

Bushbuckridge

Various forms of resettlement have been put into effect in the Bushbuckridge area for the past fifteen to twenty years. Thanks to the efforts of a former Bantu Affairs Commissioner, some of these resettled villages are as good as can be expected in the circumstances. This applies particularly to those which benefit from the Bantu Trust irrigation schemes, which cover four to six thousand acres. Though no one could claim that they are perfect, the people are probably better off than they were under the old farm-tenant system.

From Acornhoek to White River there is a huge tract of 'released area' (i.e. land which the 1936 Land Act prescribed should be added to the land set aside for African occupation by the 1913 Land Act). The Bantu Trust has now purchased almost all the White-owned farms in this released area. Some of these were game farms, others company farms with hundreds of African tenants and 'squatters'. Many of these Africans were paying between R10 and R20 per annum rent to the White owners. Once these farms had been bought by the Trust, people flocked to them from other White farms because they thought that they could at least have security of tenure there. In fact they were officially illegal squatters.

When the resettlement schemes were put into effect, the residents who were there 'legally' were re-grouped into residential sites and apportioned arable and grazing lands. But thousands of 'illegal' squatters were moved off the farms and had to find a place for themselves. The B.A.D., I was told by an ex-official, provided transport for them but charged 10 cents a mile. Others, although they were there 'illegally', were given just a residential site on the farm, since the physical demands of moving them all were too great. For example, on the farm Marite there were over a thousand 'illegal' squatters. Rather than remove them all, the Bantu Affairs Commissioner allocated them residential sites on the spot. Since then many more families have moved into Marite. It is a mixture of Bapedi, Swazis, Zulus and anybody who is not wanted by any chief. It has been described as the Alexandra township [1] of the Eastern Transvaal.

There are at least sixty or seventy resettled Trust villages in the 'released area' between Acornhoek and White River. While some people have no doubt benefited from the regrouping because of the introduction of better farming methods and, in some places, irrigation schemes, it means that thousands of other people have been forced out and that even those who remained have had the great inconvenience of demolishing their houses and rebuilding them on a new site. The amount of grazing and arable land allocated to each family depends on the number of families who were legally resident on the farm before the re-planning. Each family usually has about two acres of arable land, which is well below the economic farming unit recommended by the Tomlinson Commission. There are very few, if any, who can survive by farming alone.

The resettlement of these farms is now almost complete, though a few families from White farms are still joining the

1. Alexandra, the African township about six miles north of Johannesburg, was about the most densely populated and cosmopolitan square mile in South Africa. It consisted of freehold stands but almost every standholder had a number of tenants. Nobody knows just how many people there were. Thousands have now been moved out; the policy is to move out the family units and retain the township as a complex of hostels for migrant workers.

various Trust villages; they are usually given only a residential site. But there are still some removals pending. At the farm Maviljane, where some two hundred families from farms in the Sabie district were resettled two or three years ago, the people have been told that the Bapedi will have to move to London township, about fourteen miles away, and the Tsongas to Thulu-mahashe, about forty miles away. At Masana, an ex-Swiss Mission farm near Bushbuckridge which has been bought by the Bantu Trust, thirty-five families have been told that they will have to move because, although they are actually living on Bantu Trust land, they are within five hundred yards of a White area. Further, if the policy of settling members of each ethnic group or tribe in their own separate 'homeland' is followed through, the various groups at Marite will have to move again to their several homelands.

Apart from all these Trust villages there are three so-called townships in the Acornhoek-Bushbuckridge area: Arthur's Seat, London and Thulamahashe. In the list of townships given by the Minister of B.A.D., a fourth, Belfast, was mentioned, but in April 1969 there was no sign of it. A prominent local White described Arthur's Seat as an 'eyesore' and London as a 'white elephant'.

Arthur's Seat

Four miles from Acornhoek, which is near the boundary of the Kruger National Park, there is a large well-established agricul-tural settlement with neat houses, shops, schools, churches, herds of cattle and land under cultivation. On the edge of this settle-ment there is a cluster of about 150 houses on a small hillside. This is the 'township', Arthur's Seat. The houses are so huddled together that it is difficult to see where one person's plot begins and another ends. But the plots appear to be the usual township size of 50 ft square – there any similarity with a township ends. There are no streets and no apparent order. All around there are wide-open spaces and suddenly this cluster of hovels.

The first people arrived in 1962 and the settlement now appears to be complete. It was originally planned as a township but has in fact become a 'closer settlement', with the difference that the plots are only half the size of those in a 'closer settlement'. On 19 August 1966, the Minister of B.A.D. said that there was a population of 1,700 in Arthur's Seat township; on 27 February 1968 he said that two houses had been built by his Department.

Most of the families came from White farms in the Sabie district, fifty to sixty miles away. They were given notice by the farmers (presumably in pursuance of the five labour-tenant laws) and directed to Arthur's Seat by the Bantu Commissioner. No compensation was paid to them nor was transport provided. On their arrival at Arthur's Seat no tents were provided nor any building materials. They put together a few sheets of corrugated iron and pieces of wood which they had brought with them and lived in these shelters until they had built mud and thatch houses.

There is no work in the area except on White farms and it is difficult for the people to obtain contracts for work on the Rand or elsewhere. Even to apply for a contract they have to travel to Bushbuckridge, which costs them 90 cents return bus-fare. One borehole is the only source of water for the whole settlement. No sanitation whatsoever was provided even though the houses are much closer together than in a 'closer settlement' or Trust village; some have now made their own pit latrines on their plots. A school was opened in April 1969; previously the children had gone to school in the old settlement of Arthur's Seat about four miles away. There is one shop in the new settlement; there are also some in the old village. No fuel for cooking and heating is available in the vicinity; the women have to collect wood from the mountains about two miles away. There is no clinic or any other medical services on the spot, but there is a Mission hospital about two miles away.

There is the usual attitude of resignation and almost despair: 'How could we like to live in a place like this? How are we supposed to live? ... But there is nothing we can do.'

London

About seven miles from Bushbuckridge there is another old-established agricultural settlement, called London, in which a new township has been planted. Officially, this township is planned for three thousand families. It was started in about 1966 but at the beginning of 1969 there were only some hundred houses, and only half of them were occupied. By April 1969 there were about five hundred houses, some two-thirds of which were occupied. The people came mainly from White farms in the Sabie, Nelspruit and White River districts up to seventy miles away. Some left the farms of their own accord, while others were evicted by the farmers; but they all had to move to London at their own expense.

To speak of 'houses' is a euphemism. At first they consisted of one all-zinc room measuring 11 ft by 11 ft, and an outside toilet. This room, according to some, was meant to be a temporary structure, primarily to store belongings while building. The people found them too hot to live in anyway and preferred to build their own temporary structures. Because they could not live in the huts which were provided, some of the first arrivals moved out again and went to Trust villages in the Bushbuckridge area. Later the B.A.D. added a brick room of the same size. The all-zinc room usually becomes a kitchen and so appears to be permanent. Some of the people have also added mud rooms, which adds to the appearance of shabbiness but at least is better than the rows of little square hutches which is all that most townships have. Most of the houses are surrounded by head-high grass – not a common feature of townships. The rent for these 'houses', one all-zinc room and one single brick, is R1.83 a month.

In April 1969 there was one water point for all the houses; pipes had been laid for water but no taps had been fitted even in the 'streets'. A school was built in 1966 but was opened only in 1968.

There was no sign of any industry being established in the area or of any further extension of the township. In fact it looked more like a ghost town than the beginning of a new one.

Thulumahashe

This is a settlement of about 150 families, fifteen miles east of Acornhoek. It is officially described as a township but is yet another of those places which do not fit into any of the neat categories defined by the B.A.D.

The first people moved there in 1960. They were thirty-two families from Trust farms, which were apparently needed for an afforestation scheme. Later others arrived from White farms. All of them had to move at their own expense. The ones from the Trust farms were given two months' notice, and any houses remaining after that were demolished by bulldozers.

The first arrivals were provided with nothing, beyond being allocated a half-acre plot which they could buy for R88, or a quarter-acre which they could buy for R44 or rent for 86 cents a month. No tents were provided; they had to erect their own temporary shacks for living in while they built. They were told that they had to build according to approved plans. But while some have built good houses many have built mud huts. There are a few township-type houses built by the B.A.D. but these are only for teachers and officials.

Since 1967 those moving in have been provided with a one-roomed asbestos house measuring 11 ft by 11 ft, and an outside toilet. The cost of this is R300 or it can be rented for R1.85 a month. The people were under the impression that the rent includes buying the house and the plot over a period of thirty years. But they said they had heard that even if the house and plot were purchased they still could not be handed on to one's heirs. In April 1969 more people were being moved into these tiny one-roomed huts.

There are taps in the 'streets'; one for every four or five houses. Shops and schools in the settlement appear to be adequate and there is a clinic about two miles away. The first arrivals were told that a factory was to be built near by, but nine years later there was still no sign of it. Many of the men continue to work on the Rand; the younger men, who cannot get work on the Rand, can sometimes obtain contracts for work in the recently developed copper-mining town of Phalaborwa. But many are unemployed.

A number of people, including some old people, I was told, have been evicted from the settlement for non-payment of rent. They have to go to a chief somewhere and ask for a place to build.

After visiting Arthur's Seat and Thulumahashe I attended the opening of a new church in the Acornhoek area. Thousands of people from these places and many other villages had gathered for the occasion, so I had an excellent opportunity to check my facts and confirm my impressions. They were in high spirits for the festive occasion – plenty of food and beer were provided. (In passing, it was noticeable that none of the White clergy present partook of the food; instead they returned to the Mission some miles away and ate there. Perhaps they were frightened of breaking some law.) But, once the people had recovered from the surprise that anyone should be interested in their living conditions, they became serious and spoke with feeling of their poverty due to lack of employment and shortage of land and cattle.

It would be almost impossible to trace the history of every resettlement scheme in the Bushbuckridge/Pilgrim's Rest area. But I think that this account should be sufficient to give some impression of the vastness of it and the general conditions – thousands and thousands of people being shunted around and herded together in places with few if any of the normal amenities and with little or no hope of finding employment anywhere near their homes. It is impossible even to guess at the numbers involved and no official figures are available.

Naboomskoppie and Alverton

About twelve miles north of Burgersfort, which in turn is thirty miles north of Lydenburg, there are two adjacent resettlement villages, separated by a small river. In one, Naboomskoppie, there is an impressive new Lutheran church, but alongside it there are neat rows of obviously fairly recently built houses which are no longer occupied and have been stripped of doors, windows and roofs. These used to be the houses of the church congregation. About 140 families had been moved there in September 1964 from the Lutheran Mission three miles outside Lydenburg. This Mission was established in the 1860s and some of the families of the people moved had been there since that time, while others settled there later. But almost all of those moved had been born here. On the Mission they had very good arable land, with some under irrigation, and good grazing land, for which, in the words of their minister, 'they paid a very small rent.' The minister pointed out that these people had been in a very fortunate, if not unique, position in that they had excellent farming facilities, and were also so near the town that they could easily commute daily to work there.

But this happy situation was shattered when the people were told that the Mission was a 'Black spot' and they would have to move. They were given the choice of going into the location at Lydenburg or to Naboomskoppie. Virtually all of them went to Naboomskoppie, in the hope that they would at least have some land. In fact, a couple of families who could have stayed at the Mission chose instead to throw in their lot with those going to Naboomskoppie. Such occurrences are sometimes used as an argument to show that the people actually prefer resettlement areas. But it was really simply a case of accepting what little was offered them rather than risk being left with nothing later, knowing that the Mission could not offer them any security. If at a later date they decided to change their employment or if the Mission no longer required their services, they would have nowhere to go.

On the appointed day Government trucks transported them to Naboomskoppie, where each family was allocated a half-acre plot. Water was pumped from the river into a reservoir and from there to a few taps in the streets. The school was housed in an old farm house. There was no sanitation.

A Bantu Affairs official told them that the law demands that when the Trust buys a farm it must be left fallow for three to five years. In April 1969 there was still no sign of ploughing land being allocated. The compensation which was promised on leaving the Mission was paid a year later. For the first year the B.A.D. provided a ration of mealie meal; the Mission also sent relief.

Before being moved from the Mission the people were promised that they would not be put under a chief. But in 1965 they were informed that those who wished to stay at Naboomskoppie would have to be under Chief Sekhukhuni. So about 95 per cent of them decided to cross over the river to the other settlement, Alverton, preferring to be under Chief Manoke. After having built houses at Naboomskoppie, they stripped them and built again at Alverton. Hence the rows of gutted houses near the Lutheran church.

After the Mission people had moved into Naboomskoppie, many families from White farms in the Sabie, Ohrigstad and Lydenburg districts moved into both Naboomskoppie and Alverton and were still being moved there in April 1969. As is usually the case with people from White farms, they did not receive any compensation and were not provided with transport. They were told that ploughing land might be allocated to them but the farm has not yet been planned.

Two miles towards Burgersfort a school is being built and plots marked out for a new, huge township. Who will be moved there? The only certain thing is that there will be little or no work and it will turn out to be another depressing dormitory for the dependants of migrant workers.

Sekhukhuniland

Like the Bafurutse [1] the Sekhukhuni people resisted the imposition of the Tribal Authority system from the outset. Most of the chiefs sided with their people and the replanning and resettlement of the region has still not been carried out. Sekhukhuniland is inhabited by people of the Bapedi and the Bakone who are intermingled with sub-chiefs from both tribes. The suzerainty of the Bapedi chiefs has however become accepted by all the people.

In the mid-fifties the Government began to resettle the Bakone people on a separate area, as a preliminary to establish-

1. See pages 159–62.

ing Tribal Authorities. There was considerable opposition and at a large tribal meeting held by the Sekhukhuni Regent the people rejected the whole Bantu Authorities system. In April 1957 the Government reacted by deporting two members of the Paramount Chief's family to Natal, and proceeded to set up the Bantu Authority. The tribe petitioned for the return of their 'sons' and started a fund to 'fight the Government'.

In November the Native Commissioner, with a large body of police, suspended the Regent, arrested a number of others, and deported two men. When the Regent won an appeal against suspension, the Government deported him also, to the Transkei, and put in his place a retired policeman who was compliant to their wishes. But the people refused to cooperate, and the Tribal Authority had to be disestablished.

Resentment against the Government continued to mount however, and many refused to pay taxes. In May 1958 the police were sent to arrest three of the popular leaders. This action roused angry crowds, and the police opened fire, killing several people. The crowds rioted and murdered seven tribesmen who had collaborated with the Government. A state of emergency ensued, the police arrested about 340 people. Altogether thirty-seven were sentenced to death, but were eventually reprieved and given life sentences. A mobile police force occupied the Reserve for many months.

So far only two sub-chiefs, from the vicinity of the Jane Furse hospital, have moved voluntarily. Another chief, who accepted the Tribal Authority plan, was murdered in 1962.

The Trust acquired a number of farms many years ago, which are now well established on the usual lines. Over the past five or six years hundreds of families from White farms in the Lydenburg area have been resettled there; the labour-tenant law seems to have been enforced on almost every farm in the Lydenburg area.

The Sekhukhuni are by no means an isolated example of resistance to Government plans, but they are remarkable in the determination they have shown. Eventually, however, the Government will no doubt secure complete compliance with their wishes.

Namakgale

The Eastern Transvaal also has a few regular townships to
house the labour forces for the bigger towns. The best of them
is Namakgale, at Phalaborwa. Phalaborwa is the only industrial
centre for a wide radius, so it draws workers from eighty to a
hundred miles away.

Namakgale is planned for eight thousand families, plus single
quarters. At present there are about three thousand families.
Many of them came from the old shanty location at Phalaborwa, others were workers from further afield. The houses are
mainly four or five-roomed township-type dwellings. The four-
roomed have water and toilet outside, while the five-roomed
have a toilet and bathroom outside. The rent is R4.40 and
R5.68 respectively a month.

Like almost all such townships, Namakgale is some distance –
five miles – from the town. The bus-fare is 16 cents return or
75 cents for a weekly ticket (90 cents to further parts of the
town). But some firms provide transport, while others give a
travel allowance to their employees.

It is well equipped with shops, schools, churches and the
normal facilities of a township. Street lighting has been installed and, in April 1969, it was expected that electricity would
soon be connected to the houses.

This is one of the few townships or settlements of any kind
which has easy access to a border industry area, though, in this
case, it was of course a matter of the people coming to the industry and not vice versa.

Considering the extra expense of living in a township – rent,
bus-fares etc. – the wages in Phalaborwa are far from generous.
A labourer earns, I am told, on average, R7–R8 a week; a
semi-skilled worker, R12 a week; a skilled worker, e.g. a labora-
tory assistant, R20 a week; domestic servants, R10–R12 a
month.

Phalaborwa sprang up as a copper-mining town in the 1950s.
I tried to find out what happened to the Africans who were living on what is now the White town and in the areas which are

now being mined. It is interesting to note that these Africans, now living in a Trust village some distance away, had been mining copper on a small scale for many, many years before the White man came.

Ngodini

The African labour-force of White River has also been re-housed in a township, Ngodini, eleven miles out of town. They used to live in a municipal location in White River, where they had built their own houses. Their only expense was 50–75 cents a month for sanitation services. About six hundred families were moved from there in September 1968. They either had to provide their own transport to Ngodini or they could use Government lorries for a fee of R4.

Ngodini is planned for six thousand families, according to the Minister of B.A.D. At present there are about a thousand; four hundred of them are people endorsed out from Johannesburg, Vereeniging and other towns. The houses are mainly four-roomed township-type with water inside and an outside toilet, for which the rent is R4.50 a month. There are primary and secondary schools, and a temporary hospital staffed by the Swiss Mission.

The bus-fare into White River is R4.30 a month. Some firms have increased wages to help cover the extra costs and some others provide transport. There were many complaints from employers at having to help to meet this extra cost, which is equivalent to doubling the wages in some cases.

There is no real industry in the district. There has been a proposal to establish border industries at Kaapmuiden, thirty-one miles from Nelspruit and thirty-six miles from White River. But there is no sign of any preparations yet. It is said that the families living in compounds at sawmills and also those on White farms around White River will all be moved to Ngodini.

People living in the African locations attached to other towns in the Eastern Transvaal have been told they will be moved. A new township has been announced to serve Nelspruit, though it has not been prepared yet. The old people, widows and un-employed from the location at Ermelo have been told they will be moved either to the proposed Nelspruit township, or to Ngodini.

9. Northern Transvaal

Whenever I visited a new region, I found it necessary initially to spend some time getting the feel of the area. It also took some time to discover the pattern which the authorities were trying to establish. This was particularly difficult in the Northern Transvaal. Very few people seemed to know what was going on concerning the resettlement of Africans. Probably there was no one in a position to give a comprehensive and accurate account of the removals in this region. Two sociologists who each visited the same area wrote reports containing contradictory descriptions of the same basic facts. Of course it depends a great deal on whom one talks to, whether one gets the Government's or the people's side of the story.

Those people who should have known something proved to be extremely uncommunicative. The impression given by the clergy in near-by White towns was that nothing of any significance had happened for the past fifty years. I learned later that many of the local clergy were in fact aware of the removals in their areas and of the implications for the people involved. But, whether through a preference to see no evil, or a desire to deceive me, or a mere preoccupation with other problems, with three exceptions they gave me very little assistance or information.

The Northern Transvaal contains the 'homelands' of three cultural groups: the Tsongas (also known as Shangaans), the Vendas and the Northern Sotho (also called Bapedi); but a number of smaller tribal groups also live in the region. The largest group, the Northern Sotho, of whom there are 1·7 million, is mainly concentrated in the Pietersburg and Potgietersrus area, on the western side of this region. There are some 360,000 Vendas and 731,000 Tsongas, whose homes are mostly in the north-eastern corner of the Transvaal. Of course, not all the people included in these census counts are actually living at the present time in the Reserves.

In many places, these peoples have lived intermingled in a series of chiefdoms which displayed a considerable diversity of pattern in their settlements, economies and political organization. None of the major groups possessed a distinct territory of its own, nor was territorial exclusiveness a principle of political or social importance to these people. In some areas, Tsongas, Northern Sotho and Zulus are found living together, and elsewhere there are other permutations. The north-eastern tip of the region, predominantly Venda and Tsonga in population, is the most mixed area of all.

This intermingling is not in keeping with the policy of Tribal Authorities, and the Government have been making efforts for some time to disentangle all the ethnic groups into separate 'nations'. We have already seen in the case of the Tswanastan, which is spread out in pockets hundreds of miles apart in the Northern Cape and Western Transvaal, how little it matters to the Government whether a Bantustan can be viable. But in the case of the Vendas and Tsongas, the idea of creating nation-states seems even less plausible. The barrenness of their 'homelands' in the remotest corner of the Transvaal, one of the most inhospitable and underdeveloped parts of the whole country, makes nationhood even more of a fiction than in other cases. The effort to establish Bantustans with wholesale removals is always wholly irrelevant to the real problems of the rural African Reserves and, indeed, can only aggravate their difficulties; in the case of the Vendas and Tsongas, the irrelevance is more than usually striking.

Some idea of the poverty of the country is given by Muriel Horrell's [1] report of a visit to these areas in 1965. The report, which was based on official sources of information said:

For six years in succession there has been a most severe drought in the Northern Transvaal. Over wide areas streams and dams have

[1]. Senior Research Officer of the South African Institute of Race Relations, and author of numerous publications. The report is entitled, *A Visit to the Bantu Areas of the Northern Transvaal* (S.A.I.R.R., 1965).

dried up, crops have been lost, wild plants normally used as food have become hard to find and grazing has well-nigh disappeared. Agricultural officers state that 30 per cent of the boreholes have dried up. Whereas previously 60 per cent of the boreholes drilled were successful, this number has now been halved. About 40 per cent of the cattle have been lost (128,000 in 1964). These losses would have been fewer had more African owners accepted Departmental offers to move their stock to places where grazing was available . . .

For some time voluntary relief organizations operated in the area but from 1 June 1964 the Department extended its relief programme very widely and asked voluntary bodies to discontinue their efforts. . . . About 250,000 children and adults who are unfit for work of any sort are being fed daily on mealie-meal and pro-nutro soup.

Able-bodied men and unmarried women are expected to seek work through labour bureaux; but those who are unfit to compete in the open market are given employment, at R14 a month, on such projects as eradicating weeds, or building roads and dams in the remoter areas.[1]

The Venda and Tsonga 'nations' have no sizable town, no border industries, and not even one tarred road. There has been a certain amount of agricultural improvement work – dams, irrigation schemes, fenced enclosures and so on. But with the continual packing of more people into the Reserves, the problems are worsening. The Tomlinson Report[2] estimated that once the Released Areas had been added, the African Reserves in the whole of South Africa could support 2,142,000 people. There are almost this number in the Reserves of the Northern Transvaal alone.

The original plan was to have only one Bantustan for the Vendas, Tsongas and Northern Sotho. The change to the present plan provides a case study in itself of the peculiar logic and psychology of apartheid, breeding ever greater refinements of discrimination like the hosts of anti-Christ in medieval eschatologies. Eventually, Tsonga chiefs and headmen themselves

1. I have quoted from this report published several years ago not out of any selective bias, but because no later independent and authoritative report has been made of the area. However the conditions have not changed in any fundamental way – there has been continuing drought in the last few years and no new economic factors have been introduced.

2. Referred to on page xxi.

demanded their own separate Authority. But they say that they made this claim only because the Bantu Authorities system was being imposed by the Government. Given a policy of ethnic separation, the logical conclusion is that every chief should demand his own jurisdiction.

According to missionaries, doctors, teachers and many other people in the area, the Vendas had already been living happily and according to their own social and religious customs for a hundred years while sharing the territory with the Tsongas and Northern Sotho. They lived side by side, their children went to the same schools, there was extensive inter-marrying. There is a Venda chief, for example, who has one Venda wife, one Tsonga and one Sotho. The people were not concerned if their immediate chief or headman belonged to another tribe since they were still free to approach a chief of their own tribe with their problems. The Vendas had their own initiation schools, but the Tsongas were perfectly free not to attend them.

Friction between the two groups started with the introduction of the Bantu Authorities system. Under the Bantu Authorities Act of 1951 Tribal Authorities are first established, then Regional Authorities and finally Territorial Authorities. When the Regional Authority was established in the Northern Transvaal, the Tsongas complained that, considering their numerical superiority, they were not adequately represented. There were four Regional Authorities. In one of these all the members were Tsonga, but in the other three there was only one Tsonga member.

An official of the Tsonga Territorial Authority told me that the chiefs and the Territorial Authorities applied pressure on their people to move, so that the Government had no need to use force. People are virtually forced to move because of social pressures and fears within their own communities. He said that the Government is ultimately responsible since they started the Bantu Authorities system, which upset the good relations which had prevailed for generations between the groups; the people had been quite happy living together before. Once the separate Authorities were established, Tsongas living in Venda territory were discriminated against and victimized. For example, Vendas were always given preference when labour contracts were available; Vendas were always given the principalship of schools and all schools had to use Venda as the medium of instruction. Therefore many Tsongas, especially their leaders, were anxious to move into their own territory.

At a meeting with the Bantu Affairs Commissioner in 1960, the Tsongas demanded that when Territorial Authorities were established they should have their own separate one. Separate Authorities were then established and the boundaries between the Venda and Tsonga area fixed. The Tsongas claimed that the boundary should have followed the Levubu River (north of which is predominantly populated by the Vendas, with a preponderance of Tsongas to the south; but the boundary is still zig-zagged so that there is often a Tsonga village sandwiched between two Venda or vice versa). They also complained that Venda chiefs were appointed in predominantly Tsonga areas. Every Tsonga I spoke to claimed that the Government authorities favour the Vendas – this also increased the friction. Missionaries and teachers told me that the friction between the two groups has increased greatly since the fixing of the boundaries.

An example of how the removals took place was an exchange of Vendas and Tsongas between the Sibasa and Mavambe districts which took place in June and July 1968. It was occasioned by a dispute between two Tsonga headmen and a Venda chief. The Bantu Commissioner ordered the headmen to go with their people to a Tsonga area, and the Department in Pretoria arranged to transport Vendas from the Tsonga area back in exchange.

Officially, these moves were to be voluntary. But there can be no doubt that the Government officials decided who should move and then saw to it that they did move. Most of the able-bodied men were away working in the cities, so those present were mainly women and children who were easily intimidated. The people claim that when the lorries arrived, officials forced them to pack up and move, and armed policemen were present. In each district the people who belonged to the 'correct' ethnic group of the area had to regroup their houses into villages before the newcomers from the other district moved in. Altogether three to four thousand of each tribe were moved, and no compensation was paid to them.

A missionary described the move itself as 'completely heartless'. The people were taken and dumped in the veld without even a tent. The sick and the old were all moved in the same way. One old man suffering from pneumonia was transported on the top of a lorry. He died two days later. A pregnant woman was taken in the same way and gave birth under a tree at the new place. The people who had to stay behind to look after the cattle were also without shelter for two or three weeks as the roofs had been taken to the new place. The missionary, who has lived and worked in the area for many years, said that the people from the one side were taken from a fertile region where there was fruit and vegetables in abundance to a very arid region, where the local inhabitants had become accustomed to eating dried hairy-worms and leaves. The seeds they took with them were useless in the new region. Signs of malnutrition soon became evident and the missionary provided relief. He concluded that the move had caused great disruption in the people's lives and it would take years for the community to cohere again.

When I made my visit in April 1969, there were still many Tsongas living in the Venda area around Sibasa. Many to whom I spoke said they were quite happy where they were and had no desire to move, though they feared that they might have to.

Doctors said that the health of the people in the whole area is so bad that it is impossible to say what effect the removals have had but that the lack of sanitation must eventually have some effect. These people usually live far apart; now they are all put close together in residential settlements and no sanitation is provided.

I returned to the Northern Transvaal in October 1969 and found that about 350 Tsonga families from Tshakuma, a Lutheran Mission farm which has been bought by the Trust, and other villages in the Sibasa district had been moved into five settlements on land which had been excised from the north-west corner of the Kruger National Game Park. Water was provided for them from boreholes, as indeed it is for the animals in the Park, but nothing else. On their arrival the people built temporary shelters with the thatching grass which they had taken with them; not surprisingly there were accidents which led to some of these being burned down.

All these people came from a very lush, sub-tropical area where there was an abundance of fruit and vegetables. A large part of their income came from selling their produce by the roadside and many could support themselves by this means. The land they have now is very good cattle country but these people do not have cattle. In their old settlements they also had clinics, stores, schools and perennial streams. Now they have none of these things. If they need to call an ambulance they have to travel thirty miles to the nearest telephone – and there is no public transport.

The lorries arrived at Tshakuma for three successive years and each time the people refused to move. Eventually they gave up, thinking that sooner or later they would have to go. Those who could afford to do so provided their own transport and went to places of their own choosing the day before the lorries arrived. So it was the poorest ones who were dumped in the Game Reserve and other settlements. They were moved while the men were away working in Johannesburg and other cities. Some of these men do not seem to know where their families are, and have written to the local missionary asking him to find out.

Just outside the Game Reserve there are some other small settlements, with just a few families, which were also established in July–August 1969. In one of these, Marva, there are fifteen families, which number 175 people. Between them they have two wage-earners and two old-age pensioners. They are thus almost completely dependent on aid provided by a missionary. The missionary says that for the past four years he has had to support hundreds of such families for the first three or four months in a new settlement.

Trust villages, regrouped on ethnic lines, are scattered throughout the Vendastan and Tsongastan. It would be impossible to describe all these villages – there are over sixty in the Tsonga territory alone, but there are a number near Soekmekaar which illustrate the patchwork effect of the resettlement and the general conditions. (I cannot say exactly where these are because when going to them and when returning I became completely and utterly lost in the Reserve. The roads are that in name only and there are no signposts. I drove around, probably in circles, for hours, and eventually came to Soekmekaar. For the return journey it was dark and every time I stopped to ask groups of Africans the way they fled in terror at the sight of a White man.) Following what is a main road for those parts from Daviesville, which is about ten miles north-east of Soekmekaar, one passes through four Trust villages: Sephukubuye, Mawoweni, Barotha and Heldewater, which are, respectively, Bapedi, Venda, Bapedi and Tsonga.

At Sephukubuye there are about a thousand families, most of whom were moved in 1958 from White farms within a radius of about twelve miles. As in all these places, except Heldewater, they did not receive any compensation and they had to erect their own temporary shelters to live in while they built their houses. About a hundred of these families claim to be Venda and wish to transfer their allegiance to a Venda chief; the rest are Bapedi. About a hundred Bapedi families living on White farms in the Soekmekaar district were expected to be moved in if the hundred Venda families left. At the time of my visit, April 1969, a few families were still arriving by their own transport from White farms; they expected to be given only a residential site.

At Mawoweni there used to be an old settlement, the residents of which were about one-third Venda and two-thirds Tsonga. In 1962, the Tsongas were moved to other Trust villages; the remaining Vendas were regrouped into residential sites and other Vendas brought in from other areas. When they first came they were put into the shells of the houses which the Tsongas had vacated. About a year later they were allocated their residential sites. Some of these sites now have three or four families living on them, since the children have married and have not been given their own sites.

At Barotha many of the present thousand Bapedi families were living on the White farms which the Trust bought to establish this settlement. These were regrouped into residential sites and then others were brought in from further afield, mainly from other White farms. This process started in 1958 and continued for many years. About a hundred families refused for some time to move into the prescribed residential area. They were eventually made to move at the end of 1967. They are now huddled together in one corner of Barotha. They were each allocated only half a residential plot and were given no land for ploughing or grazing. (This is yet another example of what happens to people who do not move 'voluntarily'.) There are also a few non-Bapedi who expect to be moved from Barotha to a village of their own ethnic group.

Heldewater is rather different from these other villages. Here there are about two hundred families, under their own chief, who came from Grootfontein, near Elim. When the boundaries were fixed between the Venda and Tsonga territory, these people were told that they would be under a Venda chief. Their chief would not accept this, since he and his people were Tsongas. So he was told to move. He refused to move until some provisions had been made at Heldewater. They were eventually moved at the end of 1967. A school and boreholes were provided; they were also given tents, poles and thatching grass.

Each of these villages has boreholes and a school. Suphukubuye has a primary school with 650 pupils and four teachers; the primary school at Mawoweni has 431 pupils and only two Government-paid teachers – the community were employing another four; at Heldewater the primary school has 244 pupils and four teachers; a secondary school was opened in 1969.

Most of the men in these villages are migrant workers on the Witwatersrand, Tzaneen and other towns; very few, if any, are able to earn a living from the land. The amount of land allocated to each family and the rent for it varies. For example at Sephukubuye they pay R3 a year for six acres, while at Heldewater they have only two acres for which they also pay R3 a year.

Around Louis Trichardt there are about eighteen such villages with an average of about three hundred families each. These people told me that they did not receive any compensation when they had to rebuild; some said that they had to demolish their houses and rebuild a matter of yards away in order to fit in with the plan ('betterment scheme'). Each family now has six acres of arable land and a share in the communal grazing regardless of how much land they had before. They pay R2 a year for the arable land, 25 cents per head of large stock and 5 cents per head of small stock; every married man also pays R1 a year local tax (known as 'heart tax'), in addition to the R3.50 a year general tax for 'development' of the Reserves. If they are moved into the area of another chief they have to pay R15–20 to him.

All the people I spoke to asserted that there was no possibility of them even subsisting on the amount of land they had. According to Muriel Horrell's report, quoted above, very few people in the whole region have economic farming units. Moreover, a number of people are being moved from White farms into a residential site and no farming land. The same applies to many young men setting up their own homes.

Makwerela

The capital of the Vendastan, Sibasa, is the home of the Commissioner-General of the Vendas and other White officials. I was told that the Africans living in the town are to be moved to Makwerela Township, on the outskirts of the town.

On the maps issued by the Department of Information, Makwerela appears in large capitals as if it were a city. When I visited it in April 1969, it consisted of about a hundred four-roomed, township-type houses and looked like a location for a small rural town. These houses, I was told, were occupied by policemen and Bantu Affairs and Territorial Authority officials and workers. It is said that eight industries are to be established at Sibasa and the workers will be housed here; there will be 1,750 houses in all.

Ngiyane

The capital of the Tsongastan is Ngiyane (Bendstore), which is somewhere on the blank part of the map between the Shing-widzi and Groot Letaba Rivers. The ordinary road map does not show even a minor road or track for hundreds of square miles. But coming from Duiwelskloof I suddenly hit a new dirt road, wide enough for four lanes of traffic; though in a round trip of about 160 miles I saw not more than four vehicles. I passed a few rural African villages and eventually came to a store, a police station and a B.A.D. depot. This, I was informed, was Ngiyane.

There were obvious signs of agricultural improvements and surveying work. But I drove on for another fifteen miles, by which time I must have nearly reached the Game Reserve, without seeing any development which could relate to the capital of the Tsongastan.

I went down one of the side roads for about five miles and found nothing but a Nederduitse Gereformeerde Kerke (Dutch Reformed Church) Mission. It is notable how N.G.K. Missions always seem to be strategically placed in relation to the tribal areas. The Dutch Reformed Churches represent the religious arm of the Afrikaner people, as the Nationalist party is their political arm. The Dutch Reformed Churches have, broadly speaking, supplied the theological justification for apartheid. On the other hand, in all parts of the country Lutheran and Roman Catholic Missions have been found to be in the 'wrong' places, have lost their congregations through removals and have been left with large numbers of useless buildings.

I learned later from people in Duiwelskloof and from members of the Tsonga Territorial Authority that there are no firm plans for Ngiyane. The Minister, Mr Botha, stated that there is to be a township for a thousand families, but it has not been explained what type it would be. Mr Botha recently addressed the first session of the Tsonga Territorial Authority at Ngiyane. Some tents were erected for this occasion.

Lenyeenyee and Nkowankowa

In the Letaba district, Lenyeenyee and Nkowankowa were the only two new townships that I could find. They are thirteen and ten miles respectively south-east of Tzaneen.

When the old location at Tzaneen was moved in 1962–3, the Bapedi were sent to Lenyeenyee and the Tsongas to Nkowankowa. I was told that there are now many Zulus, Swazis and Vendas in Nkowankowa. It seems very difficult to keep them apart, though officially the people are supposed to want to live with their own separate ethnic group. The population of both places has been, and is still being, swelled by people evicted from White farms and people from the regrouped Trust villages. Some of these latter had very good houses and could not afford to build on the same scale in the new Trust villages, so they preferred to move into the townships. The rent is R4.16 a month for a four-roomed house with outside toilet. The men work mainly in Tzaneen or on the nearby citrus estates, where the women also find seasonal employment. The bus-fare to Tzaneen is R4 a month and the normal wage for a labourer in Tzaneen is R16 a month. There are three firms connected with the citrus estates near Nkowankowa who pay labourers R5.60 a week.

In April 1969 there were about 650 families in Nkowankowa and about 800 in Lenyeenyee. They are both planned to accommodate 1,500 families.

Lorraine

Lorraine is an agricultural settlement about thirty-five miles south of Tzaneen. There are about four hundred families who were previously living on their own land about a mile away. That was declared a White area so they had to move across the Makoetsi River to Lorraine. They were given land of the same size and type but, they claim, they were not paid any compensation for their houses. Most of them built their houses at Lorraine before they moved across.

In a letter to the Director of the South African Institute of

Race Relations, dated 6 June 1968,[1] the Chief Bantu Affairs Commissioner of the Northern Areas stated that Lorraine and Moetladimo (see next section) had not yet been developed. Yet the people at Lorraine moved in 1962 and the first group arrived at Moetladimo in 1957.

At the time of my visit, one or more families a week were moving into a settlement adjoining Lorraine, which would appear to be the beginning of a 'closer settlement'. The official name is 'Timamogolo' but it is known locally as 'New Line'.

Moetladimo (*Metz Farm*)

Moetladimo, the other officially undeveloped township, is in fact a fairly old agricultural settlement a few miles from Lorraine. There are about five hundred families, most of whom are members of the Mamahlola tribe, who were moved from their own farm on the other side of Tzaneen. They were told in 1953 that they would have to move because they were causing soil erosion. They refused because they claimed they had had President Kruger's assurance that the farm was theirs for ever. Nevertheless, in 1956 the ultimatum was given that they had to move on 15 June 1957. However, when the lorries arrived on 15 June only a small group under an aged headman agreed to go. These were taken by the lorries and lent a tent for three months. Besides water and a school, there was a clinic at Moetladimo when they arrived, which is most unusual, if not unique.

The chief still refused to move and collected R2,000 from his tribe to engage a lawyer from Johannesburg to fight their case. The lawyer told them that he thought the move could be prevented but first the compensation which had already been received must be returned to the Bantu Affairs Commissioner. But some had already used the compensation money for their contribution to his fee. My informants were not clear what negotiations the lawyer entered into, but he failed.

In 1959, the Bantu Commissioner arrived with a detachment

1. Quoted in South African Institute of Race Relations Information Sheet No. 36, 1968.

of soldiers, lorries and bulldozers. The people were all taken to Moetladimo and their houses demolished. Before I went there I had heard that the army had been called in to move them and this was confirmed by a number of people at Moetladimo to whom I spoke.

The group which moved at the appointed time received free grass and poles, but this group received nothing, except the cash compensation which some had already spent on the lawyer's fee. Some lived in temporary shacks for a couple of years, hoping that they would be able to return to their old farm. Ten years later they were 'beginning to settle', they said.

The settlement appears to be as developed as it ever will be. There are now three schools: a lower primary with over four hundred pupils, a higher primary with over 250 pupils and a recently opened secondary school. Each family has approximately ten acres of arable land, some of which is irrigated. This, they said, is not enough to earn a living from; most of the men work in Phalaborwa or Tzaneen. There are a number of boreholes and a river. So far they have not had to pay anything, as the land was given in exchange for their own farm. But the people said they had heard that some form of rent would soon be introduced. A few people from White farms are still joining the settlement, making their own arrangements with the chief.

Saamkorst

A further example of a Lutheran Mission being in the wrong place was the one about four miles from Louis Trichardt. About four hundred families were living on the Mission when it was declared a 'Black spot'. They were moved by the army to Saamkorst, twenty miles north of Louis Trichardt, about ten years ago. The Lutheran Minister in charge of the Mission at the time said that the removal was 'humanely' carried out but that the presence of armed soldiers and army lorries frightened the people. He also said that the people were shocked at the soldiers using the church as a mess. The soldiers who demolished the houses were either over-enthusiastic or else over-estimated the number of people they could move in one day, with the result that some of the people's houses were demolished but they were not able to be transported to Saamkorst that day and so had to spend the night in the open.

At Saamkorst the people were settled in tents and given land for ploughing. It is unusual for 'squatters' from Mission stations to be given any land, even land like this, which I am told is practically useless as it hardly ever rains in the area.

Since these people came from a Lutheran Mission they wanted a site for their own church at Saamkorst, but they had to wait a long time before it was granted. The Dutch Reformed Church had a site within three weeks and the Bantu Commissioner asked the people why they then needed another church.

The future of two other Missions, Elim Hospital and Valdezia, was still uncertain at the time of my visit. The hospital authorities were promised four years ago that it would not be moved, but now they are not so sure.

A religious community of another sort is also threatened with removal. Ten miles out of Duiwelskloof is the home of a famous 'Rain Queen', Chieftainess Modjadji, and her followers. They are members of the Balobedu tribe,[1] numbering something like ten thousand people. It is a very important religious centre; people make pilgrimages there from hundreds of miles away. So far they have refused to move, because of the importance of the mountain where they live, and certain very old sacred trees, in their religious ceremonies. After two years of drought, the Government offered them a place with water if they moved. The Chieftainess persuaded them to build a dam on the tribe's mountain instead. But the Bantu Trust has now bought 90,000 acres near their land, so it looks as though they will be moved.

1. The Lobedu religious and political system has been described in a classic of South African social anthropology: *The Realm of a Rain Queen* by E. J. and J. D. Krige (1943).

Potgietersrus District

The ruthless separation of the Tsongas from other tribes extends even to the Northern Sotho Reserve in the Potgietersrus area, a hundred miles from their own 'national' territory.

At Magongwa–Tshamahanse, nine miles from Potgietersrus, there were 1,117 families, Tsonga and Mandebele, living under a Mandebele chief, scattered over a wide area. But it was then decided that the Mandebele people must live on one side of the road and the Tsongas on the other, so hundreds of them had to swop over. After the removal the Tsongas demanded their own chief. Local clergy and others all agreed that it was only after the separation that any friction developed between the two groups; previously they were all content to be under the Mandebele chief. Those who were there at the time of the removal in 1965–6 were allocated two acres of arable land. But those who have arrived since are given only a residential plot.

Throughout the whole district almost all the tribal villages have been taken over by the Bantu Trust. As usual this meant that the people had to demolish their houses and rebuild in the specified place without compensation. In this area, in particular, the passion on the part of the authorities for straight lines seems to have been given full play. I heard of cases where people had to demolish and rebuild their house a few feet further back because part of it was over the line demarcated for the residential site. Most of these residential areas are already extremely overcrowded but people are still being moved in from European farms. In seven villages in the immediate vicinity of Potgietersrus there are 3,488 families; each family usually has two acres for ploughing. There is extreme poverty and malnutrition.

According to reports, there have also been instances of privately owned farms being taken over by the Trust. For example, at Tiberius (a farm towards the Botswana border) a number of families had contributed to the purchase of the farm. But they were told by the Bantu Affairs Commissioner that having used the farm for so long they had had the value for their money so now the farm must be shared by all. I spoke to a person from this farm and he said that he did not understand what was going on. All he knew was that his grandfather had contributed to the purchase of the farm, but now he was told that he would have a residential site and grazing and arable land would be allocated to him; the fencing, he said, had already started. I also heard of the same thing happening on other farms.

It was after visiting some of these squalid, overcrowded, poverty-stricken villages that I read of the speech of Mr G. F. van L. Froneman, Deputy Minister of Justice, Mines and Planning, on resettlement in the 'homelands'. He said that 'superfluous appendages', such as wives and children, should be returned to the homelands and it was not the Government's responsibility to provide facilities for them. I knew that he was not talking about what should happen: he was talking about what was happening and had been happening for years. I had seen the 'superfluous appendages' starving to death or resorting to prostitution to keep alive; though why they should even want to live, in such circumstances, it is difficult to see.

While the Department of Information present propaganda about the 'Bantu' who benefit from Government 'development' schemes, there are many thousands who are suffering, starving or dying as a direct result of their pursuit of the doctrine of apartheid. Many of these people have become resigned to their suffering and expect nothing better from the White man.

Pietersburg District

The Reserve in the Pietersburg district is under the jurisdiction of the Lebowa Territorial Authority. An agricultural officer told me that the plans for this Authority had been drawn up but had not yet been made public; he thought they would involve a lot more resettlement. Already many tribally owned farms have been taken over and replanned by the Trust; here too there seems to be the fetish about straight lines, with people having to move only a few yards in order to comply. Some of these villages are at least a hundred miles from Pietersburg, which is the nearest town. To go shopping or to do business is a major expedition usually taking two days or more.

Some villages are well established, but they can only be reached after driving for hours through the bush. In many of them the people have only two acres of land and four or five cattle. They say that it is completely impossible to earn a living from their plots and that it is taken for granted that every young man will go to Johannesburg to work.

In one of these villages I heard a most articulate denunciation of the whole concept of Bantustans. The speaker pointed out how the 'homelands' are completely dependent on remittances from migrant workers, who could not earn enough to contribute to development in the 'homelands'. He described the hypocrisy of talking about development when there was no work, no industry and no towns, when Africans could still not earn equal pay for equal work, and when the people in the 'homelands' had often to build their own schools and pay a third or more of the teachers themselves.

The point is reinforced by a report published by the *Johannesburg Star* on 1 July 1970 after carrying out a survey in this region. The paper said:

The homeland of the Northern Sotho consists of two jagged blocks of land lying on either side of Pietersburg. Together they span the Northern Transvaal, from the Kruger Park in the south-east almost to the Limpopo River in the north-west.

The area, like so much of the Northern Transvaal in this mid-winter drought of 1970, is practically one enormous dust bowl.

As you travel east from Zebediela towards the eastern escarpment you can almost count the blades of grass. In the west, there are villages encircled by sand several centimeters deep.

Everywhere withered mealie stalks are all that remain of the crops that failed. Most of the rivers are dry, and at a place called Mphahlele, about thirty miles east of Pietersburg, people get their water from a cloudy puddle at the bottom of an 8 foot hole in a dry river bed.

One of the most striking features of the territory was the absence of men. The spokesmen for nearly all the families interviewed were women, usually mothers or grandmothers, though in some cases the family had been left in the charge of an elder daughter.

Of the male spokesmen, one was a young man who made a living locally as a builder. His average income, he said, was about R10 a month. . . .

Only two of the males interviewed were able to make a living off the land. One had a plot on an irrigation scheme where he had grown wheat and mealies. His crop, he said, had netted him R15. He had no other source of income.

At a place called Wisconsin in the west was a man who appeared to be a substantial landowner by local standards. He had reaped 12 bags of millet. In addition he received a small remittance from two sons.

But most of the other families reported that they depended almost entirely on the money they received from an absent breadwinner. The money was usually received regularly and through the post. . . .

A widow, three adult women and three grandchildren were entirely dependent on the charity of an already impoverished tribe. The seven of them lived in a mud hut hardly bigger than the average urban storeroom. There was no door and no windows and the family slept on the floor on reed mats. There was also no furniture.

Asked whether they ever ate meat they laughed with genuine mirth. Fruit, vegetables, meat and milk were unattainable luxuries. The family apparently lived on mealie-meal and nothing else.

Ironically – and tragically – the eastern block of the homeland abuts on the vast Zebediela orange estates. At this time of year the trees are laden with fruit, yet on the other side of the fence and almost within sight of the orchards are people living who never taste an orange.

One of the most astonishing observations made during the survey was the ability of people to find fuel in what appeared to be an almost completely barren landscape. Apart from the scattered thorn trees – which the government, they said, had forbidden them to cut down – the land was bare of shrubs and bushes and it was obvious that if fuel is available at the moment it must shortly be used up. Fires were made of a few odd sticks and the wood was used very sparingly.

The fetching and carrying of water obviously played a large part in the daily activity of many people. Sometimes the nearest water source was as much as five miles away and the water had to be carried by hand – or, more accurately, by head.

The houses of the Northern Sotho consist of two or more huts forming part of a walled enclosure with a smooth mud and dung floor. Usually at least one of the huts has a tin roof, glazed windows and a proper door. Most of the huts were built of mud bricks.

Few families had any literate members, but all had children who had either been to school or were at school now. All paid school fees ranging from 80 cents to R1.40 a year.

I came across one small village, not a resettlement one, which was of particular interest. Most of the residents were people who had been discharged from the leper hospital. They were 'burn-out cases' with deformed or missing limbs. But they were about the happiest group of people I met on my whole trip. I held a service in one of their spotlessly clean huts; it was a moving and chastening experience. A blind man led the singing; many had no hands to hold a prayer book. They chatted happily before and after the service, expressing their pleasure at having someone from outside visit them, and there was no word of complaint or self-pity.

Moletse

According to the official list, there are four townships in the Pietersburg district: Mankweng, Moletse, Nanedi, Sebayeng (Solomondale). Mankweng appears to be simply an extension of the existing township at Turfloop. Moletse is a proper township five miles outside Pietersburg and is planned for nine thousand houses; Solomondale is half a 'closer settlement' and half a quasi-township; Nanedi is just a 'closer settlement'.

Moletse started in May 1967 and within two years there were already three thousand houses. Some of the people came from Roodepoort Lutheran Mission, about twenty-five families from a Coloured farm near Pietersburg; but most of them came from Pietersburg's two locations – New Pietersburg and the old location. New Pietersburg was a freehold location about three miles from Pietersburg. Some of the tenants wanted to move because of the overcrowded conditions. At the time of my visit, in March 1969, there were still many people there; the move had been halted while the old location was being cleared. The owners had not yet received their compensation although Coloured families had been moved into their houses and were paying rent to the municipality. If the authorities claim that these moves are necessitated by slum clearance, how can they justify moving Coloured families into the same place? The same thing happened, for example, at Boksburg, and, it is said, is going to happen at Queenstown.

The old location, which had been almost completely cleared, was one mile from Pietersburg. Those who had built their own houses had been removed and paid compensation; those in municipal houses were still there. The vacated houses are now being used as hostels for domestic servants, since Pietersburg is 'White by night'.[1] There were instances of up to twenty people living in the one house. There were complaints in the local press from Whites about their servants having to live in such insanitary conditions. Their main concern, no doubt, was that the servants were coming from these conditions into their masters' houses.

Only those who had been resident in Pietersburg for five years qualified for a house in the new township. The others were endorsed out to the 'homelands'. From Pietersburg's other municipal locations, the widows had been endorsed out.

There were complaints about the recreational and shopping facilities and the increased expenses. Recreational facilities consist of two soccer fields. There are three general dealers and one café all in Zone 1, which is about $1\frac{1}{2}$ miles from Zone 2.

Nanedi (Naledi)

Nanedi (or Naledi) seems to be a forgotten village. The Minister said in the House of Assembly on 4 May 1965 that it was a township planned for six hundred families; in fact it is a 'closer settlement' of ninety-odd families. Sixty-nine of the families came from Palmietfontein (cf. Solomondale, below) on 8 January 1962; the others came later from various White farms. They were moved by Government lorries and loaned tents. There was no shop, no clinic, no toilets, no school. They still share a borehole with a neighbouring village, nearly a mile away. They were put on plots, 50 yds by 50 yds, and given some land for communal grazing on which they were allowed to keep two head of cattle each; but they have since been warned that they have to get rid of these. They were first told that they had

---

1. When a town or municipality has been declared 'White by night' it means that all Africans and other non-Whites must be out of the White area at night. Domestic servants, for example, are not allowed to stay in rooms in the employers' compounds, but must travel to work each day from a location.

to buy the plots for R80; some paid the full amount in cash, the others were paying in instalments; they were then told that their money would be refunded and they would have to pay R1.60 a year rent. This was later reduced to R1 a year; but the money they had already paid had not been refunded by March 1969. By reducing the rent to R1, the authorities seem to have agreed that it is a 'closer settlement'.

The headman said that the Bantu Affairs Commissioner told him that the plan for six hundred families had been dropped, and in a letter to the Director of the South African Institute of Race Relations dated 6 June 1968 the Chief Bantu Affairs Commissioner of the Northern Areas said that Nanedi had been de-proclaimed. They also seem to have dropped the plan of building a cotton factory, which the people were promised before they moved. A few of the men work in Pietersburg, returning home monthly, but most of them work in Johannesburg and Pretoria.

The people have now built a school themselves; they also pay two of the teachers, while the Government pays the third. Their main complaints concerned the lack of medical facilities and the fact that old-age pensioners have to travel ten miles to collect their pension. A doctor visits once a week but the nearest clinic is fifteen miles away and the nearest hospital and maternity home twenty-five miles. I think that the only reason that the people spoke so freely was the hope that we would be able to help in these matters. Another difficulty is fuel. They are not allowed to collect it from the near-by Trust area but must walk a couple of miles to a chief's farm. They said that life would be completely impossible for them if their remaining cattle were taken away.

Another forgotten township is Sengwamakgope, near Soek-mekaar. It was also planned for six hundred families, but has remained a 'closer settlement'. The ninety-five families who live there were moved in in 1958 – since then no more people have come.

Solomondale

Solomondale, twenty miles east of Pietersburg, has two sections. The older part is a 'closer settlement' to which about two hundred families from Palmietfontein were moved on 8 January 1962. Palmietfontein was a farm about twelve miles from Pietersburg, which about 250 families rented from a White landowner for R24 a year per family. Some of the families had been there, they said, for about a hundred years. They were first told many years prior to 1962 that they would have to move and they engaged lawyers to argue their case, but it did not go to court.

They were given the 'choice' of going to Solomondale, Nanedi or to work on White farms. They were not paid any compensation, although they claimed that the farm had been very well developed by them, they had built a school, a dam, a dip, etc. Many claimed they were able to earn their living from the farm. They were moved by Government lorries, taking their old building materials with them. They were allowed to take two head of cattle but no sheep or goats. On arrival at Solomondale the 'accommodation offered' consisted of one or two tents per family. Each child received a two-pound jar of mealie meal for a few days. There were no shops, clinic or toilets; but water and wood were plentiful. The school was housed in large tents; later it was moved to a temporary building and now there is a proper school. They had to buy their half-acre plots for R88 and also had to pay R10 per family to the chief. As from February 1969, they have not been allowed to keep any cattle.

This is another of those places which the people have made to look decent by their own efforts. But obviously they did not want to move and did not do so voluntarily. They spoke with feeling of their old home, the fight they had put up to stay there and the hardships they have been through and are still suffering.

The other section of Solomondale consists mainly of one-roomed asbestos houses, to which some people have added shacks with the old materials which they brought with them. As happens so often, there are ten or more people in these 'houses', which are about 12 ft square; the rent for them is R1.55 a month. There are also a few three-roomed houses for which the rent is R3.40 a month. At the time of my visit there were about eighty houses occupied and people were still moving in. They had come from New Pietersburg, Rodewal Lutheran Mission, Dumasa and other places.

Rodewal Mission

Most of the people from Rodewal Mission went to Nooitgedacht, which is an agricultural settlement about twenty miles north-east of Pietersburg. The Mission was founded in 1874. In 1912 the Mission sold part of the farm to the tenants for R8 per family. About 250 of the families formed a cooperative but others bought their own portion and had their own tenants; one man had 600 acres. The Mission retained 3,600 acres on which there were about eighty tenant families.

They were told in 1961 that it was a 'Black spot' and would have to be moved. The Bantu Affairs Commissioner wanted to send the Mission tenants to a township, since as non-landowners they were not entitled to go to an agricultural settlement. But the cooperative agreed to admit them to membership for a payment of R12 per family, so that they could all move together. Most did this but about fourteen families went to Solomondale.

They were moved by Government lorries on 26 June 1967. Nooitgedacht is ninety acres bigger than Rodewal; instead of having the extra portion cut off, they bought it for R2,000. Each member received an equal share of land. There was a reservoir and water pipes; for this each family paid R5. Apart from the water and tents, there was nothing. It now looks very smart, with extremely neat houses, schools and shops. But one local missionary said that at the beginning it was terrible. He organized a supply of food and blankets since it was a very cold winter. He and the local residents said that there were a lot of deaths at that time. Another missionary agreed that there was hardship at that time but said there were no complaints from the community as a whole but only from individuals. It was conducted very smoothly and efficiently, he thought, with about four hundred families being moved by forty lorries in five days.

Their hardship and deaths were a small price to pay for the efficient elimination of another 'Black spot'.

Roodepoort Mission

Another Lutheran Mission, Roodepoort, about eight miles south of Pietersburg, was moved at about the same time. These people were not so fortunate, since they were all tenants. The Mission, which was founded in 1906, had a 3,600 acre farm with about two hundred tenant families. They were informed that it was a 'Black spot' and they would have to move. Church officials tried to negotiate with the B.A.D. so that all the people would be moved together; but they failed. About half of them went to other villages where there was a Lutheran congregation; some went to relatives in various places and others to Moletse Township. They received compensation for their houses, and if they moved in groups transport was provided; but if only one or two families were going to a particular place no transport or temporary accommodation was provided. The hardest hit were those who went to Moletse. They are still just about as far from Pietersburg, but now they have to pay R5 a month just for a house, whereas at Roodepoort they paid only R6 a year and had land for ploughing and keeping cattle.

Yet another Lutheran Mission is threatened with the same fate. This is Kratzenstein Mission, about ten miles east of Turfloop. It was founded about ninety years ago and has a farm of about 3,800 acres on which there are about two hundred families. In November 1967 numbers were painted on the doors, which is a sure sign of impending removal. A meeting was held with the Bantu Affairs Commissioner in March 1968 and the Church officials suggested that the Trust buy the farm and leave the people there since two thirds of the boundary borders the Reserve. At the time of my visit no more had been heard. But even if they are allowed to stay they will still have the inconvenience of having to move into allocated residential sites and conforming with the Trust's plans.

10. Orange Free State

The White heartland of South Africa, the Orange Free State, lies in the centre of the sub-continent, stretching from the Vaal River to the Orange, and from the border of Lesotho to the beginning of the Kalahari sands.

When the Voortrekkers crossed the Orange River in the late 1830s they found an open plateau, ideal for their herds of cattle. There was a relatively sparse population of African tribesmen and the Boers staked out large farms for themselves. In time villages and towns began to develop and there were more and more frequent clashes with the Sotho, Ndebele and other tribes.

The main concentration of African people was in the south-eastern part of the State, in the lee of the mountains of Basutoland (now the independent country of Lesotho). Today there are only two small African Reserves, at Thaba 'Nchu and at Witsieshoek, and both of them lie near the Lesotho border.

The Thaba 'Nchu Reserve had its origins in a 'sale' of land by King Moshesh I of the Basotho to the Methodist Church in the early 1880s. The 'price' was a number of cows and goats. The Methodists, working together with a local chief, Moroka, settled people in the vicinity of what is now the town of Thaba 'Nchu. These people were mostly Tswanas from the Western Transvaal. For this reason the Thaba 'Nchu Reserve is now part of the proposed Tswanastan which has its headquarters at Mafeking, over two hundred miles to the west, in the Northern Cape.

After the Basotho wars the Thaba 'Nchu area was part of the 'conquered territory' which was added to the Orange Free State. Most of the area was occupied by White farmers, and a number of small towns developed. The area occupied by the Tswanas was recognized as an African Reserve.

The present town of Thaba 'Nchu is unusual in South Africa in that the African and White areas are in very close proximity and at some points overlap each other. It is obvious that this state of affairs will not be allowed to continue indefinitely.

The Thaba 'Nchu Reserve occupies about 275,000 acres, with an official population of 30,000. Approximately 10,000 more Africans live in the 'White' area, mainly on farms. The population of the Reserve is, however, probably considerably higher than the official figure. (Muriel Horrell in *The African Reserves in South Africa*[1] gives an estimate of 50,000.) There are thirty-seven African schools throughout the area, two of which are secondary schools. The latter are at Moroka Mission, in the town of Thaba 'Nchu and in Selosesha Township, just outside the town. Children from outlying areas can only attend secondary school if they become boarders, with a consequent increase in expenditure by their parents.

The Methodists at Moroka Mission run the only hospital for the entire Reserve. There are, on average, 150–200 patients at any time. In 1967, 1,254 patients suffering from malnutrition were admitted, while an untold number of others came as outpatients or did not visit the hospital at all.

The Thaba 'Nchu Reserve has a number of other institutions: a youth camp and a children's home (euphemisms for 'reformatory') with a total of 586 inmates, a deaf and dumb school with 108 children; a TB centre catering for 250 patients; and a teachers' training school with 388 students.

As for agricultural development, the Reserve has three irrigation schemes, ten dams, one cooperative dairy and a cattle-breeding scheme.

The traditional Tswana custom was to hold land under communal tenure and for the people to live together in a 'stad' or large village. The lands and the cattle posts were situated some distance from the village. Until quite recently only a few people were to be found in the villages, besides the very old and the very young, during the harvesting season. Most of the inhabitants would go to the lands and live there during the week. Nowadays, few of the Thaba 'Nchu Tswana have any lands to

1. South African Institute of Race Relations, 1969.

which they can go, most of them having been dispossessed in 1965. They were told that if they wanted to have lands and keep cattle they had to move to Trust villages, or otherwise go to Selosesha Township, a couple of miles outside the town of Thaba 'Nchu. For some time they flatly refused to go to the township but now some of them go when they get married, as they cannot get a site in the old 'locations' adjoining the town of Thaba 'Nchu. Very few moved into Trust villages in the Reserve. The people from one of the 'locations', Mokoena, did; it involved them moving only a few miles. They had to build their own houses and provide their own sanitation; they also built their own school and are paying the teacher. No compensation was offered and one who applied for it was told that he was not entitled to anything because he had moved voluntarily! Others overcome the difficulty by sending one of their sons to establish a nominal home in a Trust village, thus becoming entitled to plough and to keep cattle there, while the real home remains in the old 'locations'. Some are now moving 'voluntarily' rather than risk being summarily evicted later. But the vast majority are still there and many of those I spoke to said they had no intention of moving. But they are under the continual threat of removal, and church sites are refused on the grounds that the people are all to be moved.

In the rest of the Reserve, the resettlement of the people into Trust villages started in the early 1950s. Thirty to forty villages have now been replanned, varying in size from fifty to two hundred families, and usually with six acres of arable land and grazing for ten head of cattle per family. The inhabitants have to build their own houses and sanitation; schools are usually built on a rand-for-rand basis, but if people are moved into an existing village they are responsible for building an extension to the school. The houses of those who refused to move were knocked down; then they presumably moved into the Trust villages 'voluntarily'. Apart from the inconvenience of having to move and rebuild, people complain of having less land and fewer cattle. Many also say that, while there may be agricultural advantages, the main reason for them being so grouped is that they can be more easily subject to control. When the villages are being regrouped, those who for any reason are not using the land full-time or who are considered incapable of doing so are sent to Bultfontein (see below).

There are still a few African-owned farms in the Thaba 'Nchu Reserve whose owners are able to live from the land, including a few of those who benefit from the irrigation schemes. But the vast majority are migrant workers in the Orange Free State goldfields, Kimberley and the Witwatersrand. Three factories are being built near Thaba 'Nchu; a furniture polish factory, a candle factory and a coffin factory. This lugubrious combination of industries will provide some employment for local Africans.

Objections to the resettlement into Trust villages have been both strong and vocal. Most people, however, eventually re-signed themselves to their fate and moved peacefully, some being encouraged by having their houses knocked down for them by the Government.

The 'betterment schemes', which involve the replanning of the Reserves and settling the people in Trust villages, are in part a genuine attempt to increase the productive capacity of the Reserves, which have been overgrazed and overworked agriculturally for many years. One could say that these schemes are justified as long as one accepts that 13 per cent of the country (and the poorest parts at that) for 70 per cent of the population is a fair distribution. Africans see it differently. They see that they are having their land reduced when they are resettled, and many thousands are being deprived of any right to land and of any kind of farming activity. Above all, Africans have developed a profound mistrust of official motives.

The plain fact is that the Reserves cannot support the present population, even without the further mass removals which are planned. The kind of agricultural improvements and other developments which the Government is trying to introduce, apart from being far too little and far too late, are simply no solution to the basic problem of poor land being made to carry far too many people.

Morajo

Wherever I went in the Thaba 'Nchu Reserve I heard about Morajo: 'Have you heard about Morajo? You see what happens if you don't agree to move?'

The first inhabitants settled in Morajo in 1914. The area was proclaimed an African Reserve in 1913 and the people were told that they could come from the White-owned farms and settle there. They said that 'during Smuts' time' they could have as many cattle as they wanted and plenty of land – some sowed ten bags each of mealie and wheat. 'But then Malan came and everything changed. We have been prisoners for 21 years.'

They were first told in 1949, when the marking-out of stands and fencing-off grazing and arable lands throughout the Reserve were started, that they would have to move but they were not told precisely where. Later some of the residents at Morajo moved into residential sites which had been allotted, but about two hundred families refused to move. Many of the men have since been arrested for ploughing illegally.

Their continued opposition to the 'betterment schemes' and to moving to Trust villages has led to many arrests. Some have been arrested many times for various offences. For example, one man was arrested and sent to prison for two months for refusing to help put up fences without pay; he later served a one month's sentence for ploughing illegally; he served another one month's sentence for refusing to cull his cattle. He was also among the twenty men, three of whom were blind, who were arrested on 5 December 1968 for still living at Morajo. These twenty men were taken to Bloemfontein to await trial and while they were there their cattle were impounded by the Bantu Affairs Commissioner. They were released, presumably on bail, on 14 December. They said that their lawyer advised them to pay R40 each and that the case would be held later in Bloemfontein; they said it was 'an appeal'. Their lawyer died soon afterwards, so they engaged another lawyer who briefed an advocate, Mr David Soggot, to appear for them. The case was heard in Bloemfontein on 11 March 1969 and they lost. Their advocate asked for them to be given an extension to allow them time to make proper arrangements to move, but this was refused.

The lorries arrived at Morajo on 20 April, loaded the people and their belongings and dumped them either in Trust villages or at Bultfontein. In many of the villages I saw groups of demoralized-looking people living under a few pieces of corrugated iron. These were the people from Morajo. This was about five weeks after the removal and none of them seemed to be making any effort to build a house. One or two of those who went to Bultfontein were loaned tents, but the others were given nothing at all. They did not receive any compensation and some of them complained that their furniture and fittings were ruined in transit. One man asked and was given permission to leave his belongings in his old house until he had re-built elsewhere. But 'G.G.' workers arrived and bulldozed his house; they left his furniture outside but smashed the doors and windows.

Even those Morajo people who have gone to Trust villages have not been allocated any land. On 25 April 1969, they were told that they had to sell all their stock before October of that year. They were told that they were 'strikers' and so were being punished. Many of them had considerable flocks of sheep and numerous cattle. One man, for example, had already sold 72 of his sheep and he still had to sell another 115 sheep and 21 cows before October.

In 1955 their passes were stamped with a number which, they say, puts them into a category where they have no rights to land or cattle. They are now condemned to live for life on a tiny plot for which they pay R1 a year, plus a levy of 25 cents for the hospital which is being built near the town of Thaba 'Nchu.

Bultfontein I and II

In the Orange Free State, some of the clergy told me: 'We have our own Limehills here,' and directed me to Bultfontein. But others, while they knew about Limehill in Natal and expressed their horror at what had taken place there, seemed to know nothing of similar places on their doorsteps.

Bultfontein I is about six miles from the town of Thaba 'Nchu. When you first go in you see a number of tents and shacks scattered around; a few people are busy building houses but dozens of others sit around looking lost. Some of the shacks consist of a few pieces of corrugated iron put together like a tent on top of a 'foundation' of mud; the back is filled in with mud, as is the front, except for an opening which serves as a door. I was told that the B.A.D. had actually put people into these hutches, which are even worse than tents.

The first arrivals came at the end of 1968 and by May 1969 there were about seventy families. Some of these were previously living in the Reserve but for some reason did not qualify to be resettled in a Trust village. Others had been evicted from White farms; some had been endorsed out of towns like Welkom, and at least one from Johannesburg; a few were from the locations at Thaba 'Nchu and there were about six families from Morajo.

Those in the tents and the mud and corrugated-iron structures were brought by Government lorries. The others had to provide their own transport, and were given nothing; many of them were also living in shacks when I visited. The earliest arrivals are a bit further on and have built their houses in neat lines on tiny plots. No sanitation was provided and in May 1969 there were very few latrines in evidence. There was one borehole with a windmill, which was the only amenity provided on an otherwise completely bare stretch of open veld. No emergency rations were provided, there was no school, no shops, no clinic – nor any sign of these being provided – and no transport to Thaba 'Nchu. The people have to do their shopping and even buy wood for their fires in Thaba 'Nchu and then carry it for six miles, or pay to have it transported by a truck.

At Bultfontein the people have no land or cattle; just the residential plots, some of which measure 22 yds square. Many of them managed to leave their cattle with friends in the Trust villages or on farms. But if old people own cattle anywhere they do not qualify for a pension.

At the time of my visit people were still arriving in ones and twos. By now how many more unwanteds have been made to go there?

Bultfontein II is about 1½ miles from Bultfontein I, towards the town of Thaba 'Nchu. There are about a dozen families living in the same conditions, except that when I visited there were no completed houses since they only started moving in in February 1969. Three families came from Morajo, one was evicted from Selosesha Township and the others came from the 'locations'. They claimed that they were told by 'G.G.' that the old and disabled should come here because the main railway line is to pass here. It was not clear how that was going to help them.

Four families had tents, the others nothing at all except the corrugated-iron shacks which they had erected themselves. Most of them had not yet even started to build. The one amenity, the windpump, is about 400 yds away. There is a track leading to the settlement but the tents and shacks are scattered among the long grass.

The people from Morajo were told that they had to make written application for compensation. One man said that when he saw the place he told the White official supervising the removal that he could not possibly stay in the bare veld. The official told him to make a written application to go elsewhere.

Selosesha

Selosesha is a Bantu Township about two miles from Thaba 'Nchu. In May 1969 there were about seven hundred houses occupied; it is planned to have 3,500, which means that there is plenty of room for those from the locations adjoining the town of Thaba 'Nchu who do not go into Trust villages.

The first houses were completed in 1964 but they stood empty for some time because the people declined to leave their old homes in the locations and refused to move into the township. In 1965, the people from Bethany Lutheran Mission near Bloemfontein were moved in. Then a number of others endorsed out from Bloemfontein and Welkom came. Finally, people from the locations have been moved in, mainly young men who are unable to get a site there to set up a home.

Most of the houses are of the ordinary four-roomed township-type, for which the rent is R4.20 a month. It looks just like any other township. There is a primary school and a secondary school. A shopping centre consisting of a 'restaurant', a fresh produce dealer and a general dealer, opened at the beginning of 1969.

The vast majority of the males are migrant workers in Bloemfontein. Many were previously living with their families in Bloemfontein. When they were endorsed out, or when the Mission was cleared, they settled their families at Selosesha and returned to Bloemfontein to work and live in hostels.

It is rumoured that if the people from the locations refuse to move into Selosesha they will be moved to join another part of the Tswanastan near Mafeking. I heard in fact that there has been a suggestion in official circles that the whole of Thaba 'Nchu Reserve might be cleared and the people removed to one of the other blocks of Tswana territory. This would mean sending them several hundred miles to the north or west where the country is far less hospitable (see for example the description of Kuruman, page 108). So far, fortunately, there is no sign of any action being taken to carry out this threat.

Witsieshoek

The other Reserve in the Orange Free State is Witsieshoek, thirty-five miles south of Harrismith. I was not able to stay long enough to investigate the whole Reserve, nor did I meet informants able to give me an authoritative and comprehensive account of the settlement schemes. So I concentrated on the new township which is a little distance from the administrative centre of Witsieshoek. In this official complex there are the B.A.D. offices, a police station, a so-called training school (actually a reformatory) and houses for White officials. It is rare to see a White person in the African Reserves, and I must have seen more Whites, albeit from a respectful distance, in Witsieshoek than I had seen in the whole of the rest of my tour of the Bantustans. The presence of so many officials was far from reassuring.

Witsieshoek Reserve has a long and turbulent history, which

213

probably accounts for the dominating presence of the police. The Reserve is all that is left of Basotho territory in the Orange Free State. Serious trouble started there even before the Nationalist Party came to power in 1948, when the people protested against the enclosure of their grazing grounds and cattle culling by the Government. Their protests were ignored; further restrictions were imposed on their use of land in the Reserve as the overgrazing got worse.

Rioting broke out in 1950, in which fourteen tribesmen were shot dead and two policemen were killed. The chief, Paulus Mopeli, and other leaders, were deported. Chief Mopeli was then already an old man. He was banished to Nebo in the Eastern Transvaal to live out a solitary and destitute life.

The main body of the township consists of about 150 two-roomed brick houses with asbestos roofs. There are about sixty more houses of asbestos with iron roofs. A couple of hundred yards away there is another group of about sixty huts made of corrugated iron only and resembling inferior garden sheds. There are outside latrines and taps in the streets. A Dutch Reformed Church Mission runs a hospital some six miles away and there are shops two miles away.

This township is for people who are being resettled from places like Thaba 'Nchu, the Eastern Cape, and all over the Transvaal, from both the farms and locations. A number to whom I spoke said they used to work on White farms but were told that they were too old to work and would have to go – 'we were thrown out with suffering and we are still suffering'. The residents seem to be mainly old people; possibly all of them are. Those with nobody in the family working do not pay rent; the others pay R2.70 a month for a two-roomed house. A number of the one-roomed huts were occupied but I could find only small children playing about the place.

Epilogue

Most of the material in this book was published in a private edition in South Africa in April 1970. Since then, the removals have been continuing unabated. I have revisited many of the settlements and have seen conditions steadily deteriorating.

The new ones started in the last few months present the same all too familiar picture. In August 1970, when I was travelling between East London and Kingwilliamstown in the Eastern Cape, I saw a new cluster of tents and shacks not far from the road. I went in and found that about sixty families had been moved from Macleantown near East London to this place thirty miles away called Chalumna. They did not understand why they had been moved. Some had been living in very good houses before, and had title deeds to them. Others had been 'squatters', and were, as usual, the worst hit, since they did not qualify for any compensation. Each family was allocated a plot 35 yds square to build a house; no cattle were allowed. There were no shops, no clinic, no sanitation, no employment. The only building in the camp was a four-roomed school.

People are still being moved into the Limehill complex, and preparations are still completely lacking. On my last visit, in October 1970, I found twenty-two families living in tents just over the road from Uitval – the settlement where the outbreak of typhoid and gastro-enteritis struck two years earlier. Most of these new families had been moved out of Indian-owned property in Wasbank, and had been living in the tents for seven months. They had not been given any compensation nor had they been provided with rations or building materials. They were forbidden to use water from the borehole for building mud huts, yet the Government tanker, the only alternative supply, had only delivered water twice in the previous five months.

I spoke to six women, none of whom had a husband. One had been living in one tent with her ten children for the whole seven months. Using all her savings, she had managed almost to complete a house, but ran out of money before it was finished. She had to travel to Wasbank every day, where she worked in a peanut factory. They paid her R3 a fortnight; R1.50 went on the bus-fares, leaving her with R1.50 a fortnight to feed eleven mouths – one cent (about half an English penny) a day per person. Another woman was living with one daughter of twelve, having sent her other children away to relatives. Their only income was the few cents that the girl could earn by drawing water for other people.

The worst long-term effects of resettlement are now beginning to appear – a dreadful apathy, families permanently broken up and petty violence. It is noticeable at Limehill that there are more idle youths for whom there is no prospect of work locally, and who cannot get contracts for migrant work.

The 'emergency' at Weenen, still unexplained, continues. The settlement is now well hidden from the road, being completely fenced off. It is more depressing than ever. I talked to an old age pensioner there who has to pay R2.50 a month for rent out of his pension of R4.

The people at Babanango are losing their fight against eviction. Three or four times this year they asked me to go down to see them. Each time I went, knowing there was nothing I could do to help. A number of them have been arrested and prosecuted for not moving. But they have absolutely nowhere to go. I had to go into the hills to see one man who was hiding there with his cattle for fear that if he returned to his home he would be arrested again. He had already spent one night in jail and had paid a fine. It looks as though these people will have to go eventually to the 'closer settlement' at Mpungamhlophe or to work on White farms. There is no hope that they will be able to keep the cattle which represent so much for them. One man had been given a letter by the Bantu Affairs Commissioner to present to another Commissioner, which sums up the official attitude:

The bearer has been given a trek pass and is referred to you for the satisfaction of your farm labour requirements or for resettlement if your farm labour requirements have been satisfied.

I attended a lecture given by the Parliamentary Under-Secretary for B.A.D. in November 1970. He argued with all appearance of sincerity that no 'Bantu' had been removed without consultation, and they were never moved from any place with which they had historical links. He evaded answering my questions about Babanango.

At Mnxesha, which is now known as Dimbaza, one of the townships for 'redundant' people in the Eastern Cape, one shop was opened on 3 August 1970. There was no sign of any other improvements, although there had been grandiose official promises of a 'shopping centre', a 'hotel', 'swimming pool' and such urban amenities. There has also been no improvement in the incidence of malnutrition and death. It was reported that there were 845 new cases of pellagra in the first seven months of 1970. In October a magazine report[1] stated that in a recent count 195 children's graves were found in the camp's burial ground. And this is a township where most of the people are either given work or rations by the Government.

Mr Botha, Minister of B.A.D., boasted at a meeting on 19 October that there was not one African in South Africa who was starving, and he added that the Nationalist Government would not let it happen. When one has seen death certificates with the cause of death given simply as 'starvation', when one has seen hundreds of children in hospitals throughout the country too weak from starvation to stand, one is no longer able to feel anger at such claims – one feels an immense pity at the wilful blindness of these men in power.

In Natal I told the people in one settlement what the Minister had said. They laughed. They were obviously starving. I asked if I could photograph some of them and they said, 'Take all of us, we are all starving. How could we be anything but starving in these conditions?' At another place, I met a woman of thirty-five who was admitted to hospital weighing 50 lb. The nurses

1. *Personality*, 23 October 1970.

told me that she had been on the point of killing and eating her sixteenth-month-old baby when she was admitted. In the same hospital I saw a fifteen-month-old baby weighing less than 10 lb. and a child of five who weighed 20 lb. There were dozens of similar cases.

No doubt there is starvation in other countries in Africa and the rest of the world. The difference in South Africa is that starvation is not due to natural disasters or the poverty of the country, but to ideology. Malnutrition is increasing and will go on increasing in the resettlement areas. This worsening situation is being imposed while Whites in South Africa enjoy conspicuous wealth and fast-increasing incomes.

The removals are, if anything, being speeded up and planned on an even bigger scale than before. Large townships are being planned in the Eastern Cape, at Kidd's Beach and Middeldrift; 600,000 people are to be resettled at these and other settlements in the Ciskei in the next ten years.

In Natal, an enormous site is being prepared (which means marking off plots with pegs) in the Ladysmith district, where the Government has proposed the establishment of 'border industries'. Another large settlement is being prepared at Nqutu in Zululand, thirty miles from the nearest industry and a place renowned for its lack of water. There are rumours also of more very big moves in the Northern Transvaal, where it is said that the Reserves to the west of Pietersburg are to be 'consolidated' with those to the east.

At Grahamstown, which was founded by the English settlers in the early nineteenth century, the Fingo village on the outskirts of the town is scheduled for removal. The land was given to the Fingos as a reward for fighting on the British side against the Xhosas. The settlers have just been celebrating their 150th anniversary, while their old allies are to be turned out.

The Government appears to be making a particular drive against African 'tenants' on White farms at present. The labour-tenant system is being abolished in one district after another, and the people are faced with the alternatives of working full-time for the White farmer (if he wants their labour) or being sent to resettlement camp without any land. Already thousands have been moved into Zululand, and even into the Msinga Reserve, which is almost completely barren.

In August 1970 an appeal was made to the Commissioner-General of the Zulu 'nation', Mr Torlage, on behalf of the people who were to be evicted from over five hundred farms. One old man said, 'Our great grandfathers were born in this area and now, at this stage of my life, we are forced to leave ... there is no place for us to move.' Other old people said that their sons were allowed to stay to work for the farmers, but they themselves were not wanted. Others, too old to work, were being evicted because their sons would not work for the farmers. One said: 'The Whites first of all told us to get rid of our cattle. We did that, and now they are getting rid of us. We think it better for all of us that we die. ... A dog was not treated like this.'[1]

It is a fact, however, that all the people I met who had been tenants on White farms said they would prefer to go almost anywhere rather than become a full-time worker on a White farm. They would have no freedom left and would be completely at the mercy of the farmer. This fear of the White farmers is based on the very widespread experience of the abuse and exploitation which flourish on the farms. Fairly typical was the group of families kept at Rorke's Drift in Zululand as a private labour pool by an Orange Free State farmer. One of the women at Rorke's Drift had three of her children taken away to the farm in the Free State, where all three had to work for six months with no wages. They were half-starved and continually beaten. When the tenant system was abolished in this district, the farmer demanded that all the tenants should work the whole year without pay under the same conditions. They all refused and were turned out of their houses. Some went to find a place in the villages in the Reserve, others had to move into the Limehill complex.

Chief Buthelezi, head of the newly constituted Zulu Territorial Authority, in a courageous inaugural speech in July 1970, made immediate demands on the Government to start honouring the sham promises of apartheid: 'The first of these, which I

1. *Natal Daily News*, 19 August 1970.

consider a priority, is for the Government to give the Zulu nation more territory, for without more territory our scheme will not make sense.' He also said: 'Even some chiefs have been ordered off land. I receive two or three deputations a week asking for land. There is nothing I can do.' But there has been no response from the Government, and no more land has been provided for the thousands evicted from their homes. Meanwhile, the new census figures show that there are more Zulus alone than Whites in South Africa.

The first South African edition of this book received wide notice in the English language press, but it made no impact on the men in power. There has been no halt and no amelioration in the removals since it appeared. The Government chose to ignore the issue. Sadly, the established Churches have also decided to remain silent on the total effect of the removals policy, though some clergymen and laymen have spoken out about aspects of the injustice or about individual cases of hardship.

Perhaps this recital of what is happening in the African Reserves can help some of those who support the regime, whether they do so with their votes or merely with a passive tolerance of conditions, to see for themselves the results of their complaisance. My own experience, since the start of my travels in the resettlement areas, has taught me, quite simply, that official explanations and reports are almost always deliberate misrepresentations. One must check and inquire personally to get behind the distortions of the facts, and the more one inquires the more layers of untruth are stripped away. Behind this record of the removals which have taken place so far lies a huge number of stories told to me by individuals, and carefully checked with others. These tragic stories left me with an ever-mounting awareness of the evil of a system which rates human beings and families so cheap.

I believe that we must ask ourselves now where this policy is leading, and we must consider this in terms of the facts, not illusions. What will happen if the Government goes on, unchecked, to implement their policy, until all Africans are either migrant workers or helpless refugees in the 'homelands'? What will happen as more and more of the 'Black spots' are wiped out and more and more 'redundant' people are cast out of the White areas?

One thing is obvious after travelling through the Reserves. Conditions are not getting better, and cannot get better as long as the removals continue. The people who live in the 'homelands' – the peasants, many of whom are now landless, and the masses of townspeople dumped there – cannot make a living. As more people are being pushed into these overcrowded, impoverished territories, they are being turned into rural ghettoes.

South Africa has a wealthy industrial and mining economy which could provide prosperity for all her people. But as long as the removals policy goes on, the majority of the people will face misery, poverty and disease. Not all the resources and wealth of the State could make the Reserves productive enough to feed the millions who are forced to live on these dry stones and exhausted soil.

No real economic development has started in the 'homelands' in spite of two well-publicized five-year plans. Rural incomes for Africans have declined even in money terms in the last ten years. The only industries in the 'homelands' (some mines and a few small factories) are White-controlled. No African can start a business that is not approved by Whites, who in practice protect their own industries and markets. While the population rises fast, the number of jobs stagnates. And no real development can begin where there is neither freedom nor self-reliance.

As the overcrowding gets worse, it is easy to project the graph for malnutrition and death from disease. But the worst effects are more subtle than statistics can show; this policy is emasculating a whole people. I have seen this effect on people whom I have known for years. They are broken, demoralized, apathetic, seeking any kind of release from stress. Many have become so cowed and brainwashed that they are ready to agree that they have no rights at all.

At the same time, the migrant labour system is destroying family and community life. The result of this breakdown in the physical and social conditions of life cannot, in the long run, be peace. However demoralized, however little there is left to live for, these people cannot escape the spread of violence. It has already started in many of the resettlement camps.

There have been rebellions against authority in the rural areas before; but as the Government sets up the screen of Bantu Authorities between itself and the people, the immediate symbols of apartheid in the Reserves will more and more be Africans. Violence directed against oppression will appear as internal tribal strife. The Government can stand back and proclaim that it is none of their business as neighbour turns against neighbour.

Apartheid is now being implemented in the guise of separate development. This concept is no more than a pretence of a solution to South Africa's problems for the outside world and a sop to White consciences inside the country, while behind its empty propaganda the system of White supremacy is perpetuated. As Dr Verwoerd, the former Professor of Psychology who invented separate development, explained: 'The Bantu will be able to develop into separate states. That is not what we would have liked to see. It is a form of fragmentation that we would not have liked if we were able to avoid it. In the light of the pressure being exerted on South Africa, there is however no doubt that eventually this will have to be done, thereby buying for the White man his freedom and the right to retain his domination in what is his country.'[1] Thus, the ideology of separate development is based on the all-pervading principle of domination. For the Nationalist Party, White supremacy is the fundamental element of policy, raised above all considerations of humanity. They hold fast to a fanatical belief in their God-given right to put their interests and their race first in everything.

But the determination to maintain White supremacy at all costs is not peculiar to the last twenty years, the Nationalist Party, or the Afrikaner Volk. Long before the Nationalists came to power, General Smuts declared: 'There are certain things on which all South Africans are agreed. The first of these is that it is a fixed policy to maintain White supremacy in South Africa.' The treatment of Africans as chattels runs right back through South African history; this is the attitude,

1. Hansard, 4 April 1961.

overriding Christian love, which has permitted and even justified the policy of forced removals and all the other injustices imposed under the false banners of 'separate development' and 'Christian civilization'.

This year thousands more of our people will be transported to some hellish replica of Morsgat, Ilingi or Kuruman. Next year there will be thousands more. How long shall we allow this to go on? How many more human cargoes must be dumped in the Reserves before we find a way of stopping this crime? If it is not stopped soon, will the rumble of the 'G.G.' lorries driving the people away from their homes haunt us all our lives?

Appendix I

The Statistics of Removals

I want to ask how much progress we have made in respect of the implementation of that aspect of our policy, i.e. the elimination of the redundant, non-economically active Bantu in our White areas. . . . Approximately 900,000 Bantu have been settled elsewhere under the National Party regime over the past few years, since 1959. Surely this is no mean achievement; on the contrary, it is a tremendous achievement. Over the same period at least 216,000 have been resettled under the National Party regime in terms of the Group Areas Act in the Johannesburg area alone.

Dr P. G. J. Koornhof, Deputy Minister of B.A.D.,
House of Assembly, 4 February 1969

Since the pace of endorsements-out and removals has been quickening during the latter years, it can be concluded that the first million Africans had been removed by 1970. This number does not include the people removed under the Group Areas Act which covers the removal of Africans, Coloureds and Asians to segregated urban areas within the White areas.

For a breakdown of this number it is impossible to obtain reliable figures from any official source, and those statistics that have been made available are frequently contradictory or inconsistent.

The following extracts from Hansard in 1970 illustrate something of the difficulty one meets in acquiring information:

(1) The Minister of B.A.D. was asked the number of Bantu families removed or required to move in terms of the Group Areas Act. The information was refused. (Hansard No. 6, col. 2485, 25 August 1970.)

(2) The Minister of B.A.D. was asked: How many Bantu males and females were removed from the major urban areas during 1969? The information was refused. (Hansard No. 6, col. 2491, 25 August 1970.)

(3) The Minister was asked: How many squatters were ejected from farms during 1969? Answer: Information not known. (Hansard No. 6, col. 2492, 25 August 1970.)

(4) The Minister was asked: How many male and female Bantu respectively were removed from White urban areas? Answer: Information not readily available. (Hansard No. 9, col. 4167, 18 September 1970.)

(5) The Minister was asked: (a) How many resettlement villages for Bantu have been established, (b) where are they situated, (c) how many adult males, adult females and children respectively are at present accommodated in each village?

Answer: It is not clear to me what the honourable member means by resettlement villages established for Bantu. In the Bantu Homelands in the Republic there are 69 Bantu Townships which are in various stages of development, whilst others are still in the planning stage. . . . Bantu from White and other areas are settled in all of these townships. I regret that the population statistics of each township is not readily available. (Hansard No. 11, col. 5263, 29 September 1970.)

However, some figures for 1968 have been released, in the Report of the Department of B.A.D. for the period 1 January 1968 to 31 December 1968.

(19) The following statistics give an indication of the progress made during the year under review with the settlement in the homelands of Bantu who were not productively employed elsewhere:

(a) From 'black spots', mission stations, etc.	17,937
(b) From White rural areas	23,730
(c) From urban areas	19,882
(d) Traders	107
Total	61,656

Under the heading 'Bantu Resettlement Board' (this operates only in Johannesburg), it states that 222 families and 1,788 'single' men were removed and resettled.

Under the heading 'Squatter Control Section' (Chapter 7, sec. 38) it gives:

(e) Labour tenants settled	6,903
(f) Squatters settled	7,301[1]

Under the heading 'Consolidation of Bantu Areas' (Chapter 10, sec. 29) it states that 2,090 families were involved in the clearing up of 'Black spots'.

This report does not include removals from 'badly situated' scheduled or released areas, e.g. Schmidt's Drift, from where about 8,000 were moved in 1968. Nor does it include the removals necessitated by the 'betterment schemes' within the Reserves; nor the removal of municipal locations. The figure of those removed from urban areas probably refers only to those removed under police surveillance.

In addition some 1968 figures were provided in the House of Assembly:

The Minister was asked: How many Bantu were removed from the municipal areas of Johannesburg, Pretoria, Durban and Cape Town respectively to their homelands in 1968?

Answer: Presumably the question refers to compulsory removals under sections 14 and 29 of Act 25 of 1945 and the figures are as follows:

Johannesburg	16,814
Pretoria	570
Durban	4,780
Cape Town	47

(Hansard No. 15, col. 6220, 20 May 1969)

This makes a total of 22,211 from four towns, a larger number than that given in the official report for the whole country. The thousands moved from Western Cape towns to Ilingi, Sada and Mnxesha are not included here. From November 1967 until April 1968 an average of 1,410 from Johannesburg, 323

---

1. This figure is the only one which tallies with figures given in Hansard. On 10 February 1970 (Hansard, No. 2, col. 618) the Minister gave figures for labour tenants and squatters resettled since 1964. He gave 7,301 as the number of squatters resettled. But he gave 4,031 as the number of labour tenants resettled.

from Durban and six from Cape Town were removed each
month under police surveillance – cf. *Survey of Race Relations 1968*, p. 173, quoting from Hansard, No. 13, col. 4766. All
this seems to confirm the suggestion that the official figures for
endorsements out only refer to those who were escorted by the
police and not to those who have their book stamped and make
their own way. Hansard, No. 1, col. 316, 7 February 1969 reported that 7,809 persons were removed from Black spots in
1968 (cf. above – 7,301). The Minister said that 119 Black
spots had been cleared since 1948, and that this involved 83,619
people (Hansard, No. 1, col. 324). However, on 17 February 1970
he said that twenty-nine Black spots and eighteen isolated
scheduled and released areas had been cleared, involving 119,693
people, and that 311 such areas remained (Hansard, No. 3, col.
1181).

Total

Dr Koornhof stated in the House of Assembly on 20 and 23
May and 16 June 1969 that altogether 450,373 Africans moved
from White areas had been resettled in townships in the 'homelands'. The discrepancy between this total and the figure of
900,000 he gave a few months earlier is, at least in part, explained by the fact that Dr Koornhof was clearly excluding
in his later statistics the 'squatters' and labour tenants from
White farms who have been moved, and was presumably also
excluding those people who have been moved from 'badly situated' Reserves.

Appendix 2

Development and Resettlement Costs in the African Reserves

South African financial statistics are not always as complete, or as easy to interpret, as one would wish. The funds received by the Bantu Trust and spent on the African Reserves are particularly difficult to disentangle, the headings in the accounts being less than totally explicit.

However, it is instructive to list the main forms of expenditure in the Reserves and consider the implications of some of the items.

During the five years 1956–61 the total funds allocated to the general purpose of development in the Reserves amounted to £7.9 million (approx. R13.5 million in present currency terms). But this money, tiny fraction of the £104 million recommended by the Tomlinson Commission as it is, does seem to have been genuinely devoted to the reclamation and improvement of land.

In 1961 the first 'Development Plan' for the Reserves was announced, to cover the quinquennium 1961–6. The total cost of the plan was R114,342,000. However, of this total, no less than R75,950,000 was to be spent on 'town planning', which means simply the building of townships in the Reserves to serve White-owned border industries, or to resettle Africans moved out of White areas. The remaining R38,000,000 was budgeted for various economic development projects, including irrigation works, dams and boreholes, soil conservation, fibre cultivation, forestry and the like. This sum is again far below the minimum set by the Tomlinson Commission as the expenditure needed to give the Reserves any hope of *maintaining* the inhabitants' living standard.

The next quinquennium, 1966–71, saw the unveiling of an apparently much more ambitious plan, budgeting for a total expenditure of R490 million. On the surface, as the 'plan' was presented, this is a generous and effective contribution to the needs of the Reserves. However, it is clear, on further examination, that the budget is of a different nature from that of the previous plan. The main items in the 1966–71 plan are:

	R million
Education	163
Physical development	162
Social development	58
Land purchase and capital needs	50
Economic development	39

But what do these headings mean? We must first look at the actual expenditure recorded in the national accounts. The following is a sample of years between 1955 and 1970, taken from publications of the Bureau of Statistics and the 1970 Budget Estimates:

Bantu Affairs (including Bantu Education)	1955	1960	1964	1965	1966	1967	1969	1970 (estimate)
Revenue a/c	28.1	29.4	36.0	47.9	54.4	56.6	60.9	74.8
Loan a/c	4.5	2.7	25.6	33.6	43.8	48.9	59.1	67.0
Total	32.6	32.1	61.6	81.5	98.2	105.5	120.0	141.8

In the 1970 estimates, the amount budgeted for Bantu education from the Revenue and Loan accounts was R32 million, to be supplemented by R11 million from Bantu taxation and R1 million miscellaneous receipts. For comparison, it may be useful to show the size of two other items in the Revenue account expenditure for the same years (see table on next page).

These figures show how the total funds spent on Bantu Affairs in the Republic are in absolute terms still very small (total central Government expenditure in 1969 was R2,114.4 million, of which the B.A.D. appropriation of R120 million

	1955	1960	1964	1965	1966	1967	1969	1970 (estimate)
Defence and Police (added together)	63.5	73.8	164.1	242.4	238.2	281.9	357.0	351.4
White higher education (not including schooling)	14.1	22.8	31.1	34.9	39.3	45.6	50.7	71.7

represents less than 6 per cent for 70 per cent of the population). Also, the totals for Bantu Affairs did not rise as fast as other significant items in the period.

There are no other appropriations in the National Accounts for items of expenditure on the African Reserves. All Goverment expenditure on the Reserves therefore falls within the totals shown above.

The principal agent for the administration of the Reserves is the South African Bantu Trust, a governmental body controlled by the Minister of B.A.D. In 1969 R25.3 million from the Revenue account under Vote 27 (Bantu Affairs) was the grant in aid to the Bantu Trust, while R4.7 million was paid to the Transkei Government. In addition there were other amounts received by the Bantu Trust from the Loan account. The Trust's other receipts come from local taxes and fees. Altogether, the Trust's budget for 1969/70 came to R66,465,000.

It is not possible to relate these expenditures directly to the current five-year 'Development Plan', but certain relationships can be deduced. Firstly, the heading 'Education' under the plan does not differ greatly from the total actual expenditure on all African education during the five years – though if the contribution from 'Bantu taxation' were excluded the total in the plan would appear to be an overestimate. This item therefore refers mainly to the ordinary recurrent costs of education, and covers all Bantu education, whether in the Reserves or in White areas.

'Physical development', which is a very large sum, does not appear to relate to any specific heading in the Budget accounts. It seems probable that it covers the major item in the first five-year plan, 'town planning'. The South African Official Year Book for 1970 states that the Township Development Committee planned to build houses in townships in the 'Bantu areas' to a total cost of R100 million, but it did not state the period of this expenditure. If this money were all spent in the 1966–71 plan period, it would still leave some R62 million under the heading 'Physical Development' unexplained. This could be the cost of health services in the African Reserves and townships. While these services are administered by the Department of Health, they are accounted for by the Bantu Trust, and the budget for them in 1969 was R18.2 million excluding the capital costs of new hospitals.

'Social Development', under which heading R58 million was to be spent, probably relates to items H to M of Vote 27 in the Budget accounts: Pensions and assistance to needy Bantu; Retreats and rehabilitation centres; Child welfare; Settlements for aged, indigent and unfit Bantu; Subsidies for general welfare and co-ordinating services. The total cost of these items in 1969/70 was R14.3 million and the estimate for 1970/71 was R13.6 million. These expenditures cover Africans in the White areas as well as in the Reserves.

'Land Purchase and Capital Needs', R50 million in the plan, comes under Loan account appropriations, and presumably refers to the purchase of land from Africans in 'Black spots' and of White land to add to the Reserves – known as 'Released areas'.

'Economic Development', for which the plan provides R39 million, may be supposed to cover the improvement works which were a feature of the first five-year plan and cost R38 million in that period, which indicates a decline in real terms. However, the categories may not overlap entirely, so comparisons cannot be definite.

One overall conclusion is clear: the R490 million 'Development Plan' in practice refers to at least most of the items of expenditure budgeted for by the Bantu Trust and also certain costs incurred directly by the Department of B.A.D. in connection with both the Reserves (including the Transkei) and African affairs in White areas. Most of the expenditure is for routine, recurrent costs and administration and in no sense would it be considered as development in any country which wished to present a genuine blueprint for developmental action.

The exact proportion of the R490 million which is spent on real development is hidden. But one measure of the priority given to development can be seen in the activities of the Bantu Investment Corporation and the Xhosa Development Corporation (which operates in the Transkei). The B.I.C. has a share capital of R18,250,000, and the Xhosa D.C. a share capital of approximately R7,000,000. All shares in both corporations are owned by the Bantu Trust.

The investments of these corporations are officially stated to have created slightly fewer than 1,000 new jobs in the past ten years, as against an officially recognized need for at least 50,000 new jobs a year to make the Reserves economically viable. The Bantu Investment Corporation disbursed R18 million in its first decade of existence, 1960–70.

A new plan for the B.I.C. was announced in April 1970, covering the next five years. During this period it will have R104 million to spend, of which R18 million is for South West Africa. Of the R86 million planned to be used in the Republic, R43 million, half of the total, will go on building physical assets (buildings and infrastructure) for White businesses to operate in the Reserves on an agency basis. This will help to ensure that 'development' in the Reserves continues to present no threat to any sector of the White economy. R22 million will be spent on the B.I.C.'s own undertakings, which include bus services, wholesale merchandizing, and twelve manufacturing plants. R20 million will be available for buildings to lease, and for loans to African businessmen. But if past experience is anything to go by, this last item is unlikely to be fully used, since most applications for loans from Africans are refused.

It is nowhere explained in official statistics, but it is a fact even more revealing of Government attitudes towards the development of the Reserves, that the 'Development Plan' includes the costs of resettling Africans who have been removed. Only one category of removals is specified in the ordinary budget accounts: the 'Removal expenses of Redundant Bantu ... of idle, dissolute or disorderly Bantu ... Bantu who have unlawfully entered an urban area ... removal of Bantu in terms of Act no. 38 of 1927 and voluntary removals' is included under item B 'Subsistence and Transport' of Vote 27 of the Budget. The cost in 1969–70 was R375,000 and in 1970–71 is estimated as R522,000.

Other costs of resettlement are in effect treated as development. 'Land purchase', mentioned above, is mainly occasioned by the removals policy. The building of townships in the Reserves – 'town planning' – is mainly for the victims of removals. Many of the boreholes, dams, roads, school buildings and some of the administrative costs in the Reserves are for the purpose of resettlement. Compensation for the victims' former property, provisions of rations and transport, though these items are not always given, add to the costs of resettlement.

The total costs of the resettlement policy cannot be estimated without a great deal more detailed information on the breakdown of items of expenditure, but it is certainly a significant proportion of the 'Development Plan'.

Removals and resettlement can be said to act in a direction contrary to development, by increasing the pressure on existing resources and by reducing the economic and social opportunities of the people. There can be no argument that resettlement, which leaves the people involved with less land, fewer goods, less access to jobs and transport, fewer facilities and lower real incomes, creates any new resources. Money is actually spent on destroying homes and liquidating peasant units of production in the 'Black spots'. Resettlement is therefore an act of dedevelopment, and the inclusion of its costs in the 'Development Plan' is another example of double-think.

From one practical point of view, though, development of the Reserves and resettlement are indeed closely interrelated. This can be illustrated by statistics on one of the major aspects of agricultural improvement, the 'planning' of rural locations in the Reserves. This involves the demarcation of arable, grazing and residential areas, the fencing of grazing camps and provisions of watering points, and, where necessary, stock limitations (cattle culling).

By the end of 1968 the following percentages of the total areas of the Reserves had been 'planned' (figures provided by the Deputy Minister of B.A.D. in the Assembly on 18 March 1969 and the Transkeian Annual for 1968):

	Percentage of total area planned
Ciskei	68.9
Natal	43·4
Northern Areas	71·1
Western Areas	41·0
Transkei	37·2

The work has included approximately:

86,000 miles of fencing

326,700 miles of grass strips to protect arable land and guide oxen for contour ploughing

20,000 miles of contour retaining banks

6,500 boreholes

5,810 minor dams

21,000 miles of roads

693 bridges

These works are clearly necessary and beneficial and can quite properly be described as 'development'. But again, the very urgency of the need for them, and the way in which the system of demarcation of rural areas is creating farming units which are too small to be viable, is a direct function of the serious over-crowding in the Reserves caused by the resettlement policy. The complete failure of the development works in the Reserves, such as they are, to prevent declining rural incomes and rising numbers of people living in abject poverty, is the result of the basic division of land in South Africa – 70 per cent of the population having only 13 per cent of the land.

Appendix 3

Doctors' Report on Limehill

This is a report (quoted from the *Rand Daily Mail*, 31 January 1969) agreed upon by four doctors who have been doing voluntary medical work at the clinic near the Limehill resettlement complex. It sets out their considered opinion on health conditions among the Africans who were moved there a year ago. For professional reasons, the doctors' names cannot be published.

This report is a factual account of the patients seen and diseases encountered by a group of doctors who visited Limehill between 28 December 1968 and 19 January 1969. It also gives the experiences of the doctors regarding the wider health problems of the people in this area.

The clinics were held at the Amakhasi Mission. We should like to emphasize that we were asked to staff the clinic as a humanitarian gesture and the following represents an objective analysis of the situation.

Records were kept of every patient seen, as is the normal medical custom, so that when the patients return for treatment the nurses know what to give and new doctors can have information about previous patients.

What must be continually kept in mind when expressing the health of a community is its total population. For example ten cases of meningitis is a minor outbreak in an army of 500,000, a a moderate outbreak among 100,000, but a disastrous one in a group of 10,000.

Therefore we would emphasize that the following diseases occurred in a population of no more than 10,000. However, at the first clinic most of the cases, that is, 95 per cent, came from only one area – Uitval – with a population of about 2,000, and at this

time sixty patients were seen, of whom five had suspected typhoid (one also having bronchial pneumonia). One had severe
kwashiorkor, five had early kwashiorkor, ten had riboflavine deficiency and seven had pellagra. This gives an indication of the
amount of diseases in just one community.

Overall, between 28 December and 19 January, doctors at the
clinic examined 760 patients.

The report lists a table of the diseases complained of and/or
diagnosed.

Diarrhoea	269	
Diarrhoea and vomiting	68	
Suspected typhoid	4	
Confirmed typhoid	8	(one subsequently died)
Pneumonia	9	(two deaths)
Tonsillitis	19	
Otitis media	8	
Eye infections	21	
Salpingitis	3	
Cystitis	43	
Pellagra	53	
Kwashiorkor	28	
Riboflavine deficiency	20	(a vitamin deficiency which causes painful cracks at the sides of the mouth and ulcers on the tongue)
Scurvy	8	
Rickets	3	
Scabies	27	
Worm infestation	7	(round and tapeworms)
Suspected tuberculosis	5	

Fifteen patients examined were pregnant.

Typhoid: Typhoid, which is a generic term for both typhoid
and para-typhoid fevers, is a bacterial infection which spreads by
faecal contamination from persons who have, or who have had,
the disease.

That it spreads in conditions of poor hygiene and when disaster strikes (for example, earthquakes) is common medical knowledge.

No inspection of an area where it occurs is necessary to indicate the hygienic standard. The disease speaks for itself.

We do not know the exact numbers of confirmed typhoid cases that have occurred in the past year. However, we do know that in three weeks, five cases which were seen were subsequently confirmed and in four weeks nine further cases were suspected.

In a normal healthy community, the acceptable incidence of typhoid is nil. Thus in a community the size of the Limehill complex to have five cases confirmed in three weeks – ignoring for the moment the suspected cases – would in any medical sense be called very serious.

Gastro-enteritis: Diarrhoea with or without vomiting was the commonest reason for consulting the doctor. Just over 50 per cent of all the patients who came had these complaints.

While this may be a relatively minor and insignificant episode in a healthy young person, it is most serious in babies and young children, who form a very large percentage of the cases.

This group withstands dehydration badly, and while the babies may seem only mildly ill to begin with, lack of effective treatment can rapidly transform the situation. Sudden deterioration and death may occur within hours.

The hallmark of good community medicine is to treat these cases early with special oral fluids to tide the child over the initial period of the illness. More severe cases require fluid replacement in other ways, usually intravenously in hospital. Both phases require the skilled management of staff nurses or doctors.

At the clinic only the mild cases were treated with oral solutions. Their mothers were shown how to look after the babies when they became sick and unable to feed normally.

The other aspect of diarrhoea and vomiting in children is that such episodes may be the start of kwashiorkor or other nutritional problems, especially if nutrition was previously poor. Repeated bouts of diarrhoea and vomiting can seriously impair a child's resistance to common diseases, such as measles, whooping cough and pneumonia.

Significantly, twenty cases of early vitamin B deficiency and many cases of early kwashiorkor have been seen over the three weeks.

Nutrition: Nutritional problems are medically regarded as reflecting social conditions. It has been well known and frequently confirmed that kwashiorkor is a social disease, occurring in poor families with two children or more. The first child contracts the disease when the mother becomes pregnant again and there is no more breast milk.

If the staple diet of an area is only mealie meal (and this was our common experience) there is inadequate protein and vitamins, so the child gets the disease. A normal healthy community understands the importance of a diet balanced with fat, carbohydrate and protein and containing adequate vitamins and minerals.

Reference to the table of diseases encountered at the clinic shows that there was a large number of pellagra and kwashiorkor cases in relation to the total population. There were also significant numbers of early vitamin B deficiency, scurvy and rickets. Impetigo and scabies were also common. These are infectious diseases which flourish in poor, dirty surroundings.

Pneumonia, bronchitis, tonsillitis and otitis media were also present in significantly large numbers. These last four illnesses are serious, especially if not treated early and adequately. As it is, two of the cases of pneumonia died.

One of the doctors adds that he had found nutrition in the Limehill complex to be better than in the area where he works.

Maternity facilities: We supplied no maternity services, but at the request of patients carried out ante-natal examinations. When we inquired where pregnant women would be delivered, there seemed to be no uniform answer. There was no definite place where they could go if in trouble.

There is a clinic at Limehill, but the nurse there was unable to undertake deliveries while we were there.

Kraal deliveries are unsatisfactory. From experience in other rural areas, we know that such babies frequently die. In this day and age ante-natal care is the norm, not the prerogative of the few.

We would like to indicate that we consider the maternity facilities totally inadequate by present-day medical standards.

Prevention of disease: No immunizations were given by the

doctors, because it was not possible to obtain the materials we needed. It should be normal to immunize against diphtheria, whooping cough, tetanus and smallpox. Our information is incomplete on this point, but it seems there is no coordinated scheme of immunization in operation at present.

Such programmes require to be started early, because inoculations are given over a period of months and years to obtain maximum protection.

One of the doctors, who went down to the area later than the others, said that inoculation facilities were probably better organized by the time he got there than when the first team of volunteers went to the area.

Tuberculosis: No attempt was made to treat suspected cases of TB. Such treatment requires hospital investigation and long-term follow-up. All the TB suspects were advised to attend the local hospital for confirmation of diagnosis and treatment.

Comparisons: In order to gain a proper impression, we are frequently asked to compare Limehill with other areas of South Africa, usually rural African areas. However, medically speaking, we can only compare the situation with what we consider to be the best possible.

Comparison with any White rural area will reveal, after a moment's reflection, the enormity of the problem at Limehill. Since one of the doctors had previously worked in a mission hospital, he can compare the Limehill situation with another rural African area.

From the figures of the hospital in which he worked, it is certain that the incidence of kwashiorkor is higher in Limehill than in Vendaland. Typhoid is also endemic in the Northern Transvaal, but keeping in mind the relative sizes of the population it seems that there is a greater incidence of typhoid at Limehill.

However, to any medical mind, these comparisons are totally ridiculous. To think that consolation for the diseases in Limehill can be found in the fact that other rural areas have serious disease problems is hardly a scientific outlook.

Rather does it point to the serious situation in the whole of rural South Africa, which is confirmed by every doctor working at a mission hospital. Any disease that kills or incapacitates is unacceptable. The whole of medicine works from this.

General conditions: We did not inspect houses, water or latrines. However, most concerned doctors are interested in how their patients live. To be normal and healthy, a community should have adequate housing, water for cooking and washing, and adequate waste-disposal facilities.

From the disease we saw it is self-evident that the water and waste-disposal facilities are inadequate.

The true nature of health conditions in the Limehill area can only be ascertained by doing sustained, on-the-spot, clinical work, as we did. Factual impressions can definitely not be gained by conducted tours of the complex by non-medical personnel.

The final factor in human life of concern to the doctor is the family unit, life as a whole. Significantly the majority of patients were women and children.

We understand that the men are to a large extent in other areas. We would indicate that this is unsatisfactory and a further factor in continuing the vicious cycle of disease, poverty, ignorance, disease.

Bibliography

(S.A.I.R.R. = South African Institute of Race Relations)

Carter, G. M., Karis, T., and Stultz, N. M., *South Africa's Transkei: The Politics of Domestic Colonisation* (Northwestern University Press, Evanston, Ill., 1967).

Christian Action, *South Africa: 'Resettlement' – the New Violence to Africans* (London, 1969).

Duncan, S., *The Plight of the Urban African* (S.A.I.R.R., 1970).
 The Disruption of African Family Life (S.A.I.R.R., 1968).

Hill, C. R., *Bantustans: The Fragmentation of South Africa* (Oxford University Press, London, for Institute of Race Relations, 1964).

Hobart Houghton, Prof. D., *Life in the Ciskei. A Summary of the Findings of the Keiskamma Hoek Rural Survey, 1947–1951* (S.A.I.R.R., 1955).
 Tomlinson Report: A Summary of the Findings (S.A.I.R.R., 1956).

Hooper, Charles, *Brief Authority* (Collins, London, 1960).

Horrell, M., *A Visit to the Bantu Areas of Northern Transvaal* (S.A.I.R.R., 1965).
 Bantu Education to 1968 (S.A.I.R.R., 1968).
 Introduction to South Africa (S.A.I.R.R., 1968).
 South Africa's Workers (S.A.I.R.R., 1969).
 The African Reserves of South Africa (S.A.I.R.R., 1969).

Laurence, J., *The Seeds of Disaster* (Gollancz, London, 1968).

Liberal Party of South Africa, *Blackspots: A Study of Apartheid in Action.*

Mbeki, G., *South Africa: The Peasants' Revolt* (Penguin Books, Harmondsworth, 1964).

Schlemmer, L., *Social Change and Social Policy in South Africa* (S.A.I.R.R., 1970).

Vigne, R., *The Transkei: South Africa's Tragedy* (African Bureau, London, 1969).

Wilson, M., and Thompson, L. M., *The Oxford History of South Africa Vol. 1 (to 1870)* Oxford University Press, Oxford, 1969).

Bibliography

Annual Reports of Department of Bantu Administration and Development (Pretoria).

Annual Survey of Race Relations in South Africa (ed. M. Horrell, S.A.I.R.R.).

Black Sash (magazine).

Financial Mail, Johannesburg.

Rand Daily Mail, Johannesburg.

Star, Johannesburg.

Maps

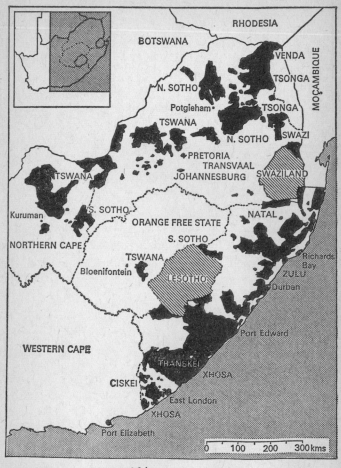

1. African areas of South Africa

Scale: 0 50 100 kms

- Osizweni
- Newcastle
- Madadeni
- Alcockspruit
- Dannhauser
- Vryheid
- Nongoma
- Dundee
- Mondlo
- Nqutu
- Vulandondo
- Babanango
- Mtubatuba
- Limehill
- Vergelegen
- Nkandla
- Melmoth
- Empangeni
- Ladysmith
- Pomeray
- Colenso
- Eshowe
- Richard's Bay
- Weenen

NATAL

- Greytown
- Impendle
- Pietermaritzburg
- Poll-tax Farm

INDIAN OCEAN

- Hammersdale
- DURBAN

TRANSKEI

- Port Edward

2. Natal

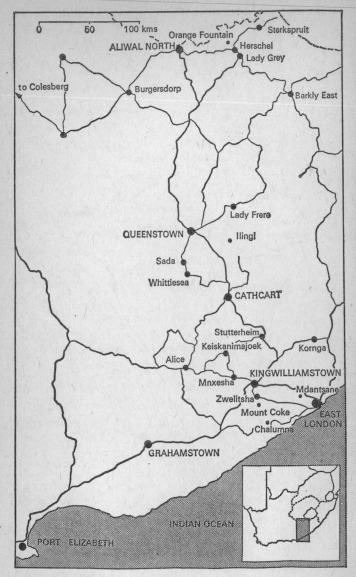

3. The Eastern Cape
246

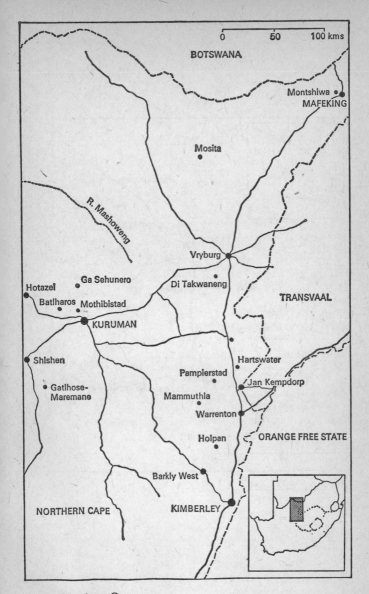

4. The Northern Cape

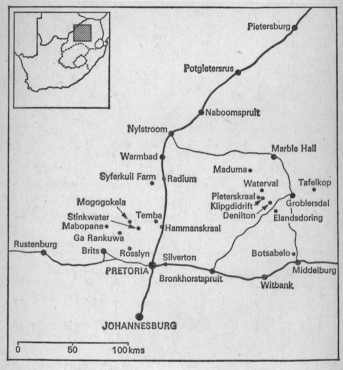

5. Central Transvaal

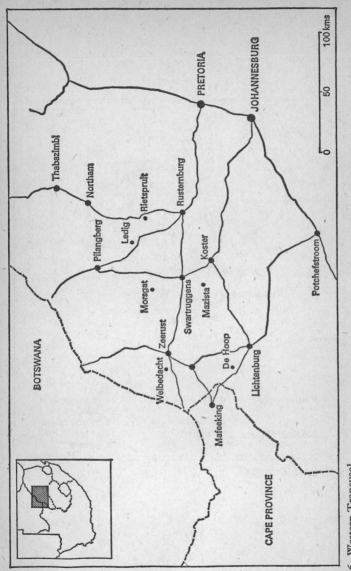

6. Western Transvaal

249

1 Namakgale	6 Thulumahashe	11 Pilgrims Rest
2 Elandsfontein	7 London	12 Sabie
3 Dientje	8 Naboomskoppie	13 Bushbuckridge
4 Acornhoek	9 Burgersfort	14 Maute
5 Arthur's Seat	10 Jane Furse Hosp.	15 Ngodini

7. Eastern Transvaal

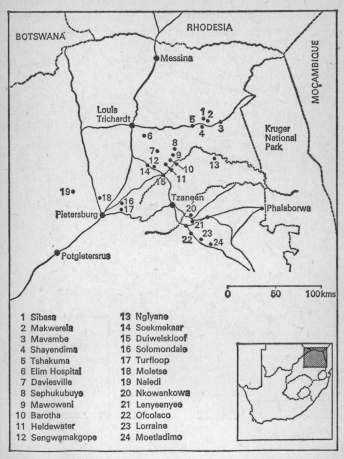

1 Sibasa
2 Makwerela
3 Mavambe
4 Shayendima
5 Tshakuma
6 Elim Hospital
7 Daviesville
8 Sephukubuye
9 Mawoweni
10 Barotha
11 Heldewater
12 Sengwamakgope
13 Ngiyane
14 Soekmekaar
15 Duiwelskloof
16 Solomondale
17 Turfloop
18 Moletse
19 Naledi
20 Nkowankowa
21 Lenyeenyee
22 Ofcolaco
23 Lorraine
24 Moetladimo

8. Northern Transvaal

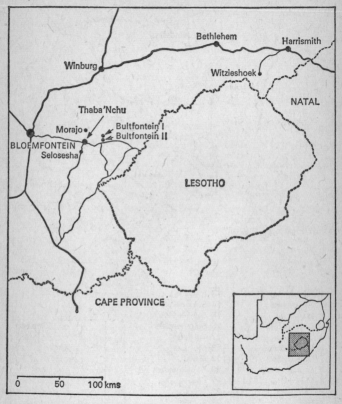

9. Orange Free State

Index